The Tao of Cooking
by Sally Pasley

Indiana University Press
Bloomington and Indianapolis

To Rudi

This book is a publication of

Indiana University Press
Office of Scholarly Publishing
Herman B Wells Library 350
1320 East 10th Street
Bloomington, Indiana 47405 USA
http://iupress.indiana.edu

First Indiana University Press reprint 1998
Originally published in 1982 by Ten Speed Press
© 1982 by Swami Chetanananda
Designed by Milton Glaser

The paper used in this publication meets the minimum
requirements of American National Standard for Information
Sciences—Permanence of Paper for Printed Library
Materials, ANSI Z39.48-1984.

Manufactured in the United States of America

Cataloging information is available from the Library of Congress.

ISBN 978-0-253-21237-5

    2   3   4   5   14

Printed on paper made from 50% post-consumer material.

Table of Contents

Acknowledgements

I wish to thank Chef Eugene Bernard for generously offering his expertise and guidance over the years; Milton Glaser for his encouragement and the willingness to share his very special talents; Nicolette Love for her invaluable editorial advice; and last but not least, Swami Chetanananda for conceiving of and sustaining this effort; and members and friends of the Rudrananda Ashrams and the Tao Restaurant Staff for their enthusiastic support.

Foreword

 In 1971, a group of young and enthusiastic yoga students came together in Bloomington, Indiana. They opened a vegetarian restaurant in order to support themselves and simultaneously reflect the quality of life underlying their spiritual practice. They named the restaurant The Tao, the Chinese word and philosophy meaning "the way" or "the path." Their progress along this path of growth and development is the basis and inspiration of this book.

But let me backtrack for a moment. As The Tao opened in 1971, another vegetarian restaurant opened in upstate New York, near Woodstock. Like The Tao, Rudi's Big Indian Restaurant was the means of support for the students of Swami Rudrananda (Rudi). When I arrived in Big Indian as a potential yoga student a few months after the inception of the restaurant, demands of the local clientele had already forced changes in the vegetarian menu. Never to be compromised, however, was our fierce commitment to quality.

We went to great lengths to uphold the highest standards possible within the limits of our experience and capabilities. We grew our own vegetables in a huge garden, baked our own wholesome whole wheat bread, made yogurt from the rich milk we collected from a nearby dairy farm, and drove miles each day to pick up fresh eggs from the "chicken lady," and mushrooms from the local mushroom farm. By early 1973, the restaurant had expanded from six to sixty seats and the staff had acquired considerable experience.

At about this time, two significant events occurred: first, Rudi's sudden and shocking death in a plane crash. Deeply saddened, many of the sixty members of the ashram moved to Bloomington, Indiana to study with Rudi's principal disciple, Michael Shoemaker, now Swami Chetanananda. Others, like myself, remained in Big Indian, determined to pursue our spiritual practice and existing lifestyle. The restaurant was just getting on its feet and there was much work to be done.

The second event took place gradually and concerned our summer neighbor, Chef Eugene Bernard. Then Chef at Manhattan's prestigious Quo Vadis Restaurant, Chef Bernard shared a deep love for Rudi. Impressed by our willingness to work and conquer our inexperience, Chef Bernard took us under his wing.

Little by little, Bernard opened our eyes to a world we never knew existed: the world of the professional kitchen. Possessing a lifetime of training and experience of a caliber rarely existing in the world today, Bernard set us straight. From the day he set foot in our kitchen, everything changed. About our business sense, he chided, "You are working for the glory, my friends. Better to close the doors and go fishing."

Luckily this wonderful, kind man kept us afloat with his knowledge and advice. To know him and learn from the ocean of experience he dispensed by droplets was a treasured privilege. For me, the time was only too short. In 1977, I moved to Bloomington, Indiana.

In the interim, the ashram in Bloomington had been active. The Tao Restaurant had developed an enthusiastic following and expanded in both size and scope. Bloomington, Indiana, the home of Indiana University, attracts people from all over the world. From places as diverse as India, Japan, Italy, and China, new acquaintances offered recipes from families and homelands, and the trend at The Tao shifted from brown rice, beans, and cheese sauces to more eclectic fare. The recent addition of wine and seafood to its menu has introduced more and more people to the pleasures of vegetarian dining, still the Tao's main focus. In this context, *The Tao of Cooking* evolved.

Introduction

The spirit behind The Tao Restaurant and the spirit that underlies the writing of this book is in every way philosophical—a spirit of openness, growth and discovery. The recipes that emerge, however, are free of philosophical constraints. I do not wish to persuade the reader to adopt a philosophy of eating. Good food must speak for itself, which I believe it does in these recipes. Through this book, I hope to encourage you to discover the rewards of vegetarian dining. For those already initiated, here is a group of recipes to add to your collection and enjoy.

Learning to cook in the context of a restaurant has its pitfalls. I have acquired a taste for foods normally outside the realm of "healthful" vegetarian food—refined white flour made into crusty French loaves, puff paste transformed into a brilliant array of luscious pastries, sauces rich with butter and cream. Can a person like myself be tempted by a soy loaf? Flavor and artistic appeal of a dish have been part of my training—a part, I confess, that still overrides what I know to be "good for me." Still, I have the stubborn idea that one can have the best of both worlds: good, healthy food that tastes good, too. Sharing in this conviction, the members of The Tao Restaurant staff continually work to uphold high standards of quality and appeal in the food they serve.

In these recipes, vegetables are presented in all their glory: fresh, delicious, exciting, fine tasting, and center stage. If you are a vegetarian for one meal or for a lifetime, you cannot argue with the inherent virtues of fresh ingredients.

And on this point all cooks, vegetarian or otherwise, must agree. The best food is produced from prime ingredients. Since nothing worthwhile is easily attained, this often implies considerable effort on the cook's part. Spinach, for example, takes patience to prepare. A large quantity must be stemmed, washed, and cooked to produce only one fourth of its original volume. Worse, for some recipes it must be squeezed dry and chopped. Too much work, you say? Cook up a batch of the frozen stuff and tell me it tastes anything like genuine spinach!

Once you discover that vegetables are exciting and taste good in their own right, not just as side dishes, you may wish to explore other aspects of the vegetarian diet. Philosophy, health, ecology, and economics are some of the bases for strong cases in favor of vegetarianism. But you should give careful consideration to changing your eating patterns. I recommend looking at some excellent books which discuss these questions in depth. *Laurel's Kitchen*, by Laurel Robertson, Carol Flinders and Bronwen Godfrey (New York: Bantam, 1978), offers a very complete section of nutritional information. A bible for anyone seriously wishing to undertake a full-time vegetarian diet, this book also contains recipes and philosophical comments. Two other books giving sound ecological arguments for vegetarianism and discussing nutritional theories are *Diet for a Small Planet*, by Frances Moore Lappe (New York: Ballantine, 1975), and *Recipes for a Small Planet*, by Ellen Bushman Ewald (New York: Ballantine, 1974).

Let these books be your guide to common sense in nutritional eating. Finally, use your intuition and sense of good taste to make eating an enjoyable experience. By keeping things simple, you may discover pleasures you never before experienced. You can celebrate minor feasts over a few fresh vegetables newly in season, steamed and lightly buttered, or dressed with soy sauce and tofu.

I have tried to keep the dishes in this book as close to their original recipes as possible. In some cases, this has precluded the most healthful solution (Polish Babka made with chocolate, white flour, and white sugar, for example), but I felt that authenticity would serve my purpose better. For once you understand the spirit of a dish, or a style of cooking, you are free to improvise and make your own choices and substitutions with great success. You have uncharted ground before you, yet you have a myriad of taste combinations to draw from. To me, this is the most exciting and inventive aspect of cooking with vegetables.

Menus

For many people, planning vegetarian meals is a new experience. A meal without meat as the central focus often requires more imaginative planning, yet can reveal some new concepts in our eating patterns. An assortment of hors d'oeuvres is one pleasant departure from the traditional menu. Whether soup, homemade bread, sweet butter, cheese, and a few raw vegetables; or a hearty antipasto composed of caponata, vegetables a la Grecque, eggplant caviar, crudites, crusty bread, and Italian cheeses, all add up to a satisfying meal. A special appetizer can be as exciting a starting point in planning a meal as the more reliable entree.

Much can still be said for the traditional menu plan centered around a main course. For example, Moussaka should be treated as the beautiful, royal dish that it is, with other dishes playing minor roles. Entrees such as Artichoke Ricotta Pie, Cabbage Brioche Loaf, Cous-Cous, and Vegetable Stew in a Pumpkin Shell deserve as much attention and can be nicely prefaced with a soup or appetizer.

To develop a sense of what foods go well together, plan a meal around a certain cuisine or style of cooking, such as Italian, Oriental, or Mediterranean. A main course of pasta, preceded by caponata, or an antipasto and crusty Italian bread, makes an excellent combination. Accompany the pasta with a green salad tossed simply with olive oil and red wine vinegar. For a finale, you might serve some fresh fruit or a chilled zabaglione. Once you have a focus in mind, the ideas begin to flow and the meal falls into place.

Try to choose your menus sensibly. Remember, a dish may take two or three times longer to prepare the first time you attempt it, so plan accordingly. Simplicity is your best ally. Too many complicated tastes together can diminish the final effect and leave you discouraged after an arduous effort. The following menus, composed almost entirely from recipes in this book, are meant to serve as guidelines. Plan ahead, leave yourself plenty of time and enjoy!

Breakfast

Half a grapefruit
Ambrosia
Orange French Toast
Coffee or Tea

Fresh Squeezed Orange Juice
Eggs Jardiniere
Little Brioche Rolls with Butter and Jam
Strawberries Romanoff
Coffee or Tea

Fresh Pineapple and Strawberries
Huevos Rancheros with Refried Beans
Warm Tortillas
Mexican Hot Chocolate

Fresh Fruit Cup
Orange Juice
Scrambled Eggs
Brioche Raisin Rolls
Assorted Cheeses
Coffee or Tea

Lunch

Split Pea Soup
Quiche Hollandaise
Tossed Salad with Vinaigrette Dressing
Cracked Wheat Bread
Plum Walnut Tart

Polish Vegetable Barley Soup
Open Heart Sandwich
Tao Salad
Poppy Seed Cake

Cuban Black Bean Soup
Guacamole and Chips
Empanadas
Fresh Coconut Layer Cake

Stuffed Vine Leaves
Felafel
Syrian Eggplant Salad
Copenhagen Nut Cake

Dinner

Chilled Fresh Pea Soup
Pasta Primavera
Broccoli Italian Style
Green Salad with Vinaigrette Dressing
French Bread
Chilled Zabaglione with Strawberries

Mulligatawny Soup
Curried Eggplant
Curried Chickpeas
Rice
Chutney
Cucumber Raita
Fresh Mangoes and Strawberries

Egg Rolls
Hot and Spicy Stir-Fried Vegetables
Fried Rice
Cucumber and Bean Sprout Salad
Strawberry Jello

Cream of Carrot Soup
Baked Stuffed Mushrooms
Rice
Tossed Salad
Carrot Cake

Garlic and Herb Cheese Spread
with Assorted Crackers
Cous-Cous with a Vegetable Stew
Arabian Salad
Onion Garnish
Honey Yogurt Pie

Caponata
Spinach Lasagna
Tossed Salad
Italian Bread
Russian Cheesecake
Espresso

Chili Pickles
Chiles Rellenos
Spanish Rice
Refried Beans
Warm Tortillas
Flan

Green Jade Soup
Nori Rolls
Vegetable Tempura
Japanese Spinach Salad with Sesame and Tofu
Green Tea
Fresh Fruit

Polish Vegetable Barley Soup
Stuffed Cabbage Rolls
Steamed Carrots
Whole Wheat Bread
Poppy Seed Cake

Turkish Boreks
Moussaka
Rice
Green Salad
Apple Custard Tart

Country Pate with a Cold Tomato Sauce
Fettucine with Cauliflower in Cream Sauce
Steamed Artichokes
Tossed Salad
French Bread
Strawberries Romanoff

Gazpacho
Tamal Pie
Refried Beans
Green Salad
Orange Ice

Turnip Sesame Cakes
Chinese Cabbage Rolls
Dry-Cooked String Beans
Fried Rice
Pineapple Sherbet

Minestrina
Baked Stuffed Eggplant
Steamed Green Beans
Baked Tomato Halves
Creme Caramel

Crudites with White Bean Dip
Artichoke Ricotta Pie
Greek Salad
Brown Rice
Honey Layer Cake

Italian Marinated Vegetables
Spinach Gnocchi with Butter and Cheese
Steamed Broccoli
Rice
Poached Pears

Avocado Gazpacho
Chilequile
Tossed Salad
Fresh Pineapple

Japanese Style Noodles in Broth
Vegetables with Tofu Sauce
Japanese Mixed Rice
Asparagus or Green Beans a la Japonnaise
Fresh Fruit
Green Tea

Butternut Squash and Leek Soup
Cheddar and Onion Pie
Tossed Salad
Steamed Broccoli
Irish Oatmeal Bread
Pumpkin Spice Cake

Chilled Cucumber and Yogurt Soup
Pastitso
Baked Tomato Halves
Syrian Salad
Plum Cake

Guacamole
Cheese Filled Tamales
Refried Beans
Spanish Rice
Fresh Strawberries

Special Events

Indian Buffet Meal

Samosas
Shahi Cauliflower
Curried Black Beans
Byriani
Cucumber Raita
Chutney
Naan Bread
Gulab Jamen
Tea

Fourth of July Picnic

Crudites with Avocado Cream
Vegetable Brochettes
Corn on the Cob
Potatoes Roasted in Foil
New Mexican Bean Salad
Scandinavian Cucumber Salad
Strawberry Rhubarb Pie

Thanksgiving Dinner

New England Corn Chowder
Vegetable Stew in a Pumpkin Shell
Steamed Carrots and Brussels Sprouts
Rice
Tossed Salad
Pecan Pie with Whipped Cream

Christmas Dinner

Antipasto (Assorted Italian Cheeses, Olives,
Radishes, Celery Sticks, Artichokes
quartered and marinated in Vinaigrette,
Hard Boiled Egg Halves, Onion Bread Ring)
Spinach Ravioli with Tomato Cream Sauce
Cauliflower Gratinata
Braised Fennel
Assorted Fruit
Michel's Kugelhopf
Espresso

Eggs and Granola

Breakfast

In addition to omelets and egg dishes, which are mentioned in a separate chapter, a few special breakfast foods deserve attention. Although the grocery shelves provide breakfast staples such as yogurt, granola, and pancake mix, you may discover several advantages to making these foods at home. By adjusting the ingredients in a recipe, you can tailor the product to your own particular taste. For example, replace whole milk with skim milk for a dieter's yogurt; add wholesome ingredients such as wheat germ, bran, or brewer's yeast to pancake mix; or adjust the sweetness of granola to suit your family's preference and add chopped dates, apricots, coconut, or other favorite ingredients. Your reward will be a superior product at a lower than supermarket or health-food store price.

Homemade yogurt is economical, simple to make and tastes better than commercially made. It is made with milk or powdered milk and a yogurt "culture," which is actually a bacteria. Left to itself under certain conditions, this culture will transform the milk into yogurt. These conditions are: warm (between 105 and 110 degrees), undisturbed, and sterilized (so that no other bacteria will interfere with the friendly one that is growing). Heating the milk to 180 degrees and cooling it to 110 wards off any unwanted bacteria strains that would prevent the yogurt from setting up and seems to give the most consistent results from fresh milk.

Powdered milk, on the other hand, needs less coddling. The heating and cooling step can be eliminated and the milk simply mixed with hot tap water and processed. When you buy powdered milk, be sure to check the date on the package, since it should be fresh for the best results. Commercial or homemade yogurt may be used for a culture.

Yogurt

Makes 1 quart

1 quart whole or skim milk
¼ cup powdered milk (optional)
3 Tbsp. yogurt for culture

1. Mix milk with powdered milk and heat to 180 degrees. Watch milk carefully as it scorches easily. Cool to 110 to 112 degrees and stir in yogurt.

2. Pour into a sterilized quart jar, cover and set in a warm, draft-free place for 6 to 8 hours, until set. Refrigerate.

2   *cups powdered milk*
4   *cups hot tap water*
    (about 110 degrees)
3   *Tbsp. yogurt for culture*

Yogurt—Another Method

1. Mix powdered milk with hot tap water and strain through a sieve. Mix in yogurt culture.

2. Pour into sterilized jars, cover and set in a warm, draft-free place for 6 to 8 hours, until set. Refrigerate.

Ambrosia can be really just about any combination of yogurt, honey and fruits. In winter, apples, bananas, pears, oranges, and pineapples are all available and provide a refreshing change of pace for breakfast. Raspberries, strawberries, or cooked, sweetened cranberries, either pureed or sliced, give the mixture an appealing color. Stewed fruits or chopped dried fruits, such as apricots and dates, are also delicious additions to ambrosia. Here is just one combination of fruit that goes nicely with yogurt.

Serves 4

1   *or 2 bananas*
2   *oranges*
⅓   *cup strawberries or*
    raspberries
6   *dates*
2   *cups plain yogurt*
½   *tsp. vanilla*
    honey to taste

Ambrosia

1. Slice bananas. Peel oranges and cut in sections. Slice or mash berries, or use frozen berries in winter. Chop dates. Mix all ingredients together and taste for sweetness.

Here is a basic method for making granola. You may increase or decrease the amount of honey and sugar according to taste. Try different amounts of seeds, or add toasted coconut, nuts, or raisins to your final mix.

Granola

Makes 12 cups, or 3¼ lbs.

1½   cups sesame seeds
1½   cups sunflower seeds
½   cup oil
1   cup honey
½   cup brown sugar
1   tsp. vanilla
¼   tsp. salt
8   cups rolled oats

1. Preheat oven to 350 degrees.

2. Spread sesame and sunflower seeds on separate baking sheets and toast in the oven for 10 to 15 minutes, until light brown.

3. Heat oil, honey, brown sugar, and vanilla together, stirring until honey is thin. Add salt.

4. Mix oats and toasted seeds together and combine with honey mixture until well coated. Spread on foil lined cookie sheets and bake until golden brown, 10 to 15 minutes. Stir once or twice during baking to brown evenly.

5. Let cereal cool on cookie sheets and store in an airtight container.

This formula for pancake mix is based on the yogurt pancake recipe and can be applied to just about any favorite recipe: mix up the dry ingredients in quantity and add eggs, milk and melted butter as you need them. Different types of flour may be substituted and other healthy ingredients, such as bran, wheat germ, and brewer's yeast may be added. You may also omit the sugar and add honey or molasses to the final batch.

Pancake Mix

8   cups flour
2   Tbsp. salt
1   cup sugar
3   Tbsp. baking powder
2   tsp. baking soda

1. Mix all ingredients together well and sift. Store in a dry place.

For 8 to 10 pancakes:

1 cup pancake mix
1 egg
2 Tbsp. melted butter
½ cup yogurt
¼ to ½ cup milk
½ tsp. vanilla

1. Beat egg with melted butter, yogurt, milk and vanilla. Stir in pancake mix and drop onto a hot, lightly oiled griddle.

You may substitute buttermilk for the yogurt and milk in this recipe.

Makes 16 to 20 pancakes

Yogurt Pancakes

2 cups white flour
1½ tsp. salt
4 Tbsp. sugar
2 tsp. baking powder
½ tsp. baking soda
2 eggs
4 Tbsp. melted butter
1 cup yogurt
½ to 1 cup milk
1 tsp. vanilla

1. Sift flour, salt, sugar, baking powder, and baking soda together.

2. Beat eggs and mix with melted butter, yogurt, milk, and vanilla. Stir in dry ingredients until well blended. Drop onto a hot, lightly oiled griddle.

Try these with molasses, or substitute buckwheat flour for the whole wheat flour.

Makes 12 to 16 pancakes

Whole Wheat Buttermilk Pancakes

1 cup white flour
2 tsp. baking powder
1½ tsp. salt
1 tsp. baking soda
1 cup whole wheat flour
¼ cup wheat germ or bran
2 eggs
3 Tbsp. honey
¼ cup melted butter
2 to 2½ cups buttermilk

1. Sift white flour, baking powder, salt, and baking soda together. Mix with whole wheat flour and wheat germ or bran.

2. Beat eggs with honey, melted butter, and buttermilk. Stir in dry ingredients until blended. Drop onto a hot, lightly oiled griddle.

A personal favorite, especially with blueberries or apples!

Cornmeal Pancakes

Makes 12 to 16 pancakes

1½ cups yellow cornmeal
1½ tsp. salt
1½ cups boiling water
¾ cup flour
1 Tbsp. baking powder
2 eggs
3 Tbsp. honey or molasses
1 cup milk
3 Tbsp. melted butter

1. Mix cornmeal with salt and stir in boiling water. Let stand while you assemble other ingredients.

2. Sift flour and baking powder together.

3. Beat eggs and mix with honey, milk and melted butter.

4. Mix liquid ingredients with cornmeal. Stir in flour and baking powder and drop onto a hot, lightly oiled griddle.

A true sourdough starter takes about a week to make and once established, it can be perpetuated for years. Here is a faster way to achieve a nice sourdough taste. A mixture of yeast, flour, and water are left to ferment overnight and the remaining ingredients are added in the morning. Real maple syrup is a must with these.

Sourdough Pancakes

**Makes about
one dozen pancakes**

1 package fresh or
   dry yeast
1 cup warm water
1 cup flour
½ cup sour milk
3 Tbsp. oil
3 Tbsp. molasses
   pinch salt
1 egg
1 tsp. baking soda
¾ cup flour

1. Dissolve yeast in water and mix with 1 cup flour. Cover and let stand in a warm place overnight.

2. Mix remaining ingredients with starter in the order given. Drop onto a hot, lightly greased griddle.

Serve these apple beignets on a snowy day with hot chocolate or steaming cups of cafe au lait.

Apple Beignets

Makes approximately 16 beignets

¾ cup water
¼ cup butter
   pinch salt
¾ cup flour
4 eggs
1 apple, peeled and
      diced
   oil for frying
   powdered sugar

1. Bring water, butter, and salt to a rolling boil in a heavy-bottomed saucepan. Stir in flour all at once, remove from heat, and beat until smooth with a wooden spoon.

2. Return pan to medium heat and cook, stirring constantly for about one minute, until dough pulls away from the sides of the pan.

3. Remove the pan from heat and beat in eggs one at a time. The dough will separate, become slippery, and finally come together again. When all the eggs have been incorporated, stir in the diced apples.

4. Heat 1½ to 2 inches of oil in a heavy iron skillet or deep fryer. Drop dough into hot oil by rounded tablespoons and cook until golden brown on both sides. Drain on absorbent paper, sprinkle with plenty of powdered sugar, and serve hot.

This is delicious made with French bread cut on the diagonal in thick slices. Serve topped with fresh strawberries for a special treat.

Orange French Toast

Serves 4 to 6

8 to 10 slices white or
      raisin bread
3 eggs
½ cup orange juice
1 tsp. finely grated orange
      rind
½ cup milk
1 tsp. cinnamon
1 tsp. nutmeg

1. Beat eggs and mix with remaining ingredients. Dip bread in French toast batter and fry in melted butter until golden brown on both sides.

Nutty French Toast

Follow the recipe for Orange French Toast; or omit the orange juice and rind and use a total of 1 cup milk and ½ tsp. vanilla. Dip bread in batter and coat on both sides with finely chopped almonds. Fry in melted butter until golden brown on both sides. Dust with powdered sugar.

Breads

Aside from enjoyment, freshly baked bread has special merits for the vegetarian. Whole grains represent a vital source of protein and may be deliciously consumed in the form of home baked bread. Since many of these recipes are ethnically rather than health-food oriented, I encourage you to substitute and add nutritious ingredients at your discretion. When you feel confident with a recipe, you may begin to improvise and create a bread to your own liking.

The following procedure is common to almost every yeast bread. When you understand the process and the interaction of the basic ingredients, you will easily succeed in tailoring a bread to your own specifications.

BASIC STEPS FOR MIXING, SHAPING AND BAKING BREAD

1. Mix fresh or dry yeast with a small amount of warm water to dissolve.

2. Mix dissolved yeast with all other liquid ingredients, shortening, sugar, and half the flour. Beat vigorously, until elastic, to start the action of the gluten.

3. Add the salt, the other dry ingredients (such as bran or wheat germ), and most of the remaining flour. Since flours vary greatly in their ability to absorb liquid, a good general practice is to reserve about ½ cup of the flour called for in a recipe. Knead this "extra" flour in gradually, and then only if necessary. As you knead the dough, stickiness is replaced by elasticity, and the amount of flour needed decreases. If you knead too much flour into the dough at the beginning, you may wind up with a stiff and heavy dough that will not rise properly in the oven. Caution at the beginning can prevent this mistake before it is too late.

4. When the dough feels smooth and elastic and no longer sticks to your hands or the countertop, it is ready for the rising period. Form it into a ball and place it in a lightly oiled bowl. Turn the ball once so that the surface of the dough is completely coated with oil. This prevents the surface from drying out and resisting expansion during the rising period.

Cover the bowl with a damp cloth and set it aside in a warm, draft-free place.

5. When the dough has doubled in bulk (from 1½ to 2 hours), punch it down with your fist. Knead it for a minute or two to release all the air bubbles. Let the dough rest for about 10 minutes to give it time to relax after kneading, and become more pliable for shaping.

6. Shape the loaves and place them in greased bread pans or on greased baking sheets to rise. The second rising period is usually shorter than the first, but varies according to recipe. Be sure to preheat the oven at this time. Most breads require a hot oven, from 400 to 450 degrees.

7. An egg wash gives the finished loaf a lovely, shiny, golden color. Just before baking, brush the top of the loaf with whole, beaten egg; or egg yolk beaten with two or three tablespoons of milk or cream. For a crisper crust, brush the loaf with water, or a solution of salt and water, once or twice during the baking period. This is especially good with "lean" breads, such as French or Italian.

8. When the bread is finished baking, it should sound hollow inside when tapped on the bottom. Both top *and* bottom crusts should be a nice, golden brown color. Remove the loaf from the pan as soon as it comes out of the oven and set it on a wire rack to cool. Air must freely circulate around the loaf as it cools for a good crust formation. When it is thoroughly cool, and only then, store the loaf in a plastic bag.

This is a basic recipe for a peasant bread. Its counterpart can be found in most European countries, variations dictated by the particular kind of flour available and the type of oven used. It is what is called a "lean" bread, containing no butter, milk, sugar, or other enriching ingredients. In Italy, it would probably not even contain salt, but I have tailored this recipe to suit American tastes. This is the kind of bread that must be eaten on the day it is made, preferably fresh out of the oven.

Makes 2 loaves

1	*package fresh or dry yeast*
1¼	*cups warm water*
3½	*cups bread or all-purpose flour*
2	*tsp. salt*

Basic Italian Bread

1. Dissolve yeast in ¼ cup warm water.

2. Mix yeast, remaining 1 cup water and 2 cups flour together in a bowl and beat until smooth.

3. Add salt and enough remaining flour to make a stiff dough. Knead until smooth and elastic.

4. Form dough into a ball and place it in a lightly oiled bowl. Turn it once to coat the surface of the dough with oil. Cover with a cloth and let rise in a warm, draft-free place until doubled in bulk, about 1½ hours.

5. Punch the dough down and let it rest for ten minutes. Divide in half and shape in two oblong loaves. Place them on a greased baking sheet dusted with cornmeal and let rise again until almost doubled, 45 minutes to an hour.

6. Make three diagonal slashes across the tops of the loaves with a razor blade. Bake in a preheated 400 degree oven for 25 to 30 minutes, until crust is golden brown and loaf sounds hollow when tapped on the bottom. If you like a crisp crust, brush loaves with water two or three times during baking.

This is a magnificent looking country bread. The slightly caramelized red onions give it a beautiful, deep, golden brown appearance. It makes a pleasant accompaniment to an antipasto.

Onion Bread Ring

Makes one large or two small loaves

1 recipe Basic Italian
   Bread
2 Tbsp. butter
1 large red onion, sliced
   small pinch sugar
   poppy and/or sesame
   seeds
1 beaten egg

1. Make Basic Italian Bread according to directions. After the first rising, shape into one large or two small rings and place on a greased baking sheet dusted with cornmeal.

2. Heat butter in a skillet. Add sliced onion and pinch of sugar and cook until onion starts to brown.

3. When loaves have doubled in bulk (45 minutes to an hour), brush top with beaten egg. Cover with cooked red onion slices and sprinkle with sesame or poppy seeds.

4. Bake in a preheated 400 degree oven for 25 to 30 minutes, until golden brown. Loaf should sound hollow when tapped on the bottom.

This is a good, basic whole wheat bread. Sesame seeds give it a nutty taste. It is excellent fresh for sandwiches or toasted. You may add one or two tablespoons of sunflower seeds for extra crunchiness.

Whole Wheat Bread

Makes one large loaf
(8¼" × 4¼")

1 cup warm water
1 package fresh or
    dry yeast
1½ Tbsp. sugar
1 Tbsp. vegetable
    shortening
2 Tbsp. sesame seeds
1¼ cups bread or
    all-purpose flour
2 tsp. salt
1½ to 1¾ cups whole wheat
    flour

1. In a large bowl, dissolve yeast in warm water. Add sugar, shortening, and sesame seeds. Add white flour and beat until smooth.

2. Add salt and enough remaining whole wheat flour to make a stiff dough. Knead until smooth and elastic.

3. Form dough into a ball and place it in a lightly oiled bowl. Turn it once to coat the surface of the dough with oil. Cover with a cloth and let rest in a warm, draft-free place until doubled in bulk, 1½ to 2 hours.

4. Punch the dough down and let it rest for ten minutes. Shape into one large loaf and place in a well greased loaf pan. Let rise again until almost doubled, 45 minutes to an hour.

5. Brush top of loaf with beaten egg and sprinkle with one or two teaspoons sesame seeds. Bake in a preheated 400 degree oven for 25 to 30 minutes, until crust is golden and loaf sounds hollow when tapped on the bottom.

Cracked wheat gives this wholesome bread a delicious crunchy texture.

Cracked Wheat Bread

Makes 2 large loaves
(1½ lbs. each)

1 cup cracked wheat
¾ cup warm water
1 package fresh or
    dry yeast
3 Tbsp. molasses
2 tsp. salt
1 Tbsp. shortening
2 cups white flour
1 cup rye flour
½ to 1 cup whole wheat
    flour

1. Soak cracked wheat in 1 cup hot water for 45 minutes to an hour, until all the water has been absorbed.

2. Dissolve yeast in warm water. Stir in molasses, salt and shortening. Add white flour and beat until smooth. Mix in soaked cracked wheat.

3. Add rye flour and ¼ cup whole wheat flour and mix and knead until dough is smooth and elastic. Add more whole wheat flour as you knead, if necessary.

4. Form dough into a ball and place in a lightly oiled bowl. Cover and let rise in a warm place until doubled in bulk, 1½ to 2 hours.

5. Punch down and let dough rest for 10 minutes. Shape in 2 loaves and place in 2 large greased bread pans. Let rise again until doubled, 1 to 1¼ hours.

6. Brush loaves with beaten egg and bake in a preheated 400 degree oven for 25 to 30 minutes, until golden brown. Loaf should sound hollow when tapped on the bottom.

The honey and cornmeal combination in this bread embodies all the good things associated with old-fashioned country living. For a darker variation (sometimes called Anadama bread) substitute molasses for the honey. Or add raisins for a delicious breakfast bread that makes superb toast.

Cornmeal Honey Bread

Makes one large loaf (8¼" × 4¼") or two small loaves (7¼" × 3½")

- 1 cup warm milk
- 1 package fresh or dry yeast
- ¼ cup honey
- 2 Tbsp. butter or shortening
- ½ cup yellow cornmeal
- 1 tsp. salt
- 2½ cups bread or all-purpose flour

1. In a large bowl, dissolve yeast in warm milk. Stir in honey and butter. Add cornmeal and 1 cup flour and beat vigorously until smooth.

2. Mix in salt and enough remaining flour to make a stiff dough. Knead until smooth and elastic.

3. Form dough into a ball and place it in a lightly oiled bowl. Turn it once to coat the surface of the dough with oil. Cover with a cloth and let rise in a warm, draft-free place until doubled in bulk, 1½ to 2 hours.

4. Punch the dough down and let it rest for ten minutes. Shape into one large or two small loaves and place in well greased loaf pans. Let rise again until almost doubled, 45 minutes to an hour.

5. Brush tops of loaves with beaten egg. Bake in a preheated 375 degree oven for 25 to 30 minutes for small loaves, 30 to 35 minutes for a large loaf, until crust is golden brown and loaf sounds hollow when tapped on the bottom.

Enriched with milk, butter, and honey, this slightly sweet bread has a hint of anise. I think the addition of grated orange or lemon rind would complement the anise nicely.

Anise Seed Bread

Makes 2 large loaves
(8¼" × 4¼")

1	cup milk
5	Tbsp. butter
¼	cup honey
1	package fresh or dry yeast
2	beaten eggs
1	Tbsp. anise seed
1	tsp. salt
4	to 4½ cups bread or all-purpose flour

1. Scald milk. Add butter and honey and cool to lukewarm.

2. In a large bowl, dissolve yeast in warm milk mixture. Add eggs, anise seed, and half the flour. Beat vigorously until smooth.

3. Add salt and enough remaining flour to make a stiff dough. Knead until smooth and elastic.

4. Form dough into a ball and place it in a lightly buttered bowl. Turn it once to coat the surface of the dough with butter. Cover with a cloth and let rise in a warm, draft-free place until doubled in bulk, about two hours.

5. Punch the dough down and let it rest for ten minutes. Shape into two loaves and place in well greased loaf pans. Let rise again until almost doubled, 45 minutes to an hour.

6. Brush tops of loaves with beaten egg. Bake in a preheated 375 degree oven for 25 to 30 minutes, until crust is golden brown and loaf sounds hollow when tapped on the bottom.

This is a long-standing favorite at the Tao Restaurant and adjoining Rudi's Bakery.

Onion Dill Bread

Makes 2 round loaves

1	package fresh or dry yeast
¼	cup warm water
2	eggs
¾	cup cottage cheese
¼	cup finely chopped onion
1	Tbsp. butter
1	Tbsp. sugar
2	tsp. dill weed
1	tsp. salt
3½	cups bread or all-purpose flour

1. Dissolve yeast in warm water.

2. Mix eggs, cottage cheese, onion, butter, sugar, and dill weed together in a bowl. Stir in dissolved yeast and 1½ cups flour. Beat vigorously until smooth.

3. Add salt and enough remaining flour to make a stiff dough. Knead until smooth and elastic.

4. Form dough into a ball and place in a lightly oiled bowl. Turn it once to coat the surface of the dough with oil. Cover with a cloth and let rise in a warm, draft-free place until doubled in bulk, about 1½ hours.

5. Punch the dough down and let it rest for ten minutes. Divide in half and shape in two round loaves. Place on a greased baking sheet and let rise again until almost doubled, 45 minutes to an hour.

6. Brush the loaves with beaten egg. Bake in a preheated 400 degree oven for 25 to 30 minutes, until crust is golden brown and loaf sounds hollow when tapped on the bottom.

This is an adaptation of an Italian idea—a kind of herbed pizza without the tomato sauce. Experiment with other herbs such as crushed fennel seeds, oregano, basil, sage, savory, and marjoram. Be sure to use good, pure olive oil and serve hot.

Herbed Flat Bread

1 package fresh or
  dry yeast
¼ cup warm water
¾ cup warm milk
1 egg
1 tsp. sugar
3 Tbsp. olive oil
2½ to 3 cups bread or
  all-purpose flour
2 tsp. salt
½ cup yellow cornmeal
2 tsp. dried rosemary

1. Dissolve yeast in warm water.

2. Combine dissolved yeast with milk, egg, sugar, and one tablespoon olive oil. Stir in 1½ cups flour and beat until smooth.

3. Add salt, cornmeal, rosemary, and enough remaining flour to make a stiff dough. Knead until smooth and elastic.

4. Form dough into a ball and place it in a lightly oiled bowl. Turn it once to coat the surface of the dough with oil. Cover with a cloth and let rise in a warm, draft-free place until doubled in bulk, about 1½ hours.

5. Punch the dough down and let it rest for ten minutes. Roll into a thin rectangle, 12 by 16 inches. Place the sheet of dough on a greased baking tray. With the tips of the fingers, make indentations over the entire surface of the dough. Sprinkle with the remaining 2 tablespoons olive oil and let rest for 15 minutes.

6. Bake in a preheated 400 degree oven for 20 to 25 minutes, until golden brown on top. Cut in squares and serve hot.

Like the Middle Eastern pita, naan "breads" puff up in the baking process to form a pocket in the center of the bread. This pocket is convenient for filling with Indian curries, dipping in sauces, or using as an edible utensil.

Naan (Indian Flat Bread)

Makes 8 to 10 flat "breads"

1 package fresh or dry yeast
1 cup warm water
1 Tbsp. sugar
3 Tbsp. oil
3 to 3½ cups bread or all-purpose flour
1 tsp. salt
¼ cup yogurt
1 Tbsp. poppy seeds

1. In a large bowl, dissolve yeast in warm water. Add sugar, oil, and 1½ cups flour. Beat until smooth.

2. Add salt and enough remaining flour to make a stiff dough. Knead until smooth and elastic.

3. Form dough into a ball and place it in a lightly oiled bowl. Turn it once to coat the surface of the dough with oil. Cover with a cloth and let rise in a warm, draft-free place until doubled in bulk, 2 to 2½ hours.

4. Preheat broiler.

5. Punch the dough down and let it rest for ten minutes. Divide in eight or ten pieces about the size of tennis balls. Form each piece into a ball and let rest for a few more minutes. With a rolling pin, flatten the balls into ovals about seven inches long and ³⁄₁₆ inch thick.

6. Brush the ovals with yogurt and sprinkle with poppy seeds. Let rest for 15 minutes.

7. Place two or three breads on an oiled baking sheet and "bake" under the broiler, 2 or 3 minutes on each side, until breads puff in the middle and tops start to brown. Serve hot.

Brioche, a light and buttery pastry, is delicious plain, with butter and jam, or filled with raisins and pastry cream. It also makes an excellent foil for cheeses and vegetables (see Cabbage Brioche Loaf in the entree section of this book).

Unlike other bread dough, brioche is very sticky and when mixed by hand must be stretched and slapped down on the work surface. This messy handling explains the aura of difficulty that surrounds brioche making in general. If patience or space is in short supply, however, a food processor or table mixer solves the problem neatly and efficiently.

If there is a trick to making brioche, it is in the shaping of the dough. It should be kept cool and handled as little as possible, since too much handling will make the dough sticky and unmanageable.

In the following recipe, I have given a different set of instructions for mixing brioche by machine and by hand.

Brioche Dough

Makes 2 lbs. dough

1 package fresh or dry yeast
⅓ cup warm water
3¾ cups bread or all-purpose flour
4 eggs
1½ Tbsp. sugar
1½ tsp. salt
½ lb. (2 sticks) unsalted butter

Mixing by Machine (Food Processor or Mixer)

1. Dissolve yeast in warm water. Add ¾ cup flour and mix and knead until smooth. Form dough into a ball and place in a lightly buttered bowl. Cover and let rise in a warm place for one hour.

2. Beat eggs into dough one at a time. Add sugar, salt and remaining 3 cups of flour and mix until smooth and elastic.

3. Beat butter until smooth and creamy, but do not let it become warm. This step is necessary for a smooth incorporation into the dough.

4. Beat butter into the dough one fourth at a time. Dough will be very soft and sticky.

5. Sprinkle a little flour in the bottom of a bowl. Place dough in bowl and sprinkle with a little more flour. Cover and refrigerate overnight.

6. The dough is ready to use any time the next day. Take only what you will be immediately using out of the refrigerator at a time. If the dough becomes warm from sitting out or too much handling, return to refrigerator for 20 minutes or so.

Mixing by Hand

1. Dissolve yeast in warm water. Add ½ cup flour and mix, beating until smooth. Cover and set aside in a warm place for one hour. This is called a "sponge."

2. With a wooden spoon, beat eggs into sponge one at a time, until smooth. Add sugar, salt and 1 cup flour and beat again until smooth.

3. Beat butter until smooth and creamy, but do not let it become warm. This step is necessary for a smooth incorporation into the dough.

4. Beat butter into the dough one fourth at a time, until completely incorporated. Add remaining flour and mix into dough.

5. Turn dough and any excess flour onto a work surface. Using a baker's scraper, knead dough until elastic by stretching it, picking it up, and slapping it down on the table. This is soft and sticky, but becomes elastic in just a few minutes, so don't be discouraged. Using a baker's scraper keeps the dough from becoming too warm from your hands.

6. Sprinkle a little flour in the bottom of the bowl. Place the dough in the bowl and sprinkle with a little more flour. Cover and refrigerate overnight.

7. The dough is ready to use any time the next day. Take only what you will be immediately using out of the refrigerator at a time. If the dough becomes warm from sitting out or too much handling, return to refrigerator for 20 minutes or so.

Makes approx. 16 rolls

Little Brioche Rolls

1 *recipe brioche dough*

1. Divide dough in half. Place one half in the refrigerator while you work with the other. Roll dough into a long coil about 1½ inches thick. Cut in 8 equal pieces and roll each piece in a ball. If the dough starts to become soft, place in refrigerator and work with the other half of the dough.

2. Flour your hands and the work surface. With the side of one hand, make an indentation to separate, but not sever, a small piece of dough (about one third) at the top of the ball. Roll your hand back and forth to make a little "neck" with a round head on top. Turn ball so that the little round head is on top. With your fingers, make depressions around the "neck" and fit the top ball into the well. When the roll bakes, it will have a little topknot which should stay attached to the bottom ball.

3. Grease a muffin tin or small deep tartlet pans. Place rolls in their pans and let rise until doubled in bulk, from 45 minutes to an hour. Brush with beaten egg and bake in a preheated 425 degree oven for 12 to 15 minutes, until golden brown.

Brioche Raisin Rolls

Makes 22 to 24 rolls

1 recipe brioche dough
¼ cup boiling water
2 Tbsp. dark rum
½ cup raisins
1 cup pastry cream
 (see recipe below)
1 tsp. cinnamon

1. Pour boiling water over raisins, add rum and let soak until raisins are plump, about 30 minutes.

2. Divide dough in half. Place one half in refrigerator while you work with the other. Roll into a rectangle 12 inches long and 8 inches wide. Spread with half the pastry cream and sprinkle with half the cinnamon. Dot with half the raisins and roll up jelly-roll fashion. Pinch the bottom flap to seal. Cut the roll in one-inch slices and place on a greased baking sheet about 1½ inches apart. Press with your hands to flatten slightly.

3. Repeat with the other half of the dough. Let rise in a warm place until doubled in bulk, from 45 minutes to an hour. Brush with beaten egg and bake in a preheated 425 degree oven for 12 to 15 minutes, until golden brown.

Pastry Cream

Makes approx. 1 cup

2½ Tbsp cornstarch
1 cup milk
1 egg
1 egg yolk
¼ cup sugar
2 Tbsp. butter

1. Dissolve cornstarch in ¼ cup cold milk. Add egg and egg yolk and mix until smooth.

2. Heat remaining milk with sugar and butter until it comes to a boil. Pour boiling milk into egg mixture in a thin stream, stirring constantly.

3. Return the mixture to the pan, continue stirring, and bring once more to a boil. Boil for 30 seconds to cook the cornstarch. Pour into a bowl and chill until needed. Just before using, beat the pastry cream with a wooden spoon, since it becomes stiff when cold.

This is a rich, moist coffee cake with the enticing addition of chocolate swirls. If you can keep them from disappearing, slices of this coffee cake make good French toast.

Chocolate Babka

Makes 2 large loaves (8¼" × 4¼")

1 package fresh or
    dry yeast
½ cup warm water
3 Tbsp. sugar
3 eggs
5 Tbsp. shortening
2 Tbsp. softened butter
3 to 3½ cups
    all-purpose flour
½ tsp. salt
    Chocolate streusel
      (see recipe below)

1. In a large bowl, dissolve yeast in warm water. Add sugar, eggs, shortening and butter and mix together. Add 1½ cups flour and beat vigorously until smooth.

2. Add salt and enough remaining flour to make a smooth, soft dough. Knead until smooth and elastic.

3. Form dough into a ball and place in a buttered bowl. Turn it once to coat the surface of the dough with butter. Cover with a cloth and let rise in a warm, draft-free place until doubled in bulk, about 2 hours.

4. Punch the dough down and let it rest for five minutes. Roll into a rectangle 9 by 18 inches. Spread all but ½ cup chocolate streusel over the dough. Roll jelly-roll fashion so that you end up with a cylinder 18 inches long. Pinch the bottom flap to seal.

5. Cut the roll in half so that you have two nine-inch rolls. With the seam side down, place each roll in a large, greased loaf pan. Divide the remaining streusel between the two loaves and sprinkle it over the top. Let rise again until almost doubled, about 45 minutes.

6. Bake in a preheated 375 degree oven for 25 to 30 minutes.

Chocolate Streusel

⅓ cup sugar
1 cup flour
2 Tbsp. cocoa
1 tsp. cinnamon
½ cup finely chopped
    walnuts (optional)
⅓ cup melted butter

1. Mix all ingredients together until well blended.

I first tasted this cake at Michel's Restaurant at The Colony Surf Hotel in Honolulu. I was sipping kona coffee and gazing at the deep blue of the Pacific just a few yards from my table. As if to mock perfection, a waiter appeared with this kugelhopf, rich in butter and studded with rum-soaked raisins.

Makes one 8-inch tube cake

¼ cup finely chopped almonds
1 cup raisins
¼ cup dark Jamaican rum
½ lb. sweet butter
1¼ cups sugar
5 eggs
1 tsp. vanilla
2⅓ cups all-purpose flour
2½ tsp. baking powder
¾ tsp. salt

Michel's Kugelhopf

1. Butter an eight-inch kugelhopf mold and coat the bottom and sides with finely chopped almonds.

2. Soak the raisins in rum for 30 minutes.

3. Cream butter, add sugar, and beat until smooth. Beat in eggs and vanilla.

4. Sift flour, baking powder and salt together in a bowl. Add to egg mixture and mix just until smooth. Do not overbeat. Stir in raisins and rum and mix until combined.

5. Pour batter into prepared cake pan. Bake in a preheated 400 degree oven for 15 minutes. Reduce heat to 350 degrees and bake 30 to 35 minutes longer, until toothpick inserted in center of the cake comes out clean. If cake browns too quickly on top, cover loosely with aluminum foil and finish baking.

6. Let cake settle in pan for 10 to 15 minutes and turn out on a plate while still warm. Dust with powdered sugar if you like.

This is an excellent cornbread with a sweet taste of honey.

Makes one 9-inch square pan

1 egg
1 cup milk
⅓ cup honey
2 Tbsp. melted butter
1 cup all-purpose flour
¾ cup yellow cornmeal
1 Tbsp. baking powder
½ tsp. salt

Honey Cornbread

1. Beat egg. Mix with milk, honey, and melted butter.

2. Sift dry ingredients together and mix with liquids just until blended. Do not overmix.

3. Pour batter into a greased, nine-inch square pan. Bake in a preheated 425 degree oven for 18 to 20 minutes.

Since it can be made in a relatively short time, this lovely, golden brown cake is a good breakfast treat. The cake is cut in wedges before baking but maintains its original shape in the oven. After baking, it can be pulled apart in nice, neat pieces. You may increase the portions to twelve if you like since it is a rather large cake.

Raisin Scones

Makes one round loaf

3¼ cups all-purpose flour
5 tsp. baking powder
1 tsp. salt
5 Tbsp. sugar
5 Tbsp. butter
1 egg
1 cup milk
½ cup raisins
a little beaten egg

1. Sift flour, baking powder, salt, and sugar together in a bowl. Cut in butter until mixture looks like coarse meal.

2. Beat egg with milk and stir into dry ingredients with raisins. Mix until ingredients are well combined. You will have a soft, sticky dough.

3. Pat the dough into a nine-inch round, approximately ¾ inch thick. Place on a greased baking sheet and cut in eight wedges as you would a pie, but do not separate the pieces. Brush top with beaten egg.

4. Bake in a preheated 450 degree oven for 10 minutes. Reduce heat to 375 degrees and bake 15 to 20 minutes longer, until top is golden brown.

When I think of Ireland, I think of the fresh, wholesome food served at bed and breakfast inns in the Irish countryside. Most memorable is this coarse bread with a nutty whole wheat flavor, served with plenty of fresh, sweet butter and hot tea.

Irish Oatmeal Bread

One round loaf

⅔ cup steel-cut oatmeal
1¾ cups whole wheat flour
2 tsp. baking powder
1 tsp. salt
1 Tbsp. butter
½ cup milk
⅔ cup water

1. Preheat oven to 450 degrees.

2. Mix oatmeal, whole wheat flour, baking powder, and salt together in a bowl. Rub butter into dry ingredients with your fingers. Stir in milk and water and mix just until well blended. You will have a very sticky dough.

3. Pat dough into a greased 8- or 9-inch round cake pan and place in preheated oven. After 10 minutes, reduce oven temperature to 375 degrees and bake for 30 more minutes.

Bread is done when a toothpick inserted in the center comes out clean. Serve warm. This bread is also delicious one day old if it is toasted.

Note: If you cannot obtain steel-cut oatmeal, you may substitute 1 cup rolled oats. Pulverize them partially in a food processor or blender, just long enough to cut the oats into coarse meal.

Whole wheat flour gives these muffins a wholesome flavor.

Blueberry Muffins

Makes one dozen

1 cup all-purpose flour
4 tsp. baking powder
½ tsp. salt
½ cup sugar
¾ cup whole wheat flour
2 beaten eggs
1 cup milk
2 Tbsp. melted butter
1 cup blueberries

1. Sift white flour, baking powder, and salt together. Mix with sugar and whole wheat flour.

2. Mix eggs, milk, and melted butter together and stir into dry ingredients. Do not overmix.

3. Fold blueberries into batter. Fill greased muffin cups three-fourths full. Bake in a preheated 400 degree oven for 18 to 20 minutes.

These delicious muffins are packed with healthful ingredients.

Bran Muffins

Makes one dozen

½ cup all-purpose flour
½ tsp. salt
1¼ tsp. baking soda
1½ cups bran
½ cup whole wheat flour
1 egg
¾ cup yogurt
½ cup milk
½ cup molasses
2 Tbsp. melted butter
1 Tbsp. grated orange rind
⅓ cup raisins

1. Sift all-purpose flour, salt, and baking soda together in a bowl. Mix in bran and whole wheat flour.

2. Beat egg and combine with yogurt, milk, molasses, melted butter, and orange rind. Stir into dry ingredients just until blended. Do not overmix. Stir in raisins.

3. Fill greased muffin cups three-fourths full. Bake in a preheated 400 degree oven for 18 to 20 minutes.

This cake is best served warm. Other fruits such as peaches, plums, or pears are good, too.

Grandmother's Apple Cake

Makes one 9-inch cake

- 1   cup all-purpose flour
- 1   tsp. baking powder
- ⅛   tsp. salt
- 6   tsp. butter
- ¼   cup sugar
- 1   egg
- 3   to 4 Tbsp. milk
- 3   medium-sized apples, peeled and thickly sliced
- 3   Tbsp. sugar
- ½   tsp. cinnamon

1. Sift flour, baking powder, and salt together in a bowl. Cut in 4 teaspoons butter until mixture looks like coarse meal. Stir in ¼ cup sugar.

2. Beat egg with milk and combine with dry ingredients. Mix just until blended. Spread batter in a greased and floured nine-inch cake pan.

3. Arrange sliced apples in a circular pattern on top of the cake. Mix cinnamon with 3 tablespoons sugar and sprinkle over apples. Dot with remaining two teaspoons butter.

4. Bake in a preheated 425 degree oven for 20 to 25 minutes, until apples are tender and top is brown.

Brown sugar, whole wheat flour, and sour cream lend an exceptionally rich flavor to this moist banana bread.

Banana Nut Tea Bread

Makes 2 small loaves (7¼" × 3½") or 1 large loaf (8¼" × 4¼")

- 1   lb. ripe bananas (3 to 4 medium sized)
- ⅓   cup butter
- ¾   cup brown sugar
- 2   eggs
- 1   tsp. vanilla
- ½   cup sour cream
- ¾   cup whole wheat flour
- ¾   cup all-purpose flour
- ¾   tsp. baking powder
- ¾   tsp. baking soda
- ¼   tsp. salt
- ½   tsp. nutmeg
- ½   cup coarsely chopped walnuts

1. Mash bananas in a mixer, or puree in a food processor.

2. Cream butter with brown sugar and beat until light. Add mashed bananas, eggs, and vanilla. Beat until well blended. Stir in sour cream.

3. Sift dry ingredients together and combine with banana mixture, stirring until well blended. Fold in nuts and pour into greased and floured loaf pans.

4. Bake in a preheated 350 degree oven for 35 to 40 minutes for small loaves, 50 to 60 minutes for one large loaf. The top should be a deep brown color and a toothpick inserted in the center of the loaf should come out clean. Turn breads out of pans while still warm and cool on a wire rack.

Because of its long keeping qualities, this is a good bread for holiday gift giving.

Apricot Tea Bread

Makes 2 small loaves
(7¼" × 3½")

4	ounces dried apricots
1	whole orange
⅔	cup raisins
⅔	cup walnuts
1	cup sugar
2	cups all-purpose flour
1	tsp. baking soda
2	tsp. baking powder
	pinch salt
1	egg
2	Tbsp. melted butter
½	cup orange juice
½	tsp. vanilla

1. Coarsely grind apricots, the whole orange (including peel), raisins, and walnuts together in a grinder, or chop coarsely in a food processor. Stir in sugar.

2. Sift flour, baking soda, baking powder, and salt together.

3. Beat egg and add melted butter, orange juice, and vanilla. Stir in ground apricot mixture until well blended. Combine with sifted dry ingredients.

4. Divide batter between two greased and floured loaf pans. Bake in a preheated 350 degree oven for 25 to 30 minutes until tops are brown and a toothpick inserted in the center of the loaf comes out clean. Turn out of pans while still warm and cool on a wire rack.

This bread may also be baked in a small kugelhopf mold or ring pan for a pretty holiday cake. Glaze it with a mixture of powdered sugar and orange or lemon juice.

Cranberry Nut Bread

Makes 2 small loaves
(7¼" × 3½") or
1 large loaf (8¼" × 4¼")

2	cups all-purpose flour
1½	tsp. baking powder
½	cup sugar
⅓	cup butter
1	egg
¾	cup orange juice
1	tsp. grated orange rind
1	cup coarsely chopped cranberries
½	cup chopped pecans

1. Sift flour, baking powder, and sugar together in a bowl. Cut in butter until mixture looks like coarse meal.

2. Beat egg and combine with orange juice and orange rind. Stir into dry ingredients until just blended. Fold in cranberries and nuts and pour into greased and floured loaf pans.

3. Bake in a preheated 400 degree oven for 10 minutes. Reduce heat to 350 degrees and bake 15 to 20 minutes longer for small loaves, 25 to 30 minutes longer for one large loaf. Breads are done when tops are brown and a toothpick inserted in the center of the loaf comes out clean. Turn out of pans while still warm and cool on a wire rack.

Pineapple and zucchini are an unusual yet pleasing combination.

Pineapple Zucchini Bread

Makes 2 small loaves
(7¼" × 3½")

¾ cup butter
1 cup sugar
2 eggs
1 cup shredded zucchini
1 cup crushed pineapple
½ cup whole wheat flour
1½ cups all-purpose flour
1 tsp. baking soda
½ tsp. baking powder
¾ tsp. cinnamon
¼ tsp. nutmeg
½ tsp. salt
½ cup coarsely chopped walnuts
½ cup raisins

1. Cream butter with sugar and beat until light. Beat in eggs. Stir in zucchini and pineapple.

2. Sift dry ingredients together and stir into pineapple zucchini mixture. Mix until well combined. Fold in nuts and raisins and pour into greased and floured loaf pans.

3. Bake in a preheated 350 degree oven for 40 to 45 minutes, until tops are golden brown and a toothpick inserted in the center of the loaf comes out clean. Turn out of pans while still warm and cool on a wire rack.

Eggs, Omelets and Quiches

Although we generally reserve eggs for the breakfast table, they play an important role in the vegetarian diet. As a solid source of protein, egg dishes are satisfying for lunch and supper, too. A simple cheese omelet accompanied by a salad, French bread, and a glass of white wine; or a rolled souffle and a green vegetable, make light and informal meals. Huevos Rancheros, Egg Foo Yung, and Cheddar and Onion Pie are among the more substantial egg dishes.

The challenge of omelet making often discourages beginning cooks. Still, with practice, no trick will escape your mastery. Three elements of successful omelet making are the pan, the butter, and the eggs. The pan should be a special omelet pan and used only for this purpose. Season it according to the manufacturer's directions; and never, but never, wash it with soap and water. Simply wipe the pan clean with a paper towel after use and store it in its special place until next time. Clarified butter is many a chef's secret to a perfect omelet. Since all the liquids and solids have been removed from the butter, it may be heated to a very high temperature without burning. In the absence of clarified butter, a few drops of oil added to raw butter will improve the odds against sticking and burning. As for the eggs, beat them well with a fork until no separate traces of white or yolk remain. Overbeating or adding milk will produce tough results. Finally, remember, practice makes perfect.

An elegant spring breakfast or brunch idea. Serve with a chilled glass of rosé or dry white wine.

Eggs Jardinière

Serves 4

4 pieces of white toast, cut in quarters
1 lb. asparagus, blanched until tender
8 poached eggs
Hollandaise sauce

1. For each serving, place one piece of toast, cut in quarters, on a plate. Arrange asparagus over the top. Place two poached eggs over the asparagus and cover with Hollandaise. Garnish with chopped parsley.

Hollandaise Sauce

4 eggs yolks
4 tsp. water
1 cup melted butter
1 tsp. lemon juice
  salt and white pepper
    to taste

1. Combine egg yolks and water in the top part of a double boiler. With a wire whisk, beat until thick over hot water. Remove from heat and beat in melted butter a few table-spoons at a time, until all the butter has been absorbed. Beat in lemon juice, salt, and white pepper and taste for seasoning.

A substantial lunch or supper dish. Serve with Mexican hot chocolate and extra warmed tortillas.

Huevos Rancheros

Serves 6 to 8

12 corn tortillas
4 cups refried beans
12 fried eggs
2 cups Mexican tomato
    sauce
  thinly sliced Monterey
    jack cheese
  sliced avocado (optional)

1. Heat tortillas on a hot, ungreased griddle until warm. Spread a spoonful of beans on each tortilla and top with a fried egg. Cover with hot tomato sauce and a thin slice of cheese. Garnish with avocado slices.

Refried Beans

Makes 4 cups

1½ cups pinto beans
1 tsp. salt
  small piece of dried hot
    red pepper, such as
    pequin
5 Tbsp. oil
1 cup finely chopped
    onion
1 tsp. finely chopped
    garlic
1 medium tomato, finely
    chopped

1. Combine beans, salt, pepper, 1 tablespoon oil, and ½ cup of the chopped onion in a saucepan and cover with water. Bring to a boil, reduce heat, cover, and simmer until tender, about 1½ hours. Check beans every 30 minutes or so and add more water if necessary.

2. When beans are soft, taste and add more salt if needed. Cook for another 30 minutes, but do not add any more water.

3. Heat remaining ¼ cup oil in a skillet. Add the rest of the onions and the garlic and cook for about 3 minutes. Add chopped tomato and cook, stirring, for 5 more minutes.

4. Add beans to skillet in batches of about one cup and mash to a paste with a fork or the back of a wooden spoon. Continue to mash and cook the beans until thick. Taste again for salt.

Makes 2 to 2½ cups

4 ancho chiles
1 or 2 pequin chiles
    (optional)
1 cup boiling water
2 cups canned tomatoes,
    with juice
1 cup chopped onion
1 clove garlic, peeled
    and smashed
½ tsp. oregano
2 Tbsp. oil
    salt and pepper to taste
    small pinch sugar
1 Tbsp. finely chopped fresh
    coriander
1 Tbsp. red wine vinegar

Mexican Tomato Sauce

1. Wash ancho chiles in cold water and remove seeds and veins. Cover with boiling water and let soak for 25 to 30 minutes, until chiles are soft. If you like a very hot sauce, prepare a few pequin chiles in the same way and soak with the other chiles. Wash hands well with soap and water.

2. Combine soaked chiles in blender with the tomatoes, onion, garlic and oregano. Puree until smooth.

3. Heat oil in a skillet and add blended sauce. Cook, stirring often, for 5 minutes. Season with salt, pepper, sugar, chopped coriander and vinegar.

This also makes a delicious omelet filling, plain, or with a slice of Swiss cheese.

Serves 6

2 Tbsp. olive oil
1 tsp. finely chopped garlic
2 cups thinly sliced onions
2 cups green or sweet, red
    peppers, sliced in
    thin julienne
2 cups canned tomatoes,
    with juice
½ tsp. basil
    salt and pepper to taste
    bay leaf
12 eggs
12 slices French bread,
    toasted
    black olives
    chopped parsley

Eggs Piperade

1. Heat oil in a skillet. Add garlic and onions and cook until onions start to wilt. Add peppers and tomatoes. Break up tomatoes with a wooden spoon as mixture cooks. Add basil, bay leaf, salt, and pepper and continue to cook until vegetables are tender, 15 to 20 minutes. Taste for seasoning.

2. Poach or fry eggs and arrange on toast on individual serving dishes. Cover with sauce and garnish with halved black olives and chopped parsley.

8 poached eggs
4 *english muffins, halved*
   and toasted
2 Tbsp. oil
½ tsp. finely chopped garlic
4 Tbsp. finely sliced
   scallions
½ lb. sliced mushrooms
1 large tomato, peeled
   and chopped
2 Tbsp. dry white wine
½ cup water
1 tsp. lemon juice
2 tsp. tomato paste
   pinch thyme
   salt and pepper to taste
1 Tbsp. chopped parsley

A hearty Sunday breakfast:

Eggs New Orleans

1. Heat oil in a skillet. Add garlic and scallions and cook 3 minutes. Add mushrooms and cook until they begin to brown. Add chopped tomato, white wine, water, lemon juice, tomato paste, thyme, salt, and pepper. Simmer for 10 minutes and stir in chopped parsley. Taste for seasoning.

2. Arrange poached eggs on toasted muffins on individual serving plates (2 eggs per person). Pour the sauce over the eggs and sprinkle with more chopped parsley.

The following instructions apply to all omelets. Be sure to have your eggs well scrambled, your filling hot and ready, and the serving plates standing by.

GENERAL OMELET INSTRUCTIONS

1. Beat 2 to 3 eggs well with a fork, until there are no separate traces of white or yolk. Have the filling ready.

2. Heat 2 tablespoons *clarified butter*, or a mixture of butter and oil, in an omelet pan over medium to high heat, until almost smoking. (Use a 7-inch omelet pan for a two-egg omelet, a 10-inch pan for a larger one.)

3. Pour eggs into pan and start scrambling (use a plastic fork to keep from scratching the pan). Scramble while you shake the pan back and forth, until the eggs start to set but are still slightly soft.

4. Spread the filling or cheese down the center of the omelet and continue to shake the pan back and forth until the eggs are set.

5. Fold one third of the omelet over the filling. Slide the remaining "flap" onto the serving plate and quickly tilt the pan upside down so that the folds of the omelet are on the bottom.

Oriental Omelet

Filling for 4 omelets

2   Tbsp. oil
½   tsp. finely chopped garlic
1   Tbsp. finely sliced
        scallions
⅓   cup celery, sliced
        on the diagonal
¼   lb. spinach, washed and
        stemmed
1½   cups sliced mushrooms
¼   cup sliced water
        chestnuts
¼   cup sliced bamboo shoots
1   Tbsp. soy sauce
1   tsp. cornstarch
2   Tbsp. water
½   tsp. Chinese sesame oil
¼   cup sliced, toasted
        almonds

1. Heat oil in a skillet. Add garlic and scallions and cook 2 minutes. Add celery, spinach, and mushrooms and continue to cook over high heat, stirring constantly, until vegetables are almost tender.

2. Add water chestnuts, bamboo shoots, and soy sauce. Dissolve cornstarch in water and add to vegetables. Cook 1 minute and stir in sesame oil. Remove from heat and keep warm until ready to use.

3. Using two eggs per omelet, follow instructions for general omelet making. Sprinkle each omelet with toasted almonds.

This omelet filling is full of the fresh taste of the garden.

Summer Garden Omelet

Filling for 4 omelets

½   lb. green beans, cut in
        one-inch pieces
        (about 1½ cups)
2   Tbsp. olive oil
1   tsp. finely chopped garlic
2   Tbsp. chopped onion
½   pint cherry tomatoes,
        halved
1   Tbsp. chopped fresh basil
        salt and pepper to taste
        sliced Monterey jack or
        Muenster cheese
        (optional)

1. Blanch green beans in boiling, salted water until tender.

2. Heat oil in a skillet. Add garlic and onion and cook 2 minutes. Add blanched green beans, cherry tomatoes, and basil. Reduce heat, cover, and cook gently for about 5 minutes, until tomatoes are soft. Add salt and pepper and taste for seasoning.

3. Using two eggs per omelet, follow instructions for general omelet making. Place one or two slices of cheese over filling if you like.

Here is another delicious garden-to-table omelet. Try it with a slice of Swiss cheese.

Omelet Provencal

Filling for 4 omelets

3 cups diced eggplant
2 Tbsp. olive oil
¾ tsp. finely chopped garlic
¾ cup finely chopped onion
2 small tomatoes, peeled and chopped
1 Tbsp. finely chopped parsley
  salt and pepper to taste

1. Cut eggplant in ½-inch dice, sprinkle with salt, and let drain on paper towels for 15 to 20 minutes.

2. Heat oil in a small skillet. Add garlic and onion and cook for 3 minutes. Add eggplant, cook 5 minutes and add chopped tomatoes. Add parsley, salt, and pepper and simmer for 10 to 15 minutes, until vegetables are tender. Taste for seasoning.

3. Using 2 eggs per omelet, follow instructions for general omelet making.

A few tablespoons of sherry or white wine cooked with the mushrooms add a nice touch to this simple but always popular omelet.

Mushroom and Sour Cream Omelet

Filling for 4 omelets

2 Tbsp. butter
½ lb. sliced mushrooms
  salt and pepper to taste
4 heaping Tbsp. sour cream
  chopped parsley for garnish

1. Heat butter in a small skillet. Add sliced mushrooms and cook until mushrooms start to brown. Season with salt and pepper.

2. Using two eggs per omelet, follow instructions for general omelet making. Spoon one fourth of the sauteed mushrooms in the center of the omelet. Garnish with a generous spoonful of sour cream and chopped parsley.

Italian in origin, this versatile "pancake" omelet incorporates the filling right into the eggs. A frittata can be made in individual size servings, or in one large pan and cut in wedges convenient for serving a large number of people. Here are just a few of the possible vegetable combinations.

Spinach Frittata

4 frittatas

1   10-ounce package fresh
     spinach
     salt and pepper
8   eggs
8   Tbsp. butter
4   tsp. finely minced shallots
4   Tbsp. freshly grated
     Parmesan cheese

1. Wash and stem spinach. Blanch in boiling, salted water until tender and drain well. Chop coarsely and season with salt and pepper.

2. Beat eggs well and add chopped, cooked spinach.

3. Heat 2 tablespoons butter in a 7-inch omelet pan. Add 1 teaspoon shallots and cook 1 minute. Add one fourth of the spinach and egg mixture and scramble, shaking the pan back and forth, until the eggs begin to set. Sprinkle with 1 table-spoon grated Parmesan and run under a hot broiler for a few moments to melt the cheese and finish cooking the eggs. Keep warm while you repeat procedure to make the remaining frittatas. Serve open-faced.

If you like, omit the Swiss cheese in this recipe and broil the omelet plain until puffed and golden. Garnish with sour cream and chopped parsley.

Potato Frittata

Makes 4 frittatas

2   medium size potatoes
     salt and pepper
8   eggs
8   Tbsp. butter
4   Tbsp. finely chopped
     scallions
4   ounces grated Swiss
     cheese, or 4 heaping
     Tbsp. sour cream
     chopped parsley for
     garnish

1. Boil potatoes until tender. Peel and grate coarsely. Season with plenty of salt and pepper.

2. Beat eggs well and mix with grated potatoes.

3. Heat 2 tablespoons butter in a 7-inch omelet pan. Add 1 tablespoon chopped scallions and cook 1 minute. Add one-fourth of the egg and potato mixture and scramble, shaking the pan back and forth, until the eggs begin to set.

4. Sprinkle the top with grated cheese and run under a hot broiler for a few moments, to melt the cheese and finish cooking the eggs. Keep warm while you repeat procedure to make the remaining frittatas. Sprinkle with chopped parsley and serve open-faced.

Egg Foo Yung

Serves 4

3   dried Chinese
      mushrooms
2   Tbsp. oil
½   cup shredded bamboo
      shoots
⅓   cup sliced water
      chestnuts
⅓   cup finely shredded
      scallions
½   cup green peas
8   eggs
1   Tbsp. soy sauce
8   Tbsp. butter or oil

1. Cover mushrooms with boiling water and soak until tender, 25 to 30 minutes. Slice in thin slivers.

2. Heat oil in a skillet. Add mushrooms, bamboo shoots, water chestnuts, scallions, and peas, and cook, stirring occasionally for 4 to 5 minutes. Cool briefly.

3. Beat eggs with soy sauce and add cooked vegetables.

4. Heat 2 tablespoons butter in a 7-inch omelet pan. Add one-fourth of the egg and vegetable mixture and scramble, shaking the pan back and forth, until the eggs begin to set and the bottom starts to brown. Turn over and brown on the other side. Keep warm while you repeat procedure to make the remaining omelets.

You may adopt this basic formula for quiche to your own choice of filling. Some good combinations are: Swiss cheese with sautéed mushrooms and shallots; sharp Cheddar cheese with broccoli or cauliflower; and Gruyère cheese with blanched and chopped spinach. Even though they bake in the quiche, the vegetables will not be tender unless they are blanched first. A tablespoon of flour mixed with juicy vegetables, such as spinach and mushrooms, will help bind the filling and produce a firmer quiche.

Basic Quiche

Makes one 9-inch pie

½   recipe plain or
      whole wheat pastry
3   eggs
1   cup cream
1   cup milk
¾   tsp. salt
      pinch pepper
4   ounces grated cheese,
      approximately 1¼
      cups
1¼ cups blanched vegetables,
      cut in bite-sized
      pieces

1. Line a nine-inch pie pan with pastry. Cover with a sheet of aluminum foil and fill the pie with dried beans. Bake the crust in a preheated 350 degree oven for 15 minutes. The beans will help the crust hold its shape while baking. Remove the foil and beans. The beans may be set aside and reused for other pie shells.

2. Beat eggs. Add milk and cream. Add salt, pepper, and grated cheese and mix together.

3. Line the bottom of the prebaked pie crust with vegetables. Pour in the cheese and egg mixture and bake in a preheated 350 degree oven for 35 to 40 minutes, until top is light brown and custard is set (knife inserted in center comes out clean). Cool quiche for 10 to 15 minutes before slicing and serving.

This quiche is rich and creamy.

Three Cheese Quiche with Herbs

One nine-inch pie

½ recipe plain or
  whole wheat pastry
1 Tbsp. butter
⅓ cup finely chopped
  scallions
3 eggs
1 cup milk
1 cup cream
¾ tsp. salt
  pinch pepper
1 Tbsp. finely chopped
  parsley
½ tsp. basil
⅓ cup freshly grated
  Parmesan cheese
¾ cup grated
  Fontina cheese
3 ounces cream cheese,
  cut in small cubes

1. Prebake pie shell as described in step number one of basic quiche.

2. Heat butter in a small skillet and sauté scallions 1 minute.

3. Beat eggs. Add milk and cream. Stir in salt, pepper, parsley, basil, cooked scallions, and three cheeses.

4. Pour into prebaked pie shell and bake in a preheated 350 degree oven for 35 to 40 minutes, until top is light brown and custard is set (knife inserted in center comes out clean). Cool for 10 to 15 minutes before slicing and serving.

Rich with tomatoes, onion, and cheese, this quiche lives up to its nickname of "pizza" quiche.

Quiche Nicoise

One nine-inch pie

½ recipe plain or
  whole wheat pastry
2 Tbsp. olive oil
1 tsp. finely chopped garlic
4 cups thinly sliced onions
1 cup canned tomatoes
1 Tbsp. tomato paste
1 egg
¾ cup cream
½ tsp. salt
  pinch pepper
1 Tbsp. finely chopped
  parsley
4 ounces grated Swiss
  cheese
  about 10 black olives,
  halved

1. Prebake pie shell as described in step number one of basic quiche.

2. Heat oil in a skillet. Add garlic and cook for 1 minute. Add onions and cook over medium heat, stirring occasionally, until onions are tender, 8 to 10 minutes. Add canned tomatoes and break them up with a wooden spoon. Add tomato paste and cook for 5 more minutes. Remove from heat.

3. Beat egg in a bowl. Mix in cream, salt, pepper, parsley, and grated cheese. Stir in tomato mixture. Pour into partially baked pie shell and dot with halved olives. Bake in a preheated 350 degree oven for 40 to 45 minutes.

This quiche has an interesting texture since the "buttery" cheese sinks to the bottom, leaving a smooth and light custard on the top.

Quiche Hollandaise

Makes one 9-inch pie

½ recipe plain pastry
1 Tbsp. caraway seeds
1 Tbsp. butter
½ cup finely chopped onions
3 eggs
1 cup milk
1 cup cream
½ tsp. salt
  pinch pepper
4 ounces Edam or Gouda cheese, cut in small dice, about 1 cup
4 tsp. Dijon mustard

1. Roll pastry into a circle and sprinkle with caraway seeds. Press the seeds into the dough with a rolling pin and line a 9-inch pie plate with the dough. Prebake pie shell as described in step number one of Basic Quiche.

2. Heat butter in a skillet. Add onions and cook until clear, about 3 minutes. Remove from heat.

3. Beat eggs in a bowl. Add milk, cream, salt, and pepper and blend well. Stir in diced cheese and cooked onions.

4. Spread mustard on the bottom of the partially baked pie shell and pour in the filling. Bake in a preheated 350 degree oven for 40 to 45 minutes, until lightly browned on top and knife inserted in center of the custard comes out clean.

This filling and delicious quiche has a rich crust that does not have to be rolled out.

Cheddar and Onion Pie

One nine-inch pie

Crust:

¼ lb. butter
1 cup flour

Filling:

1 Tbsp. butter
3 cups thinly sliced onions
1 Tbsp. flour
1¼ cups milk
2 eggs
½ tsp. salt
  pinch pepper
½ lb. sharp cheddar, grated

1. Cut butter into flour until well blended. Press into bottom and sides of a nine-inch pie pan.

1. Heat butter in a skillet. Add onions and cook until soft but not browned, about 10 minutes.

2. Mix flour with cold milk until smooth. Stir in eggs, salt, pepper, and grated cheese. Add cooked onions and pour into pie shell. Bake in a preheated 350 degree oven for 40 minutes, until top is nicely browned.

Zucchini Quiche

Makes one nine-inch pie

½ recipe plain or whole
  wheat pastry
2 Tbsp. oil
1 tsp. finely chopped garlic
4 Tbsp. finely chopped
  onion
2½ cups grated zucchini
2 tsp. flour
2 eggs
¾ cup milk
¾ cup cream
½ tsp. salt
  pinch black pepper
½ cup grated Swiss cheese
½ cup grated Parmesan
  cheese

1. Prebake pie shell as described in step number one of the basic quiche.

2. Heat oil in a skillet. Add garlic and onion and cook 3 to 4 minutes. Add grated zucchini and cook gently for 5 to 8 minutes. Stir in flour.

3. Beat eggs in a bowl. Add milk, cream, salt, and pepper and blend well. Stir in grated cheeses and cooked zucchini.

4. Pour filling into pie shell and bake in a preheated 350 degree oven for 40 to 45 minutes.

In spite of the mystique that surrounds them, soufflés are simple to make. The basis is a thick béchamel sauce enriched with egg yolks and combined with cheese or a vegetable puree. Beaten egg whites are gently folded in at the last minute and the soufflé is baked in a hot oven for about a half an hour. The base may be prepared ahead and the egg whites beaten and added just before baking time.

Cheese Soufflé

Serves 4 to 6

¾ cup milk
3 Tbsp. butter
4 Tbsp. flour
6 egg yolks
½ tsp. salt
  pinch cayenne pepper
4 ounces grated cheese
  (Parmesan, Swiss, or
  a combination)
1 tsp. dry mustard
6 egg whites

1. Preheat oven to 375 degrees. Butter and flour a 2-quart soufflé mold.

2. Bring milk to a boil in a small saucepan.

3. Melt butter, stir in flour, and cook for 2 minutes without browning the flour. Add boiling milk, ¼ cup at a time, and stir until thick and smooth with a wire whisk.

4. Beat in egg yolks one at a time, until smooth. Stir in salt, cayenne, cheese, and mustard.

5. Beat egg whites until stiff, but not dry. Gently fold one-half beaten egg whites into yolk mixture. Fold in remaining whites and pour into prepared soufflé dish. Bake 30 to 35 minutes. Serve immediately.

The unusual combination of fresh pumpkin and cheese in this soufflé has a lovely and delicate flavor.

Pumpkin Soufflé

Serves 4 to 6

¾ cup milk
3 Tbsp. butter
¼ cup flour
5 egg yolks
¾ cup freshly grated
   Parmesan cheese
1½ cups fresh pumpkin
   puree
½ tsp. salt
   pinch cayenne pepper
5 egg whites

1. Preheat oven to 375 degrees. Butter and flour a 2-quart soufflé mold.

2. Bring milk to a boil in a small saucepan.

3. Melt butter, stir in flour, and cook 2 minutes without browning the flour. Add boiling milk, ¼ cup at a time, and stir until thick and smooth with a wire whisk. Remove from heat.

4. Beat in egg yolks one at a time, until smooth. Stir in grated cheese, pumpkin, salt, and pepper.

5. Beat egg whites until stiff but not dry. Gently fold one-half beaten egg whites into yolk mixture. Fold in remaining whites and pour into prepared soufflé dish. Bake 30 to 35 minutes. Serve immediately.

Rolled soufflés may be prepared in advance and offer an interesting change of pace from the traditional soufflé. The batter is spread on a cookie sheet, baked flat, filled, rolled, and served with a complementary sauce. Here are but two examples of this type of soufflé: an elegant asparagus-filled soufflé with a Mornay sauce and a robust zucchini soufflé with a tomato sauce.

Rolled Asparagus Soufflé

Serves 4 to 6

¾ cup milk
3 Tbsp. butter
3 Tbsp. flour
6 egg yolks
½ tsp. salt
   pinch cayenne pepper
½ tsp. dill weed
3 Tbsp. freshly grated
   Parmesan cheese
6 egg whites
¼ lb. asparagus
4 ounces grated Swiss
   cheese
   Mornay sauce

1. Preheat oven to 375 degrees. Butter and flour a jelly roll pan or cookie sheet, approximately 12 by 18 inches, and ½ inch deep. Line it with buttered paper.

2. Bring milk to a boil in a small saucepan.

3. Melt butter, stir in flour, and cook for 2 minutes without browning the flour. Add boiling milk, ¼ cup at a time, and stir until thick and smooth with a wire whisk.

4. Beat in egg yolks one at a time, until smooth. Stir in salt, pepper, dill weed, and Parmesan cheese.

5. Beat egg whites until stiff, but not dry. Gently fold one half beaten egg whites into yolk mixture. Fold in remaining whites and spread out evenly on prepared pan. Bake in preheated oven for 12 to 15 minutes, until lightly browned on top. Cool 5 minutes.

6. Cook asparagus in boiling, salted water until tender. Drain.

7. Invert pan on counter and remove paper. Sprinkle with grated Swiss cheese and lay the asparagus along the shorter edge of the rectangle. Roll jelly-roll fashion.

8. With the seam on the bottom, place the roll in a buttered baking dish. Pour the hot Mornay sauce over it and run under a hot broiler until sauce puffs and starts to brown. Slice and serve.

Mornay Sauce

2 cups milk
3 Tbsp. butter
3 Tbsp. flour
  salt and pepper
1 egg yolk
½ cup heavy cream,
  whipped

1. Bring milk to a boil in a small saucepan.

2. Melt butter, stir in flour, and cook for 2 minutes without browning the flour. Add boiling milk, ¼ cup at a time, and stir until thick and smooth with a wire whisk.

3. Break egg yolk into a bowl and beat in the hot sauce little by little (to avoid cooking the egg too quickly and curdling).

4. Fold in whipped cream and taste for seasoning.

Serves 4 to 6

1 Tbsp. oil
½ tsp. finely chopped garlic
1½ cups grated zucchini
½ tsp. oregano
¾ cup milk
3 Tbsp. butter
3 Tbsp. flour
6 egg yolks
½ tsp. salt
  pinch pepper
⅓ cup freshly grated
  Parmesan cheese
6 egg whites
2 cups tomato sauce
  (See following page.)

Zucchini Soufflé Roll

1. Preheat oven to 375 degrees. Butter and flour a jelly roll pan or cookie sheet, approximately 12 by 18 inches and ½ inch deep. Line it with buttered paper.

2. Heat oil in a skillet. Add garlic, zucchini, and oregano and cook for 5 minutes over low heat, stirring occasionally.

3. Bring milk to a boil in a small saucepan.

4. Melt butter, stir in flour and cook for 2 minutes without browning the flour. Add boiling milk, ¼ cup at a time, and stir until thick and smooth with a wire whisk.

5. Beat in egg yolks one at a time, until smooth. Stir in salt, pepper, Parmesan, and zucchini. *(See following page.)*

6. Beat egg whites until stiff, but not dry. Gently fold one-half beaten egg whites into yolk mixture. Fold in remaining whites and spread out evenly on prepared pan. Bake in preheated oven for 12 to 15 minutes, until lightly browned on top. Cool 5 minutes.

7. Invert pan on counter and remove paper. Spread with ¾ cup tomato sauce and roll jelly-roll fashion.

8. With the seam on the bottom, place the roll in a buttered baking dish and cover with foil. Bake in a preheated 350 degree oven for 10 to 15 minutes, until hot all the way through. Remove from oven and cover with remaining hot tomato sauce. Sprinkle with chopped parsley, slice, and serve.

Tomato Sauce

Makes 2 cups

2	Tbsp. olive oil
½	cup chopped onion
½	tsp. finely chopped garlic
2	cups canned tomatoes, with juice
½	tsp. oregano
½	tsp. basil
	small pinch sugar
1	bay leaf
	pinch crushed fennel
	salt and pepper to taste

1. Heat oil in a saucepan. Add chopped onion and garlic and cook 5 minutes, until onion is tender. Coarsely chop tomatoes, or break up with a wooden spoon. Add to onions with oregano, basil, pinch of sugar, bay leaf, fennel, salt, and pepper. Simmer for 25 minutes and taste for seasoning.

Sandwiches and Snacks

 The invention of the sandwich revolutionized traditional eating habits in America. Luncheon as known at the beginning of this century is now reserved for weddings, special occasions, or a small segment of society with time on their hands.

Today, the average working American spends from thirty minutes to an hour for lunch, just enough time to "grab a sandwich." The vegetarian must solve the dilemma of what to put between those two slices of bread aside from egg salad. The following group of recipes explores America's grilled cheese theme, from the popular avocado-sprout-and-cheese sandwich to a pepper and onion smothered "paisano." Foreign neighbors inspire other sandwich ideas such as Mexican chimichangas, Israeli felafel, and Italian calzone. Although these require more preparation time, some may be made in advance and assembled at the last moment.

This cheese sandwich is a favorite at the Tao Restaurant.

Open Heart Sandwich

whole wheat bread
sliced avocado
thinly sliced red onion
alfalfa sprouts
sliced colby cheese
lettuce
tomato
mayonnaise

For each sandwich, toast or grill 2 slices of bread. Arrange sliced avocado on one piece of toast and top with onion, sprouts and cheese. Run under a hot broiler until cheese is melted. Spread mayonnaise on the other piece of toast and top with lettuce and tomato. Serve open-faced.

Melted Cheese Sandwich Landaise

2   Tbsp. oil
1   tsp. finely chopped garlic
1   large onion, sliced
1   large green pepper, sliced
1   bay leaf
    salt and pepper to taste
1½ cups canned tomatoes,
        with juice
    sliced French bread
    sliced Swiss cheese

1. Heat oil in a skillet. Add garlic, onion, pepper, bay leaf, salt, and pepper. Mash tomatoes against the sides of a strainer to break them up. Add tomatoes and juice to peppers and onions. Simmer 10 to 15 minutes, until thick.

2. Toast French bread and spoon the Landaise sauce over the top. Cover with sliced cheese and melt under the broiler.

The Big Veg was the mainstay of the Tao menu in its early years. All manner of leftovers can be incorporated into the mix. I like mine on toast with sliced tomato, Bermuda onion and ketchup!

Makes 8 veggie burgers

"Big Veg"

1½ cups soy beans
1   cup finely chopped
        onions
1   tsp. finely chopped garlic
¾   cup grated carrots
¼   cup ketchup
1   egg
1   tsp. salt
    pinch cayenne pepper
1   Tbsp. Worcestershire
        sauce, or soy sauce
½   tsp. thyme
1   cup bread crumbs
    flour for breading
    bread crumbs for
        breading
    beaten egg
    oil for frying

1. Cover soy beans with water and soak overnight. Cook until tender, about 1½ hours. Drain and mash to a paste with a food mill or food processor.

2. Mix beans with remaining ingredients and taste for seasoning. Form into eight patties.

3. Dredge patties lightly in flour, coat with beaten egg and roll in breadcrumbs. Heat about ¼-inch oil in a heavy iron skillet or frying pan and fry until crisp and brown on both sides.

A delicious and filling hot sandwich. Use a thick tomato sauce, such as a pizza sauce.

Eggplant Sub

eggplant
flour
beaten egg
breadcrumbs
oil for frying
French bread
garlic cloves
tomato sauce
sliced mozzarella cheese

1. Slice eggplant lengthwise into ½-inch thick slices. Score with the point of a sharp knife, sprinkle with salt and let drain on paper towels for ½ hour. Dredge eggplant in flour, coat with egg, and roll in breadcrumbs. Fry in ¼-inch hot oil until crisp and brown on both sides. Drain on absorbent paper.

2. Cut French bread in 8-inch lengths and split in half. Toast under the broiler and rub with garlic cloves.

3. Arrange eggplant slices on toasted bread, cover with hot tomato sauce and top with sliced mozzarella. Heat for a few minutes under the broiler to melt the cheese.

Another notable rendition of the grilled cheese sandwich.

Paisano Sandwich

Serves 4

2   Tbsp. oil
2   green peppers, cut
        in julienne
1   large red onion, sliced
1   tsp. finely chopped garlic
½   tsp. basil
½   tsp. oregano
    whole wheat or French
        bread
    sliced mozzarella cheese

1. Heat oil in a skillet. Add peppers, onions, garlic, basil, and oregano and cook until vegetables are tender, 8 to 10 minutes.

2. Toast bread; or cut French bread into 6-inch lengths, split and toast under the broiler. Spoon peppers and onions over toasted bread, top with sliced mozzarella, and melt cheese under the broiler.

Here is a pizza sandwich. Like pizza, the filling may be varied—for example, try a Bologna style calzone filled with artichoke hearts and hard-boiled eggs, baked, and topped with a robust tomato sauce.

Calzoni

Serves 8

1 recipe Basic Italian
    Bread
    olive oil
2½ cups sliced red onion
¼ cup capers
10 to 12 sliced black olives
1 or 2 sliced tomatoes
½ lb. thinly sliced
    mozzarella cheese
    rosemary

1. Make bread dough according to directions and let rise once. Punch down, divide in 8 pieces, and roll each piece into a ball. Let rest while you assemble the ingredients for the filling.

2. Cook red onions in 2 tablespoons olive oil until tender. Assemble capers, black olives, tomatoes, and cheese.

3. With a rolling pin, flatten each ball of dough into a 9-inch circle. Brush with olive oil and sprinkle with rosemary. Place some cooked, red onion, capers, and black olives on one half of the circle. Cover them with tomato slices and mozzarella cheese.

4. Fold the circle in half and pinch the edges together securely. Place on an oiled baking sheet, brush with more olive oil, and prick with a fork. Repeat with remaining dough and filling. Bake in a preheated 450 degree oven for 25 to 30 minutes, until crust turns a golden brown.

Panzarotti are deep fried ravioli usually made with cheese. Here they are made larger with the addition of spinach.

Panzarotti

Makes 18 turnovers

¼ lb. diced mozzarella
    cheese, about ¾ cup
¾ cup ricotta cheese
⅓ cup freshly grated
    Parmesan cheese
1 egg
1 Tbsp. finely chopped
    parsley
½ tsp. salt
    pinch pepper
¼ tsp. finely chopped garlic
½ cup cooked, chopped
    spinach
1 recipe semolina pasta
    oil for frying

1. Mix cheeses, egg, parsley, salt, pepper, and garlic together until smooth. Stir in spinach and taste for seasoning.

2. Roll pasta dough into a thin sheet and cut in 4½-inch circles. Spread a rounded tablespoon of filling on half of each circle. Moisten the edges with water and press firmly together. Deep fry in hot oil until golden brown.

These deep fried morsels are Israeli in origin and are made from a spicy chick pea paste. They may be served as an appetizer, an accompaniment to drinks, or a sandwich—enclosed in pita bread and garnished with Tabasco, tahini sauce and sliced cucumbers.

Felafel

Serves 6 to 8

½ lb. or 1¼ cups dry chick peas (garbanzo beans)
1 tsp. finely chopped garlic
¾ cup finely chopped onion
1 tsp. ground cumin
2 Tbsp. chopped fresh coriander or parsley
1 tsp. salt
pinch cayenne pepper
2 Tbsp. lemon juice
½ tsp. baking powder
approximately ½ cup flour
oil for frying

1. Soak chick peas overnight. Cook in boiling, salted water until tender, 1 to 1½ hours. Drain and mash to a paste in a food mill, blender or food processor.

2. Combine chick pea paste with remaining ingredients and form into balls about the size of walnuts. You should have approximately 35 balls.

3. Heat 2 inches oil in a heavy iron skillet or deep fryer. Test one ball and if it does not hold together well, add a little more flour to the mixture. Fry until golden brown.

For a Sandwich:

1. Warm pita bread in oven and cut in half. Fill pockets with hot felafel and garnish with a few drops of Tabasco, tahini sauce and sliced cucumbers.

Tahini Sauce

Makes one cup

½ cup sesame paste (tahini)
¾ tsp. finely chopped garlic
3 Tbsp. lemon juice
salt to taste
approximately ⅓ cup water

1. Mix all ingredients together until smooth. Taste for seasoning and serve with felafel.

These Mexican treats have often been compared to Chinese egg rolls but are really far more filling. The tortilla wrapper must not be fried too crisply or the crust will be tough.

Filling:

1½	*cups pinto beans*
1	*tsp. salt*
¼	*cup oil*
1½	*cups finely chopped onions*
1	*tsp. finely chopped garlic*
2	*tomatoes, peeled and chopped*
2	*or 3 dried, crumbled pequin peppers*
1	*cup grated Monterey jack cheese*

Chimichangas

1. Combine beans and salt in a saucepan with water to cover and bring to a boil. Reduce heat, cover and simmer until tender, about 1½ hours. Check beans every 30 minutes or so and add more water if necessary.

2. Heat oil in a large skillet. Add onions and garlic and cook until tender, about 5 minutes. Add tomatoes and crumbled peppers and cook 5 more minutes.

3. Add beans to skillet in batches of about 1 cup and mash to a paste with a fork or the back of a wooden spoon. Continue to mash and cook the beans until thick. Taste for seasoning. Stir in grated cheese.

½	*cup chopped onion*
2½	*cups canned tomatoes, with juice*
1	*clove garlic, peeled*
1	*tsp. ground cumin*
1	*tsp. oregano*
2	*Tbsp. oil*
1	*Tbsp. finely chopped parsley*
2	*dried, crumbled pequin peppers*
	salt and pepper
	small pinch sugar
1	*Tbsp. vinegar*

Tomato Sauce:

1. Combine onion, tomato, garlic, cumin, and oregano in a blender and puree until smooth. Heat oil in a skillet, add sauce, parsley, crumbled peppers, salt, pepper, and sugar and cook, stirring occasionally, for 5 minutes. Add vinegar and taste for seasoning. Thin with water if necessary. Keep warm while you fill tortillas.

Serves 6 or more

12 flour tortillas
    bean filling
    oil for frying
    tomato sauce
2   cups grated Monterey
    jack cheese
1   cup sour cream

To Assemble:

1. Place about ⅓ cup filling in the center of each tortilla. Fold the bottom flap up. Fold the sides in toward the center and roll up to form an envelope. Fasten securely with bamboo skewers or toothpicks.

2. Heat one inch oil in a heavy iron skillet or frying pan. Fry chimichangas, a few at a time, for about 2 minutes on each side, just until they start to brown. Do not fry too long or tortillas will be too crisp. Drain on paper towels and keep warm in the oven while you fry the rest.

3. Arrange the chimichangas on individual plates. Cover with sauce, sprinkle with grated cheese, and garnish with a spoonful of sour cream.

These pastries would usually be served as part of an Indian meal, which is not divided into courses. However, they are filling enough to be eaten alone as snacks, or as part of a light meal.

Samosas (Indian Deep Fried Pastries)

Makes 12 pastries

Dough:

1½ cups flour
½   tsp. salt
1   Tbsp. melted butter
½   cup water

Filling:

1   lb. potatoes
2   Tbsp. oil
⅓   cup chopped onion
1   tsp. grated fresh ginger
1   tsp. ground cumin
2   tsp. Indian curry spice
    mix (curry powder)
½   tsp. turmeric
1   tsp. salt
1   Tbsp. chopped fresh
    coriander
1   Tbsp. lemon juice
½   cup blanched green peas
    oil for frying

1. Combine flour and salt in a bowl and rub in melted butter with your fingers, until mixture is crumbly. Stir in water and knead dough until smooth. Cover and set aside while you make the filling.

1. Boil potatoes in their skins until tender. Cool. Peel and cut in ½-inch cubes.

2. Heat oil in a skillet. Add onions and cook until soft. Add cooked potatoes, spices, and lemon juice and cook 3 minutes, stirring to coat the potatoes with the spices. Stir in peas and taste for seasoning.

To Assemble:

1. Divide dough into 12 balls. With a rolling pin, flatten each ball into a 5-inch circle on a lightly floured surface. Brush half of each circle with oil and spread 2 tablespoons of filling over it. Fold the other half of the circle over the filling and press the edges together firmly to seal. Deep fry in hot oil until golden. Serve hot with chutney and raita.

Serve these Latin American treats with steaming bowls of black bean soup.

Makes 15 to 16 turnovers

Empanadas

Dough:

- 2 cups flour
- 1 tsp. salt
- 4 Tbsp. butter
- 4 Tbsp. shortening
- 5 Tbsp. water

1. Sift flour and salt together in a bowl. Cut in butter and shortening until well blended. Add water and mix to make a smooth dough. Cover and set aside while you make the filling.

Filling:

- 1 medium size acorn squash
- 2 Tbsp. oil
- 1 cup chopped onions
- ½ cup diced green pepper
- 1 cup corn, off the cob
- 1 tsp. paprika
- 1 tsp. ground cumin
- ½ tsp. chili powder
  salt and pepper to taste
- 2 or more dried hot red peppers, such as pequin
- 2 Tbsp. raisins
- 2 Tbsp. pitted green olives, cut in quarters
- 2 hard boiled eggs, cut in eighths

1. Cut squash in half lengthwise, scoop out seeds, and sprinkle with salt. Place in a baking dish with the cut side up. Pour ¼ inch water into the bottom of the dish and cover loosely with foil. Bake for 30 to 35 minutes, until the squash is tender but on the firm side. Cool.

2. Heat oil in a skillet. Add onions, green pepper, corn, paprika, cumin, chili powder, salt, and pepper. Crumble red peppers and add. Cook until vegetables are tender. Stir in raisins.

3. Peel cooled squash and cut in one-inch cubes. You should have about 3 cups.

4. Add squash and olives to skillet and stir until well mixed. Taste for seasoning.

To Assemble:

1. Roll dough into a thin sheet, slightly less than ⅛ inch thick. Cut in 5-inch circles. Spread about 2 Tbsp. filling over half of each circle and top with a wedge of hard boiled egg. Fold in half and press edges firmly together to seal.

2. Place empanadas on an ungreased baking sheet, brush with beaten egg, and bake in a preheated 400 degree oven for 15 to 20 minutes, until lightly browned.

Appetizers

In a time when the ever escalating pace of our lives has eclipsed the art of dining, the appetizer represents a moment of luxury: a pause to awaken our taste buds as well as our appetites, a moment to slow down and appreciate good food and good company.

Part of our enjoyment stems from the sheer visual beauty of the food as it is presented on the plate. In the haste of delivering the food to the table, too many cooks neglect this most important aspect. The simple touches—the frill of lettuce, the splash of cherry tomato, the gleam of lemon wedge—please the eye and raise the spirits. In choosing an appetizer, try to envision the color and texture of the dish as well as the taste. A large array of crudités served with eggplant caviar or white bean dip makes a pleasing accompaniment to a substantial main course such as Spinach Lasagne or Artichoke Ricotta Pie. The appetizer should complement, never overshadow, the meal that follows.

Although the recipes in this section make wonderful starters, do not limit yourself to serving them only as appetizers at the beginning of a meal. A hearty antipasto composed of caponata, vegetables a la Grecque, crudités, cheese, and crusty bread accompanied by bowls of gazpacho, makes a satisfying supper in the heat of the summer. Nori rolls or turnip sesame cakes served with a thick soup and a salad constitute yet another meal composed of appetizers.

Crudités are an assortment of raw vegetables that may be served as the crisp part of an hors d'oeuvre plate, with olives, pickles, devilled eggs, cheeses, or marinated vegetables. They may also be served with a sauce or a dip, such as this creamy avocado dip.

Makes 1 cup

> 1 ripe avocado
> 1 Tbsp. lemon juice
> 1 tsp. finely chopped onion
> ⅛ tsp. finely chopped garlic
> ½ cup sour cream
> salt and pepper to taste.

Crudités with Avocado Cream

1. Peel avocado and combine with remaining ingredients in a blender. Puree until smooth. Serve in a flat dish surrounded by vegetables.

Crudités

Choose vegetables for contrast in color and texture, as well as in taste. Cut them in sticks or bite-size pieces and crisp them in ice water for about a half an hour before serving.

Use any combination of the following: blanched broccoli, cauliflower, or green beans; carrots, cucumbers, zucchini, celery, or red and green peppers, cut in sticks; radish roses, cherry tomatoes, snow peas, frilled scallions, small whole mushrooms and watercress sprigs.

Often the simplest dish is the most difficult to prepare. To my mind, guacamole falls in this category. The avocado must be perfectly ripe and mashed to a paste with a fork, never reduced to the consistency of baby food in a food processor or blender. Although the Mexicans do not use it, I find lemon juice brings out the richness of the avocado and is as important as salt in seasoning the guacamole. Finally, the tomato must not be left in large chunks, but chopped to blend in with the texture of the rest of the dip.

Guacamole

Makes 1¼ cups

2   ripe avocadoes
1   tsp. finely chopped onion
2   Tbsp. olive oil
1ʹ small tomato, peeled and
      chopped
½   tsp. or more Tabasco, or
      finely chopped
      jalapeno pepper
2   Tbsp. lemon juice
      salt and pepper to taste

1. Peel avocadoes and mash with a fork. Stir in remaining ingredients and taste for seasoning.

Here is a dip that would go well in an hors d'oeuvre platter, with an antipasto, or with an assortment of crudités. Be sure that the beans are fully cooked so that the dip will be creamy.

White Bean Dip

Makes 3 cups

1 cup navy or other dry, white beans (2½ cups, cooked)
⅓ cup tahini (sesame paste)
½ tsp. finely chopped garlic
¼ cup lemon juice
¼ cup finely chopped onion
½ cup sour cream
¼ cup olive oil
1½ tsp. salt

1. Soak beans overnight. Cook until tender in boiling salted water. Drain and cool.

2. Combine all ingredients in a blender or food processor and puree until smooth. Taste for seasoning. Garnish with chopped parsley and serve with warmed pita bread.

This cold eggplant salad may be served as a component of an antipasto, or eaten plain with some good Italian bread.

Caponata (Italian Eggplant Salad)

Makes 3½ cups

2 medium eggplants (about 1 lb. each)
¼ cup olive oil
3 Tbsp. finely chopped onion
2 Tbsp. capers
¼ cup coarsely chopped black olives, preferably Greek
1 rib celery, diced
¼ cup tomato puree
2 tsp. tomato paste
2 Tbsp. red wine vinegar
1 Tbsp. chopped parsley
2 tsp. sugar
2 bay leaves
1 tsp. salt
½ cup water

1. Cut eggplant in ½-inch cubes. Sprinkle with salt and let drain on paper towels for ½ hour.

2. Heat olive oil in a large skillet. Add onion, eggplant, capers, olives, and celery and cook until onion is clear, about 7 minutes.

3. Add tomato puree, tomato paste, vinegar, chopped parsley, sugar, bay leaves, salt, and water. Cook over low heat, stirring occasionally, until tomato sauce turns a nice dark brown color, 30 to 40 minutes. Taste for seasoning.

4. Chill several hours or overnight. Serve cold with crusty French or Italian bread. Caponata will keep at least a week in a covered jar in the refrigerator.

Rich with olive oil and garlic, this dip is not for the faint-hearted. It is delicious with French bread or an assortment of crudités—as a first course or an accompaniment to drinks.

Eggplant Caviar

Makes 2½ cups

- 2 eggplants, about 1 lb. each
- 2 tsp. chopped onion
- 2 or more cloves garlic, finely chopped
- 1 large ripe tomato, peeled and seeded
- ½ cup olive oil
- 2 Tbsp. lemon juice
- 1½ tsp. salt
- ½ tsp. oregano

1. Slice eggplant in thick, lengthwise slices. With the point of a sharp knife, score the slices and sprinkle them with salt. Drain on paper towels for 30 minutes.

2. Place drained eggplant slices on an oiled baking sheet and broil for 15 to 20 minutes, until tender.

3. When cool enough to handle, pass the cooked eggplant through the medium blade of a grinder with onion, garlic, and tomato. (Or, chop finely with a knife or in a food processor.)

4. Combine chopped ingredients in a bowl and beat in olive oil in a thin stream. Beat in lemon juice, salt, and oregano. Taste for seasoning. Serve cold.

This is a Syrian eggplant dip flavored with sesame paste and lemon juice.

Baba Ganouj
(Syrian Eggplant and Tahini Dip)

Makes 2 cups

- 1 large eggplant (about 1½ lbs.)
- ½ cup tahini (sesame paste)
- 2 cloves garlic, finely chopped
- ¼ cup lemon juice
- 2 tsp. chopped onion
- salt to taste

1. Slice eggplant in thick, lengthwise slices. With the point of a sharp knife, score the slices and sprinkle with salt. Drain on paper towels for 30 minutes.

2. Place the drained eggplant slices on an oiled baking sheet and broil for 15 to 20 minutes, until tender.

3. Remove skins and combine eggplant in blender or food processor with remaining ingredients. Puree until smooth. Serve in a flat dish garnished with chopped parsley and accompanied by warm pita bread.

This chick pea spread makes a nice first course for a Syrian or Middle Eastern meal. Serve with pita bread and Greek olives.

Hummus

Makes 1½ cups

1 cup cooked chick peas
½ cup tahini (sesame paste)
2 garlic cloves, peeled and
    finely chopped
¼ cup water
¼ cup lemon juice
¾ tsp. ground cumin
¾ tsp. salt

1. Combine all ingredients in food processor or blender and puree until smooth. Taste for seasoning. Serve in a flat dish sprinkled with chopped parsley.

This is a delicious formula for marinating all sorts of vegetables. Artichokes, celery, fennel, leeks, small onions, cauliflower, broccoli, green beans, and zucchini are just some of the other possibilities. Most vegetables take longer to cook than mushrooms and should be blanched briefly before undergoing the marinating process.

Mushrooms a la Grecque

Makes 2 cups

1 lb. mushrooms
½ cup olive oil
¼ cup lemon juice
1¼ cups water
5 or 6 parsley stems
½ tsp. salt
8 to 10 peppercorns
¼ tsp. crushed fennel seeds
2 bay leaves
  zest of ½ lemon, cut in
    matchstick
¼ tsp. thyme

1. Wash mushrooms and cut off the tough ends of the stems. Halve or quarter them.

2. Combine remaining ingredients in a saucepan and bring to a boil. Simmer, covered, for 15 minutes.

3. Strain liquid through a fine sieve and return to saucepan. Bring to a boil again and add mushrooms. When liquid returns to the boil for the third time, stir and cook mushrooms for 3 more minutes.

4. Remove mushrooms with a slotted spoon and set aside in a bowl. Over high heat, reduce cooking liquid by one third. Cool to lukewarm and pour over mushrooms. Chill a few hours before serving, or serve at room temperature. Sprinkle with chopped parsley.

These Indian snacks are vegetables, deep-fried in a spicy batter made from chick pea flour. The following recipe for batter is somewhat mild. However, the hotness may be adjusted according to taste by the amount of red pepper used. Zucchini, cauliflower, spinach and potato are the vegetables most commonly used in making pekoras. You may use one or a combination of vegetables. Pay attention to the cooking time, since some vegetables will take longer than others.

Serves 6

2 cups chick pea flour
     (gram flour)
1 cup water
2 Tbsp. chopped fresh
     coriander
1 tsp. ground cumin
½ tsp. turmeric
    pinch cayenne pepper
    pinch baking soda
    juice of ½ lemon
    approx. 2 cups prepared
      vegetables (spinach,
      zucchini, cauli-
      flower, potato)
    oil for frying

Pekoras

1. Mix chick pea flour, water, coriander, cumin, turmeric, cayenne pepper, baking soda, and lemon juice together in a bowl. Set aside while you prepare the vegetables.

2. Cut zucchini in ¼-inch thick rounds. Break cauliflower in small florets. Clean spinach and break up the very large leaves. Peel potatoes and slice thin.

3. Heat 1½ to 2 inches oil in a heavy iron skillet or deep fryer. To test for the proper temperature, drop a little batter in the hot oil. If it rises to the top in about 15 seconds, the oil is ready. If the oil is too hot, the vegetables will brown on the outside without cooking on the inside. If it is too cool, they will absorb too much oil.

4. Dip the vegetables in batter and fry a few at a time in the hot oil, until golden brown. Keep the fried pekoras warm in a 300 degree oven while you finish frying. Serve hot with a garnish of chutney or raita.

I like this pâté because it looks pretty and has substance, too.

Country Pâté with a Cold Tomato Sauce

Makes 1 small loaf
(7¼″ × 3½″)

1   10-ounce package fresh
      spinach
1   Tbsp. butter
1   tsp. finely chopped garlic
¼   cup finely chopped
      onion
½   cup mozzarella cheese,
      cut in small cubes
½   cup freshly grated
      Parmesan cheese
⅓   cup carrots, diced small
      and blanched
2   Tbsp. diced pimiento
1   cup ricotta cheese
¼   cup cream
1   egg
      salt and freshly ground
      pepper

1. Wash and stem spinach. Steam just until wilted and squeeze dry in a towel. Chop coarsely and set aside.

2. Heat butter in a skillet and add garlic and onion. Cook briefly, until onions are clear.

3. Mix chopped spinach, onions, garlic, mozzarella, Parmesan, carrots and pimiento together in a bowl.

4. Combine ricotta, cream, and egg in a blender and puree until smooth. Fold mixture into vegetables and season with salt and pepper.

5. Pour the mixture into a well buttered loaf pan. Cover with a piece of buttered paper, then cover tightly with aluminum foil and place in a baking dish. Pour in enough water to come two thirds up the sides of the loaf pan. Bake in a preheated 350 degree oven for 45 minutes, until the pâté is firm. Chill several hours or overnight.

6. To unmold, dip the loaf pan in hot water for a few seconds and turn upside down on a plate. Slice and serve cold surrounded with tomato sauce.

Cold Tomato Sauce

3   tomatoes, about 1 lb.,
      peeled and
      finely chopped
½   tsp. finely chopped garlic
¼   tsp. basil (or 1 tsp. fresh
      basil, finely chopped)
2   Tbsp. olive oil
      salt and freshly ground
      pepper

1. Mix all ingredients together in a bowl and taste for seasoning. Serve chilled.

An elegant starter for an elegant meal, this terrine of spinach is subtly flavored with Pernod and a hint of Parmesan cheese. The lemon mousseline sauce is a creamy complement.

Terrine of Spinach with Sauce Mousseline

One small loaf
(7¼" × 3½")

1½ 10-ounce packages fresh spinach
2 Tbsp. butter
1 Tbsp. finely chopped shallots
½ cup ricotta cheese
2 eggs
⅓ cup cream
1 Tbsp. lemon juice
1 Tbsp. Pernod
1 Tbsp. flour
1 Tbsp. chopped parsley
½ tsp. salt
pinch white pepper
¼ cup freshly grated Parmesan cheese
3 peeled hard-boiled eggs

1. Clean and stem spinach. Blanch until tender in boiling, salted water. Squeeze dry in a towel.

2. Heat butter in a skillet. Add shallots and cook 2 minutes.

3. Combine spinach, butter, shallots, and remaining ingredients, except the hard-boiled eggs, in a blender and puree until smooth. Taste for seasoning.

4. Butter a small loaf pan and pour in half the spinach puree. Place the hard-boiled eggs down the center of the pan and cover with the remaining spinach puree.

5. Cover with a piece of buttered paper. Cover tightly with aluminum foil and place in a larger baking pan. Pour in enough water to come two thirds up the sides of the loaf pan. Bake in a preheated 350 degree oven for 45 minutes to an hour, until the pâté feels firm to the touch. Chill several hours or overnight.

6. To unmold, remove paper and dip the bottom and sides of the loaf pan in hot water for a few seconds. Reverse on a serving platter. Slice and serve cold surrounded by Mousseline Sauce.

Mousseline Sauce

Makes 1¼ cups

2 egg yolks
2 tsp. water
½ cup melted butter
2 tsp. lemon juice
salt and white pepper to taste
⅓ cup heavy cream

1. Combine egg yolks and water in the top of a double boiler. Beat over hot water until thick. Remove from heat.

2. Beat melted butter into egg yolks a few tablespoons at a time, until all the butter has been absorbed. Add lemon juice, salt, and white pepper.

3. Whip cream until it holds soft peaks. Fold into sauce and taste for seasoning.

Here is another Indian vegetable fritter that is made with pekora batter. These are called vadas, "little cakes," and are made with a spicy potato filling.

Batada Vadas

Serves 4 to 6

1 recipe pekora batter
(see recipe on page 64)
1 lb. potatoes
3 Tbsp. peanut oil
¼ cup finely chopped
onion
2 small canned, green
chiles, chopped
2 Tbsp. chopped fresh
coriander
1 tsp. grated fresh ginger
1 tsp. salt
½ tsp. turmeric
½ tsp. coriander
1 Tbsp. lemon juice
oil for frying

1. Make batter according to the recipe for pekoras on the preceding page. Let stand while you make the filling.

2. Boil potatoes in their skins, drain, and cool. Peel and dice.

3. Heat peanut oil in a skillet. Add onions, cook briefly and add diced, cooked potatoes. Add chopped chiles, fresh coriander, ginger, salt, turmeric, ground coriander, and lemon juice. Cook over low heat for a few minutes while you stir and mash the potatoes with the spices. Taste for seasoning. Remove from heat and cool.

4. Take a piece of potato mixture about the size of a walnut and shape into a small disk. Shape the remaining potato mixture in this way.

5. Heat 1½ to 2 inches oil in a heavy iron skillet or deep fryer. To test for the proper temperature, drop a little batter in the hot oil. If it rises to the top in about 15 seconds, the oil is ready.

6. Dip the potato cakes in batter and fry a few at a time in the hot oil, until golden brown. Keep the fried vadas warm in a 300 degree oven while you finish frying. Serve hot with a garnish of chutney or raita.

This is an elaborate hors d'oeuvre that can be made ahead and baked in the oven at the last minute. The mushrooms are also delicious filled and baked without the phyllo.

Spinach Stuffed Mushrooms Wrapped in Phyllo

Serves 6 as an appetizer

1 10-ounce package fresh
    spinach
3 *Tbsp. butter*
1 *lb. mushrooms*
2 *Tbsp. minced shallots*
1 *Tbsp. flour*
¼ *cup milk*
½ *cup freshly grated*
    Parmesan cheese
    salt and pepper
    pinch nutmeg
½ *cup melted butter*
½ *lb. phyllo dough*

1. Wash spinach and remove stems. Heat 1 Tbsp. butter in a small skillet and add spinach leaves. Cook gently until leaves are wilted. Drain and press out excess liquid in a sieve, reserving the liquid. Chop spinach.

2. Wash mushrooms and separate stems from caps. Set caps aside and finely chop the stems.

3. Heat 1 Tbsp. butter in skillet. Add shallots and chopped mushroom stems. Cook 3 to 4 minutes and remove from heat. Stir in chopped spinach.

4. Melt remaining 1 Tbsp. butter in a small saucepan. Stir in flour and cook briefly. Add milk and ½ cup of the reserved spinach stock. Cook and stir with a wire whisk until mixture is thick, about 5 minutes.

5. Mix sauce with spinach and mushrooms. Add grated cheese, salt, pepper, and nutmeg. Taste for seasoning.

6. With a spoon, or a pastry bag fitted with a large tip, fill mushroom caps with spinach mixture.

To Assemble:

1. Brush two sheets of phyllo with melted butter and lay one on top of the other. With a sharp knife, divide sheet into 6 sections by cutting in half lengthwise and then in thirds horizontally.

2. Take each square of phyllo and turn it over so that the unbuttered side is up. Brush lightly with a little more butter and place a mushroom cap in the center. Fold the corners toward the center, one after the other in a clockwise direction. Smooth the last flap of phyllo over the top of the mushroom with your hands, gently pressing in place.

3. Arrange pastries on a baking sheet and bake in a pre-heated 400 degree oven for 15 to 20 minutes, until golden brown.

Here is a vegetarian adaptation of a classic favorite. Serve as a snack or appetizer; or with soup and stir-fried vegetables.

Egg Rolls

Makes one dozen

2 Tbsp. peanut or vegetable oil
½ tsp. finely minced garlic
¼ cup finely sliced scallions
1 finely chopped green pepper
¾ cup finely chopped celery
¼ lb. sliced mushrooms
½ cup shredded bamboo shoots
1 cup thinly sliced Chinese cabbage
1 Tbsp. grated fresh ginger
2 Tbsp. soy sauce
½ cup mung bean sprouts
1 tsp. cornstarch dissolved in 2 Tbsp. cold water
1 Tbsp. Chinese sesame oil
12 egg roll wrappers
oil for frying

1. Heat oil in a wok or skillet. Add garlic, scallions, green pepper, and celery and stir-fry for 2 minutes. Add mushrooms, bamboo shoots, cabbage, ginger, and soy sauce and stir-fry a few more minutes, until vegetables are wilted. Add bean sprouts and cornstarch paste and cook 3 minutes, until liquid in pan comes to a boil and cornstarch thickens. Add sesame oil and taste for seasoning. Cool to room temperature.

2. Place an egg roll wrapper on your work surface with one point of the square facing you. Place a rounded tablespoon of filling in the lower center of the square. Fold the bottom "point" up over the filling and fold the side flaps in toward the center. Holding the side flaps in place with your fingers, roll away from you into a snug roll. Brush the loose flap of the egg roll with a little water and press gently to seal. Finish filling the remaining wrappers.

3. Heat 1½ inches oil in a heavy iron skillet or wok. Fry the egg rolls until golden brown on all sides. Drain on absorbent paper. Serve with Chinese duck sauce and hot mustard.

One story behind these "Pot Stickers" is that an enterprising chef, inadvertently browning his dumplings in the process of steaming them, claimed to have invented a new cooking technique which combined steaming and frying. In any case, the result is irresistible. The wrappers may be purchased ready-made in Oriental food stores.

Pot Stickers (Chinese Steamed-Fried Dumplings)

18 to 20 dumplings

4 Chinese dried
    mushrooms
2 Tbsp. vegetable oil
1½ cups finely shredded
    Chinese cabbage
1 cup finely shredded fresh
    spinach leaves
½ cup finely sliced scallions
1 tsp. finely chopped garlic
1 Tbsp. grated fresh ginger
½ cup chopped, cooked
    noodles (Chinese
    noodles or
    spaghetti)
1 Tbsp. soy sauce
2 Tbsp. toasted sesame
    seeds
2 tsp. Chinese sesame oil
    salt to taste
⅓ package dumpling
    wrappers (3-inch
    rounds)

1. Soak mushrooms in 1 cup boiling water for 20 to 30 minutes, until soft. Drain and slice thin. Reserve mushroom stock for use in soup.

2. Heat oil in a wok or skillet. Add cabbage, spinach, and scallions and cook until wilted. Stir in remaining ingredients and cook, stirring, for 3 minutes. Taste for seasoning and cool.

3. Fill four or five dumplings at a time. Lightly brush the upper half of each circle of dough with water and place a rounded teaspoon of filling in the center. Fold circle in half and pinch together in the center. Make one or two pleats on either side of this center mark and press the edges together to seal. Repeat until all the filling is used.

4. Heat 2 Tbsp. oil in a large skillet and place the dumplings in the pan with the flat side down. Cook, shaking the pan back and forth to keep the "pot stickers" from sticking, until the bottoms are golden brown. Pour in one cup of water and cover the skillet. Let the dumplings steam for 5 minutes, until most of the liquid in the pan evaporates. Transfer to a serving platter and serve with a dipping sauce.

Dipping Sauce

3 Tbsp. soy sauce
1½ tsp. white vinegar
1 tsp. Chinese sesame oil
    few drops chili oil

1. Mix all ingredients together and serve with dumplings.

Sushi is the name given to many Japanese hors d'oeuvres or snacks that have as their base a cold, delicately seasoned, vinegared rice. You may encounter sushi in many different forms—from an egg shaped rice ball topped with sashimi (thin slices of raw fish) and seasoned with hot mustard, to a seaweed encased cylinder filled with rice and crunchy vegetables or sashimi. In this recipe, the vinegared rice is wrapped in nori (sheets of dried seaweed) and filled with vegetables. Serve nori rolls as a first course in a Japanese meal; or as a component of a meal with soup, tempura, or cucumber and bean sprout salad.

Sushi gohan is the name given to the vinegared rice that is the basis for the many varieties of sushi. Japanese short grained rice may be purchased in groceries where Oriental food is sold.

Serves 4 to 6

1½ cups Japanese rice
1½ cups water
⅓ cup seasoned rice wine vinegar
4 sheets nori
½ small carrot, peeled and cut in thin strips
½ small cucumber, seeded and cut in thin strips
  few slices red pickled ginger
  few pieces dried Japanese mushrooms, soaked until soft in boiling water
  few sprigs watercress

Nori Rolls

To Make Vinegared Rice:

1. Wash rice five times in cold, running water, until water runs clear. Drain.

2. Combine rice and water in a saucepan and bring to a boil. Reduce heat, cover pan tightly, and simmer 10 minutes, until rice has absorbed all the water. Turn off heat and let rice steam with the cover on for 15 minutes.

3. Transfer rice to a non-metallic bowl and toss with seasoned rice wine vinegar. Cool to room temperature.

To Roll the Sushi:

1. When the rice has cooled, divide it into four portions. Lay a sheet of nori on a bamboo sushi mat or kitchen towel and spread it with one portion of rice. (If you dip your hands in cold water first, the rice is easier to spread.)

2. Arrange a few pieces of carrot and cucumber, or the vegetable combination of your choice, in a strip across the rice, about one inch away from the edge nearest you. Holding the vegetables in place with your fingers, roll away from you and lift the mat as you continue to roll. Repeat with the remaining sheets of nori, rice and vegetables.

3. With a sharp knife, cut nori rolls into 6 pieces. Arrange on a plate with the cut side up. Serve with a dish of soy sauce for dipping.

Vine leaves may be purchased in jars—packed in bunches in a salty brine. One jar usually contains 5 bunches of 20 to 24 leaves each. Bottled leaves must be rinsed under cold water before using. If you are lucky enough to have access to a grape arbor, you may use the leaves fresh from the vine. Simply cut the stems from the leaves and blanch in boiling water until tender.

These tasty bundles may be made a few days in advance and served either hot or cold. Reheat in a skillet with a little water on the bottom and serve glazed with melted butter and accompanied by a lemon wedge. To serve cold, glaze with a little olive oil and serve with some yogurt on the side.

Stuffed Vine Leaves

Serves 4

1	*bunch vine leaves*
⅔	*cup rice*
⅔	*cup water*
½	*tsp. salt*
1	*Tbsp. butter*
2	*Tbsp. olive oil*
	juice of 1 lemon
¼	*tsp. cinnamon*
¼	*tsp. allspice*
1	*Tbsp. chopped parsley*
⅓	*cup cooked chick peas*
¼	*cup raisins*

1. Combine rice, water, and salt in a saucepan and bring to a boil. Simmer 4 to 5 minutes and drain well. Mix with remaining ingredients.

2. Rinse store-bought vine leaves under cold running water. Lay flat on work surface with the shiny side down and stem on the bottom, facing you. Place a heaping teaspoon of rice mixture in the center of each leaf. Fold the bottom part of the leaf up over the filling and fold the sides in toward the center. Roll into a compact cylinder. Pack the rolled and filled leaves close together in a skillet, with the seam on the bottom. Barely cover with water and weight down with a heatproof plate. The plate will keep the leaves from unravelling while cooking.

3. Cover the pan with a lid and simmer gently on the top of the stove for one hour, until most of the liquid has been absorbed. Serve hot or cold.

Here is a simple and attractive cheese appetizer.

Garlic and Herb Cheese Spread

Serves 4 to 6

6 Tbsp. butter
8 ounces cream cheese
¼ tsp. finely minced garlic
1 Tbsp. chopped parsley
1 Tbsp. minced chives
    or scallions
¼ tsp. salt
    freshly ground pepper
¼ cup finely chopped
    parsley for garnish

1. Cream butter with cream cheese and blend in garlic, parsley, chives, salt, and pepper. Taste for seasoning.

2. Wet hands with cold water and shape cream cheese into a four-inch, round disk. Chill until firm.

3. Cover top and sides of cheese round with chopped parsley, gently pressing to coat. Serve with crackers.

The borek is a pastry of Turkish origin, made with a variety of fillings in a variety of sizes and shapes. Here is a cheese filled borek, sometimes called tiropeta, flavored with fresh dill and parsley.

Turkish Boreks

Serves 4 to 6

6 ounces cream cheese
3 ounces feta cheese
    (½ cup, crumbled)
1 egg
1 Tbsp. finely chopped
    parsley
1 tsp. chopped, fresh dill
    salt and freshly
    ground pepper
½ lb. phyllo dough
½ cup melted butter
    sesame seeds

1. Mix cream cheese, feta cheese, and egg together until creamy. Stir in parsley and dill. Season with salt and pepper.

2. Brush two sheets of phyllo with melted butter and lay them one on top of the other. With a sharp knife, cut in 4 lengthwise strips. Place a rounded teaspoon of filling on the bottom of each strip. Pick up the lower right hand corner of the strip and bring it across to the left edge to form a triangle. Fold the dough in a triangular fashion as you would a flag, so that you wind up with a neat little triangle encasing the filling. Repeat until all the filling is used.

3. Brush the tops of the pastries with more melted butter and place them on a buttered baking sheet. Sprinkle with sesame seeds and bake in a preheated 400 degree oven until golden brown, 15 to 20 minutes. Serve hot.

These Syrian cheese pastries may be served alone with drinks; or along with hummus or baba ganouj as a prelude to a Middle Eastern meal. They may also be frozen and baked at a later date. If this is the case, do not defrost them but spread them on a cookie sheet and place directly in a preheated oven.

Samboussak

1. Mix semolina, flour, and salt together in a bowl. With your fingers, rub in melted butter until mixture looks crumbly. Add water and knead until smooth.

2. In a separate bowl, beat egg and mix with grated cheese.

3. Divide dough in half and roll out on an unfloured board. It should be about the thickness of a nickel. With a round cutter, cut in 3-inch circles. Place 1 teaspoon of the cheese mixture in the center of each circle and fold in half. Press edges firmly together to seal. Repeat until all the filling is used.

4. Brush pastries with beaten egg and sprinkle with sesame seeds. Bake on an ungreased cookie sheet in a preheated 400 degree oven for 15 to 20 minutes, until light brown. Serve hot.

3 dozen small pastries

¾	cup semolina
1½	cup all purpose flour
½	tsp. salt
½	cup melted butter
½	cup water
1	egg
½	lb. grated Muenster cheese
	sesame seeds
	beaten egg

Quesadillas are Mexican cheese-filled pastries that are deep fried. The dough is made from a specially treated corn meal called *masa harina,* the same used to make corn tortillas. Working with the masa dough requires some patience, but you will soon get the knack of it if you persevere. A tortilla press is an invaluable tool for this operation.

Quesadillas

1. Grate cheese and mix with chopped jalapeno pepper. Set aside.

2. Mix masa with flour, salt, and baking powder. Add oil, egg, and milk and mix with your hands until you have a stiff dough. Shape into balls about the size of walnuts.

3. Roll dough in 4½-inch circles between two sheets of plastic wrap, or press into a circle using a tortilla press. Hold a circle of dough in one hand and place a rounded table-spoon of cheese in the center. Carefully fold in half and press

Makes 16 to 18 pastries

6	ounces Monterey jack cheese
2	or more tsp. finely chopped jalapeno pepper
1½	cups masa harina
1	Tbsp. flour
1	tsp. salt
½	tsp. baking powder
1	Tbsp. oil
1	egg
	approx. ⅓ cup milk

edges together to seal. Continue until all the dough and filling are used.

4. Heat ½ inch oil in a heavy iron skillet or frying pan. Fry quesadillas until golden brown on both sides. Drain on absorbent paper and serve hot, sprinkled with a little salt.

Leave it to the food-loving Chinese to invent dim sum, a "tea meal" consisting of a wondrous assortment of steamed and fried dumplings and filled cakes. A favorite is the turnip sesame cake. These sesame cakes, usually served as part of a dim sum meal, make great snacks, hors d'oeuvres or accompaniments.

Makes 12 small cakes

Dough:

2½ cups flour
1 tsp. salt
⅓ cup vegetable shortening
⅓ cup boiling water

Filling:

2 cups coarsely grated
      turnip
1 tsp. salt
2 Tbsp. finely sliced
      scallions
1 Tbsp. soy sauce
1 tsp. Chinese sesame oil

1 beaten egg
½ cup plus 2 Tbsp.
      sesame seeds
   oil for frying

Turnip Sesame Cakes

1. Mix flour with salt and cut in shortening until well blended. Stir in boiling water and mix to a smooth dough. Let rest 10 minutes.

1. Mixed peeled and grated turnip with salt and let stand 10 minutes. Squeeze dry in a towel and mix with scallions, soy sauce, and sesame oil. Taste for seasoning.

Assembling, Frying and Baking:

1. Roll dough into a coil 1½ inches thick. Cut in 12 equal pieces and roll each piece into a circle 4 ½ inches in diameter. Since dough is quite oily, you won't need any flour for rolling. A tortilla press makes quick work of this step.

2. Place a rounded teaspoon of filling in the center of each circle. Gather the edges in toward the center and pinch together to form a pouch. Gently press and flatten pastries into 3-inch circles with your hands. Try not to tear the dough as you do this.

3. Dip pastries in beaten egg and coat with sesame seeds, pressing gently so that seeds will adhere to the dough.

4. Heat ¼ inch oil in heavy skillet. Fry pastries 2 or 3 minutes on each side, until golden. Drain on absorbent paper. Bake in a preheated 350 degree oven for 10 minutes. Serve hot.

Soups

There is no end to the wonderful combinations of vegetables we can enjoy as liquids. From the light and appetizing cream soups to the hearty and filling vegetable stews, homemade soups have a certain incomparable magic. What could delight the senses more than a delicate cream of asparagus soup in early June, or a cool and tangy gazpacho in the hot summer months? Polish vegetable barley soup, minestrone, and vegetable borscht fill our stomachs and warm our insides on brisk winter days, while we can savour creamy butternut squash and leek soup but briefly in the autumn months.

Apart from these seasonal distinctions, soups hold an important place in the spectrum of eating. A bowl of hearty soup coupled with a loaf of homemade bread and a glass of wine provides a special blissful contentment. Japanese noodle soup, nori rolls, and pickled vegetables; or Syrian red lentil soup, crudités, white bean dip and pita bread comprise informal meals and offer a welcome change of pace. As a refreshing break in the summer, or a warm and nourishing respite in the dead of winter, homemade soups rank high on the list of comfort foods.

Contrary to popular notion, most soups, especially vegetarian soups, do not take hours and hours of simmering atop the stove. In fact, most of the recipes in this section take from 30 to 45 minutes to cook. Soup stocks, on the other hand, take longer since the flavor and goodness of the ingredients must be slowly extracted and concentrated in the form of a broth. As a component of homemade soup, stock enriches the final product in nourishment and flavor and is well worth the extra effort. Onion skins, carrot peels, the tops of scallions and leeks, mushroom trimmings, and tomato ends all contribute to the stock pot and may be saved until you have a quantity worth simmering.

For all its enrichment value, soup stock is not an essential component of all vegetarian soups. The chilled soups such as avocado gazpacho, beet soup, and cucumber and yogurt soup are quick and simple. In fact the beauty of these soups *is* their simplicity, which allows the sometimes subtle flavor of a vegetable to shine through clearly.

Experience in tasting and cooking meatless soups is the best proof that there is nothing lacklustre about them.

Creamy split pea soup flavored with cheese instead of ham, or vegetable soup enriched with soy sauce instead of beef stock, are classic examples of thoroughly satisfying soups made without meat or meat stocks. If you are a "beginning" vegetarian, I am confident that you will soon discover the many merits of vegetarian soups.

To the surprise of many, soups made without meat are full of flavor. The basis of this flavor is a good soup stock. Like meat stocks, vegetable stocks use many of the throw away items from the kitchen: carrot peels, onion peels, celery leaves, and parsley stems. All these form the body and soul of this essential element of soup making.

The following recipe for vegetable stock is only meant to serve as a guideline for the novice stock maker. If you plan ahead, you can start saving little tidbits in a container in your refrigerator (they will keep for several days). I have outlined some of these ingredients in the recipe. Avoid vegetables with a very strong flavor, such as broccoli, cauliflower, spinach, or cabbage. These will overpower the other vegetables in your stock and therefore in your soup.

When you have accumulated a potful, take inventory and round out your collection with more onions and carrots, or whatever you think might be lacking. Add water and simmer slowly for one to two hours.

Leftover, cooked vegetables are better added to the finished soup than to the stockpot, since most of their flavor has already been extracted in the first cooking. Still, they can add interest and filler to a soup, and are often most palatable in this form.

For about 4 quarts stock:

2 Tbsp. butter
3 or 4 sliced shallots
1 small turnip (use in moderation, since it has a strong flavor)
1 or 2 celery stalks, with leaves
   handful of parsley stems
2 onions
2 carrots
1 bunch leeks or scallions, green part only
1 cup mushroom trimmings
   a few tomato ends
   about 10 peppercorns

Vegetable Stock

1. Heat butter in a stock pot and add sliced shallots. Cook over low heat until they start to brown. Slice remaining vegetables and add to the pot. Cover with water and simmer 2 to 3 hours. Strain.

Here is a rich and delicious version of gazpacho. Cut all the vegetables the same size and shape for the best visual appeal.

Avocado Gazpacho

Makes 5 cups

1 cucumber, peeled and seeded
1 green pepper, seeded
2 tomatoes, peeled
1 avocado, peeled
1 Tbsp. finely chopped Bermuda onion
2 Tbsp. lemon juice
1 cup water
1 cup tomato juice
salt and pepper to taste
Tabasco sauce to taste

1. Cut cucumber, green pepper, tomatoes, and avocado in small cubes and combine in a bowl with remaining ingredients. Thin with equal parts of tomato juice and water, if necessary. Taste for seasoning. Serve chilled garnished with chopped parsley.

This cold and creamy beet soup is shocking pink!

Chilled Beet Soup

Makes 4 cups

2 Tbsp. butter
1/3 cup chopped onions
2 cups sliced beets, fresh or canned
1 cup tomato juice
1 cup water
3 or 4 thinly sliced radishes
1/2 cucumber, peeled, seeded and diced
2 Tbsp. vinegar
salt and white pepper to taste
1½ cups milk or cream

1. Heat butter in a saucepan. Add onions and cook until they are soft but not browned. Add sliced beets, tomato juice, water, radishes, cucumber, and salt. Simmer over medium heat until vegetables are tender, 15 to 20 minutes. Stir in vinegar. Puree soup in blender until smooth. Chill in refrigerator.

2. When soup is cold, stir in milk or cream and taste for seasoning. Serve cold with a garnish of sour cream and chopped fresh dill weed.

Here is an unusual borscht that makes use of the beet greens.

Chilled Borscht

Makes 5 cups

greens from 4 fresh beets
2 cups cooked, diced beets (approx. 4 beets)
½ cucumber, peeled, seeded and diced
3 or 4 thinly sliced radishes
1 Tbsp. thinly sliced scallions
¾ cup tomato juice
1½ cups water
3 Tbsp. red wine vinegar salt and pepper to taste
½ tsp. dill weed
¾ cup cream

1. Wash and stem beet greens. Steam in a small amount of water until tender. Squeeze dry in a kitchen towel and chop.

2. Combine cooked beet greens in a bowl with diced beets, cucumber, radishes, and scallions. Add tomato juice, water, vinegar, salt, pepper, and dill weed. Stir in cream and taste for seasoning. Serve ice cold.

Chilled Cream of Cucumber Soup

Makes 4 cups

2 Tbsp. butter
⅓ cup finely chopped onion
2 large cucumbers
2 cups vegetable stock
1 Tbsp. chopped parsley
½ tsp. dill weed
½ tsp. finely chopped chives or scallions
salt and white pepper to taste
½ cup cream

1. Heat butter in a saucepan. Add onions and cook 5 minutes without browning.

2. Peel cucumbers, slice in half lengthwise and scrape out seeds with a spoon. Cut in medium dice and add to saucepan with onions. Stir in vegetable stock and simmer over medium heat until cucumbers are soft, 20 to 25 minutes.

3. Puree soup in a blender until smooth. Add parsley, dill weed, chives, salt, and white pepper. Chill in refrigerator.

4. When soup is thoroughly chilled, stir in cream and taste for seasoning.

The walnuts add an unexpected richness to this tangy and refreshing soup.

Chilled Cucumber and Yogurt Soup

Makes 6 cups

2½   cups yogurt
¼   cup olive oil
¼   cup finely chopped
       walnuts
¼   tsp. minced garlic
1   Tbsp. wine vinegar
1   tsp. dill weed
2   large cucumbers
       approximately 1 cup milk
       salt and freshly
         ground pepper

1. Pour yogurt in a bowl and whisk in olive oil. Stir in walnuts, garlic, vinegar, and dill weed.

2. Peel cucumbers, slice in half lengthwise, and scrape out seeds with a spoon. Cut in small dice. You should have about 3 cups.

3. Stir cucumbers into yogurt and add enough milk to thin to desired consistency. Add salt and pepper to taste.

This quick and simple soup could also be served hot. Garden fresh peas are best, but frozen may also be used.

Chilled Fresh Pea Soup

Makes 4 cups

1   Tbsp. butter
½   cup chopped onion
3½   cups fresh or frozen
       green peas
1½   cups vegetable stock
1   cup milk
½   cup cream
       salt and pepper to taste

1. Heat butter in a saucepan. Add onions and cook over medium heat for 5 minutes, until they are soft but not browned. Add peas and stock and bring to a boil. Remove from heat, cover and let steam 8 to 10 minutes, until peas are tender but not overcooked. Puree in blender until smooth. Chill in refrigerator.

2. When soup is thoroughly chilled, stir in milk, cream, salt, and pepper. Taste for seasoning. Serve with a garnish of sour cream and chopped fresh dill weed.

Matchstick carrot slivers make a pretty garnish for this classic favorite.

Vichyssoise

Makes 4½ cups

1 lb. potatoes, peeled
    and diced
1 cup sliced leeks
    salt and white pepper
    to taste
2½ cups vegetable stock
1 small carrot
1 cup cream
1½ cups milk

1. Combine potatoes and leeks in a saucepan with salt, pepper, and vegetable stock. Simmer over medium heat until potatoes are tender, 20 to 25 minutes.

2. Puree soup in a blender until smooth. Chill in refrigerator.

3. Peel carrot and cut in fine matchstick. Blanch until tender in boiling, salted water. Drain and chill.

4. When soup is thoroughly chilled, stir in cream and milk and taste for seasoning. Garnish with carrot slivers.

This soup has a lovely, delicate color and flavor. It is also nice served cold on a hot summer day.

Cream of Yellow Squash Soup

Makes 8 cups

2 Tbsp. butter
½ cup finely chopped
    onion
½ cup finely chopped celery
2 Tbsp. flour
2 lbs. yellow summer
    squash, cut in cubes,
    about 7 cups
3 cups vegetable stock
1 cup heavy cream
1 tsp. salt
    pinch white pepper
    pinch nutmeg

1. Heat butter in a stock pot. Add onions and celery and cook until tender, about 5 minutes. Sprinkle flour over vegetables and cook, stirring, for another 2 to 3 minutes. Do not let the flour brown.

2. Add cubed squash, stock, and salt and simmer 20 to 25 minutes, until squash is tender.

3. Puree the soup in the blender until very smooth. Return to pot and stir in cream, salt, pepper, and nutmeg. Reheat and taste for seasoning.

If you are using a food processor or blender to make gazpacho, finely chop the vegetables but take care not to reduce them to a puree.

Gazpacho

Serves 6

1 lb. ripe tomatoes (about 3 medium-sized)
1 large cucumber
1 large green pepper
¼ cup coarsely chopped onion
2½ cups tomato juice
2½ to 3 Tbsp. red wine vinegar
  salt and pepper to taste
¾ tsp. Tabasco

1. Core tomatoes and plunge them in boiling water for one minute. Remove, cool slightly, and peel. The skins should be loose enough to peel easily.

2. Peel and seed cucumber. Remove seeds from green pepper. Pass tomatoes, cucumber, green pepper, and onion through the large blade of a grinder (or chop in a food processor or blender).

3. Stir in tomato juice, red wine vinegar, salt, pepper, and Tabasco. Taste for seasoning and chill. Serve ice cold garnished with a sprinkle of chopped parsley.

Chilled Tomato Soup with Buttermilk

Makes 4 cups

3 medium-sized ripe tomatoes
2 Tbsp. thinly sliced scallions
  salt and pepper to taste
1 Tbsp. chopped parsley
½ cup tomato juice
2 cups buttermilk
½ tsp. crushed fennel seeds

1. Core tomatoes and plunge them in boiling water for one minute. Remove, cool slightly, and peel. The skins should be loose enough to peel easily.

2. Cut peeled tomatoes in eighths and puree in blender with scallions, salt, pepper, and parsley.

3. Pour pureed tomatoes in a bowl and stir in tomato juice, buttermilk, and crushed fennel seeds. Taste for seasoning. Serve cold with a sprinkle of chopped parsley.

Here are two creamy versions of a chilled fruit soup that could be served at the beginning or end of a summer meal. The first is laced with sherry, while the second has the tangy flavor of buttermilk.

Fruit Soup I

Makes 3 cups

- 1   orange
- 1   cup sliced strawberries
- ½   small cantelope, cut in chunks
- ½   cup raspberries
- 1   Tbsp. honey
- 1   Tbsp. lemon juice
- ⅓   cup sherry
- 1   cup cream

1. With a sharp knife, cut peel away from orange and eliminate all traces of white part. Cut in pieces and combine in a blender with strawberries, cantelope and raspberries. Blend until smooth.

2. Strain fruit puree through a sieve to remove seeds and pithy part of fruit. Stir in honey, lemon juice, sherry, and cream. Taste for seasoning. Garnish with a spoonful of unsweetened whipped cream.

Fruit Soup II

Makes 4 cups

- 1   orange
- ½   small cantelope, cut in chunks
- 1   cup raspberries
- ½   cup blueberries
- 2   Tbsp. honey
- 1   Tbsp. lemon juice
- ½   cup cream
- 2   cups buttermilk

1. With a sharp knife, cut peel away from orange and eliminate all traces of white part. Cut in pieces and combine in a blender with remaining fruit. Puree until smooth.

2. Strain fruit puree through a sieve to remove seeds and pithy part of fruit. Stir in honey, lemon juice, cream and buttermilk. Taste for seasoning. Garnish with a spoonful of sour cream.

A filling and sustaining soup for a cold winter day.

French Onion Soup

Makes 5 cups

1 Tbsp. oil
2 Tbsp. butter
8 cups thinly sliced onions
1 tsp. sugar
4 cups vegetable stock
2 Tbsp. soy sauce
   salt and white pepper
      to taste
¼ cup red wine
1 Tbsp. finely chopped
      parsley
   sliced French bread
   grated Swiss or
      Parmesan cheese

1. Heat oil and butter in a saucepan. Add onions and sugar and cook gently until onions are golden brown, about 35 minutes. Stir occasionally.

2. When onions are a nice caramel color, add stock, soy sauce, salt, pepper, red wine, and parsley. Simmer 25 minutes and taste for seasoning.

3. Ladle soup into oven-proof serving bowls. Top with a slice of stale or toasted French bread and cover with a generous sprinkle of grated cheese. Run under a hot broiler until cheese melts and starts to brown.

For a delicious variation, substitute cauliflower for the broccoli in this soup.

Cream of Broccoli Soup

Makes 4 cups

½ bunch broccoli
3 Tbsp. butter
¾ cup finely chopped
      onions
½ cup finely chopped celery
2 Tbsp. flour
3 cups vegetable stock
   salt and pepper to taste
1 cup heavy cream
   grated cheddar cheese
      for garnish

1. Remove leaves and tough ends of the broccoli stems and cut in ¼-inch thick slices. You should have enough broccoli to measure about 4 cups.

2. Heat butter in a saucepan. Add onions and celery and cook until tender, about 5 minutes. Sprinkle with flour and cook for another 3 minutes, stirring to keep the flour from browning. Add broccoli, stock, salt, and pepper and simmer for 20 to 25 minutes, until broccoli is tender.

3. Puree soup in blender until smooth. Strain through a sieve to remove pulpy bits of broccoli and return to saucepan. Add cream and reheat. Taste for seasoning. Garnish with grated cheddar cheese.

For a beautiful presentation, reserve some of the cream and trail it over the top of the soup before serving.

Cream of Carrot Soup

Makes 7 cups

- ⅓ cup finely chopped onions
- 4 cups carrots, peeled and sliced in ⅛-inch thick slices
- 2 Tbsp. uncooked white rice
- 1 Tbsp. tomato paste
- 4 cups vegetable stock or water
  salt and white pepper to taste
- 1 cup milk
- 1 cup heavy cream

1. Combine onions, carrots, rice, tomato paste, water, salt, and pepper in a saucepan and bring to a boil. Reduce heat and simmer for 25 minutes, until rice is cooked and carrots are tender.

2. Puree soup in a blender until smooth. Return to saucepan and stir in milk and cream. Reheat and taste for seasoning.

New England Corn Chowder

Makes 7 cups

- 2 Tbsp. butter
- ½ cup diced onion
- ¾ cup diced celery
- 2 cups corn, off the cob or frozen
- ½ cup diced green pepper
- 1 cup peeled and diced potatoes
- ¾ cup diced carrots
- ⅓ cup diced sweet red pepper
  salt and pepper to taste
- 2½ cups water
- 2½ cups milk

1. Heat butter in a saucepan. Add onions and cook over medium heat until clear, about 5 minutes. Add celery, corn, green pepper, potatoes, carrots, red pepper, salt, pepper, and water. Bring to a boil, reduce heat and simmer for 20 to 25 minutes, until vegetables are tender. Add milk and reheat. Do not boil or soup will curdle.

Mexican Corn Soup

Makes 5 cups

2	*Tbsp. butter*
½	*cup chopped onions*
4	*cups corn, off the cob or frozen*
2½	*cups vegetable stock salt and pepper to taste*
3	*Tbsp. tomato paste*
½	*cup heavy cream*
¼	*tsp. Tabasco*

1. Heat butter in a saucepan. Add onions and cook 5 minutes, until clear. Add corn, stock, salt, pepper, and tomato paste and simmer for 20 to 25 minutes.

2. Puree half the soup briefly in a blender. Return to saucepan and add cream and Tabasco. Reheat without boiling and taste for seasoning.

This is a French style cream soup in which the vegetables are pureed until very smooth.

Cream of Mushroom Soup

Makes 5 to 6 cups

2	*Tbsp. butter*
½	*cup chopped onion*
1½	*lbs. sliced mushrooms*
2	*Tbsp. flour*
2	*cups vegetable stock salt and pepper to taste*
1	*cup milk*
1	*cup heavy cream*

1. Heat butter in a saucepan. Add onion and cook 5 minutes, until clear. Add mushrooms and cook 3 more minutes. Stir in flour and continue to cook, stirring often, for 8 to 10 minutes. Add stock, salt, and pepper and simmer over low heat for 20 minutes.

2. Puree soup until smooth in a blender. Return to saucepan and reheat with milk and cream. Taste for seasoning.

Here is a cold weather favorite, thick with barley and enriched with the flavor of soy sauce.

Mushroom Barley Soup

Makes 5 cups

2	*Tbsp. butter*
½	*cup finely chopped onions*
½	*cup barley*
½	*lb. sliced mushrooms*
4	*cups vegetable stock*
3	*Tbsp. soy sauce salt and pepper to taste*

1. Heat butter in a large saucepan. Add onions and cook until tender, about 5 minutes. Add barley and mushrooms and cook 5 more minutes, stirring often.

2. Add stock, soy sauce, salt, and pepper and simmer for 45 minutes to an hour, until barley is fully cooked. Taste for seasoning.

Sour cream and caraway seeds give this mushroom soup an unusual yet delicious twist. Take care not to boil the soup or it will curdle.

Czechoslovakian Mushroom Soup

Makes 7 cups

2　Tbsp. oil
¼　tsp. finely chopped garlic
1½　lbs. sliced mushrooms
1　tsp. oregano
1　tsp. salt
　　pinch cayenne pepper
1　tsp. caraway seeds,
　　　crushed with a
　　　rolling pin
1½　Tbsp. flour
1　tsp. paprika
4　cups vegetable stock
2　tsp. lemon juice
2　Tbsp. tomato paste
2　egg yolks
1½　cups sour cream
½　cup finely chopped
　　　parsley

1. Heat oil in a large saucepan. Add garlic and mushrooms and cook 5 minutes, stirring occasionally. Stir in oregano, salt, cayenne, crushed caraway seeds, flour, and paprika. Cook over medium heat for 5 minutes, stirring occasionally. Add stock, lemon juice, and tomato paste and simmer for 20 to 25 minutes.

2. With a wire whisk, beat sour cream into egg yolks until smooth. Gradually beat in hot soup. Return to saucepan and reheat without boiling. Stir in chopped parsley and taste for seasoning.

Curry powder, cream, and white wine distinguish this soup from the more conventional onion soup.

Cream of Curried Onion Soup

Makes 6 cups

3　Tbsp. butter
7　cups thinly sliced onions
1½　tsp. curry powder
¼　cup dry, white wine
1　Tbsp. uncooked white
　　　rice
4　cups vegetable stock
1　bay leaf
1　Tbsp. tomato paste
　　salt and white pepper
　　　to taste
1　cup heavy cream

1. Heat butter in a saucepan. Add onions and cook, stirring occasionally until clear, about 5 minutes.

2. Add curry powder, white wine, rice, stock, bay leaf, tomato paste, salt, and white pepper. Bring to a boil, reduce heat and simmer for 20 minutes.

3. Puree half the soup in a blender and return to saucepan. Reheat with cream and taste for seasoning.

Old-Fashioned Potato Soup

Makes 8 cups

2   Tbsp. oil
2   cups thinly sliced leeks,
       scallions or onions
1   cup diced celery
3   Tbsp. flour
1   lb. potatoes, peeled and
       diced
4   cups vegetable stock or
       water
    salt and pepper to taste
1   cup milk
1   cup cream

1. Heat oil in a saucepan. Add leeks and celery and cook over low heat for 5 minutes. Sprinkle with flour and cook for 5 minutes, stirring to keep the flour from browning. Add potatoes, stock, salt, and pepper and bring to a boil. Reduce heat and simmer for 20 to 25 minutes. Stir occasionally to keep vegetables from sticking to the bottom of the pan.

2. When potatoes are tender, stir in milk and cream and reheat. Taste for seasoning. Serve garnished with a sprinkle of chopped parsley.

There can never be too many recipes for potato soup. This one is creamy and filling, with an added bonus of Parmesan cheese.

Cream of Potato and Onion Soup

Makes 6 cups

2   Tbsp. olive oil
1   cup finely chopped
       onions
2   cups water
    salt and white pepper
       to taste
4   cups peeled and diced
       potatoes
½   cup heavy cream
½   cup milk
½   cup freshly grated
       Parmesan cheese

1. Heat oil in a saucepan. Add onions and cook 5 minutes, until clear. Add water, salt, pepper, and half the diced potatoes. Simmer for 20 minutes, until potatoes are tender.

2. Blanch remaining potatoes in boiling, salted water until tender. Drain and set aside.

3. Puree potato and onion mixture in a blender until smooth. Return to saucepan and add cooked, diced potatoes, cream, and milk. Reheat. Just before serving, stir in grated Parmesan cheese.

Butternut Squash and Leek Soup

Makes 8 cups

  1 butternut squash,
      weighing about 3 lbs.
  4 cups vegetable stock
  2 Tbsp. butter
1½ cups thinly sliced leeks
 ¾ cup milk
 ¾ cup cream
    salt and freshly ground
    pepper

1. Peel squash, remove seeds and cut in one-inch cubes. You should have from 6 to 7 cups of cubed squash. Combine in a saucepan with vegetable stock and bring to a boil. Reduce heat and simmer, covered, for 15 to 20 minutes, until squash is tender. Puree in a blender until smooth. Return to saucepan.

2. Heat butter in a skillet. Add leeks and cook until tender but do not brown. Add to squash puree with milk, cream, salt, and pepper. Reheat and taste for seasoning.

Cream of Tomato Soup

Makes 3½ cups

1½ lb. tomatoes, peeled
    and sliced
  3 Tbsp. butter
 ⅓ cup chopped onion
 ⅛ tsp. finely chopped
    garlic
 ¾ cup diced celery
  1 Tbsp. uncooked white
    rice
  1 Tbsp. chopped parsley
    salt and pepper to taste
    small pinch sugar
 ½ cup water
  1 cup cream

1. Core tomatoes and plunge them in boiling water for one minute. Remove, cool slightly and peel. The skins should be loose enough to peel easily. Slice.

2. Heat butter in a saucepan. Add onions, garlic, and celery and cook gently for 5 minutes. Add tomatoes, rice, parsley, salt, pepper, sugar, and water and simmer for 25 to 30 minutes.

3. Puree soup in a blender until smooth. Strain through a sieve and return to saucepan with cream. Reheat and taste for seasoning.

You may substitute 1 cup cooked, leftover rice for the uncooked rice in this recipe.

Mediterranean Tomato Rice Soup

Makes 7 cups

2   Tbsp. oil
1   cup finely chopped
      onions
½   tsp. finely chopped
      garlic
¼   lb. thinly sliced
      mushrooms
4½ cups peeled and chopped
      tomatoes, fresh or
      canned
2½ cups vegetable stock or
      water
1   bay leaf
⅓   cup uncooked white rice
1   Tbsp. chopped parsley
¼   tsp. thyme
¼   tsp. basil
¼   tsp. crushed fennel seeds
      salt and pepper to taste
1   tsp. sugar or honey

1. Heat oil in a saucepan. Add onions and garlic and cook 5 minutes over medium heat, until clear. Add mushrooms and cook 5 more minutes. Add tomatoes, stock, bay leaf, rice, parsley, thyme, basil, fennel, salt, pepper, and sugar. Bring to a boil, reduce heat and simmer for 35 to 40 minutes. Taste for seasoning and serve.

Serve this simple, clear soup with nori rolls or tempura. You may also add thin Japanese noodles for a more filling soup.

Green Jade Soup

Makes 4½ cups

3   Chinese dried
      mushrooms
4   cups vegetable stock
⅓   cup carrots, peeled and
      cut in one-inch
      matchstick
¼   cup thinly sliced scallions
½   cup thinly sliced
      mushrooms
      about 10 spinach leaves
3   Tbsp. soy sauce

1. Soak dried mushrooms in 1 cup boiling water for 20 to 30 minutes, until soft. Drain and reserve stock. Slice in thin strips.

2. Bring reserved mushroom stock and vegetable stock to a boil in saucepan. Add carrots, scallions, and both kinds of mushrooms and simmer for 3 minutes. Add spinach leaves and soy sauce and cook for a few more minutes, until spinach is just wilted. Taste for seasoning.

Served with fresh homemade wheat bread, this soup makes a hearty and heart-warming meal all by itself.

Polish Vegetable Barley Soup

Serves 8 to 10

2 Tbsp. oil
½ tsp. finely chopped garlic
1½ cups finely chopped onions
⅓ cup barley
1 cup diced carrots
1 cup diced celery
¼ lb. thinly sliced mushrooms
1 medium potato, peeled and diced
8 to 10 cups vegetable stock or water
½ tsp. thyme
5 Tbsp. soy sauce
salt and pepper to taste
sour cream for garnish

1. Heat oil in a stock pot and add garlic and onions. Cook until tender over medium heat, stirring occasionally, for about 5 minutes. Add barley and cook 3 minutes more.

2. Add remaining vegetables, stock, and seasonings and bring to a boil. Reduce heat and simmer for 45 to 50 minutes. Taste for seasoning and serve with a generous spoonful of sour cream.

This is a favorite wintertime soup.

Vegetable Borscht

Makes approx. 7 cups

¼ tsp. finely chopped garlic
¾ cup chopped onion
¾ cup carrots, peeled and diced
¾ cup diced celery
1 medium-sized potato, peeled and diced
1 cup beets, cut in julienne
approx. 4 cups water
salt to taste
1 tomato, peeled and chopped
1 cup thinly sliced green cabbage
3 Tbsp. tomato paste
2 tsp. sugar
pepper to taste

1. Combine garlic, onion, carrots, celery, potato, and beets in a large saucepan with salt and enough water to cover. Bring to a boil, reduce heat, and simmer for 20 minutes.

2. Add tomato, cabbage, tomato paste, sugar, and pepper and simmer for 20 more minutes. Taste for seasoning. Garnish with a spoonful of sour cream.

Be careful not to let this soup boil once the cheese has been added, or it will curdle.

Vegetable Cheese Soup

Makes 6½ cups

2 Tbsp. butter
¼ cup finely chopped onion
2 Tbsp. flour
½ cup diced celery
½ cup diced carrots
½ cup diced green pepper
1½ cups peeled and diced potatoes
2 cups vegetable stock or water
salt and pepper to taste
2 cups milk
1 cup green peas
1 tsp. Dijon mustard
2 Tbsp. sherry
1 cup cherry tomatoes, halved if large
1½ cups grated sharp cheddar cheese

1. Heat butter in a saucepan. Add onion and cook gently for 5 minutes, until clear. Sprinkle with flour and cook, stirring, for 3 to 4 minutes.

2. Add celery, carrots, green pepper, potatoes, stock, salt, and pepper. Stir and bring to a boil. Reduce heat and simmer for 15 to 20 minutes, until vegetables are tender. Add milk, peas, mustard, sherry, and cherry tomatoes and simmer for 5 minutes. Taste for seasoning.

3. Remove from heat and stir in grated cheddar cheese. Serve.

This slightly spicy curry soup has sweet overtones of apple and honey.

Mulligatawny

Makes 7 cups

2 Tbsp. butter
1 cup diced onions
1½ cup diced carrots
1 cup diced green pepper
1 cup peeled, diced apples
1 cup diced celery
2 Tbsp. flour
4 cups vegetable stock or water
2 tsp. curry powder
¼ tsp. cardamon
1½ Tbsp. tomato paste
2 Tbsp. honey
1 tsp. tamarind extract (opt.)
salt and pepper to taste
approx. 1 cup yogurt

1. Heat butter in a saucepan. Add onions, carrots, green pepper, apples, and celery. Cook over medium heat for 5 minutes, stirring occasionally. Sprinkle with flour and cook, stirring, for another 3 minutes. Do not let the flour brown.

2. Add stock, curry powder, cardamon, tomato paste, honey, tamarind extract, salt, and pepper. Simmer for 30 to 35 minutes. Taste for seasoning. Garnish each bowl with a generous spoonful of yogurt.

Literally, minestrone means "big soup." Filled with all kinds of vegetables, this example of minestrone makes a meal in itself.

Minestrone

Makes 10 to 12 cups

- 2 Tbsp. olive oil
- 1 cup finely chopped onion
- ½ tsp. finely chopped garlic
- 1 cup diced carrots
- ½ cup diced celery
- 2½ cups diced zucchini
- 1 cup shredded cabbage
- 1 tsp. basil
- 1 Tbsp. chopped parsley
- 4 cups peeled and chopped tomatoes, fresh or canned
- 4 cups water
  salt and pepper to taste
- ¾ cup cooked chick peas
- ¾ cup pastina
- 1 cup green peas

1. Heat oil in a large saucepan or stock pot. Add onion, garlic, carrots, celery, zucchini, cabbage, basil, and parsley and simmer for 5 to 8 minutes. Add tomatoes, water, salt, pepper, chick peas, and pastina and bring to a boil. Reduce heat and simmer for 30 to 35 minutes. Add peas and cook for 5 to 10 minutes, until peas are tender. Taste for seasoning and serve.

The opposite of minestrone, minestrina means "little soup." This "little soup" makes a fine beginning for an Italian meal.

Minestrina

Makes 5 ½ cups

- 1 large potato
- 2 cups water
- 1 tsp. salt
- 2 Tbsp. olive oil
- 1 cup finely chopped onion
- 1 cup diced celery
- 1 cup diced carrots
- 2 cups milk
- ¾ cup freshly grated Parmesan cheese
  pinch black pepper
- 1 Tbsp. finely chopped parsley

1. Peel and dice potato. Combine in a saucepan with water and salt and bring to a boil. Reduce heat and simmer for 10 to 15 minutes, until potatoes are tender. Puree in blender until smooth.

2. Heat olive oil in a saucepan. Add onion and celery and cook 5 minutes, until onions are clear. Add carrots and potato puree and simmer for 10 to 15 minutes, until vegetables are tender.

3. Add milk and reheat. Taste for seasoning. Remove from heat and stir in Parmesan cheese, pepper, and chopped parsley.

This is a personal favorite. Make plenty, since it is even better on the second or third day.

Cuban Black Bean Soup

2 cups black beans
2 Tbsp. oil
1½ cups finely chopped onions
1 tsp. finely chopped garlic
1 large green pepper, diced
1 Tbsp. oregano
4 tsp. ground cumin
6 cups water
2 tsp. salt
5 tsp. vinegar

1. Cover beans with water and soak overnight. Drain.

2. Heat oil in a saucepan. Add onion, garlic, green pepper, oregano, and cumin. Cook, strirring occasionally, for 5 minutes.

3. Add soaked beans, water, salt, and vinegar and bring to boil. Reduce heat and simmer for 1½ to 2 hours, until beans are tender. Add more water from time to time if necessary. Taste for seasoning and garnish with marinated rice and chopped onion.

Rice Garnish

½ cup cooked white rice
½ cup chopped onion
2 tsp. olive oil
4 tsp. white vinegar

Toss cooked rice with onion, olive oil, and vinegar. Serve a generous spoonful with soup.

Makes approx. 8 cups

¾ cup diced zucchini
¾ cup diced carrots
1 potato, peeled and diced
½ cup finely chopped onion
¾ cup green beans, cut in ¾-inch pieces
1 tsp. salt
8 cups water
1 cup cooked navy beans, or other white beans
3 Tbsp. tomato paste
⅓ cup freshly grated Parmesan cheese
½ tsp. chopped garlic
⅓ cup fresh basil leaves, or 1 Tbsp. dried basil
¼ cup olive oil

This is a kind of French minestrone—a hearty and filling soup made with lots of different vegetables. The soul of this soup is a *pistou,* a thick paste of garlic, basil, cheese, and olive oil that is stirred into the soup just before serving.

Soupe au Pistou

1. Combine zucchini, carrots, potato, onion, green beans, salt, and water in a large saucepan and bring to a boil. Reduce heat and simmer for 20 minutes. Add navy beans and cook for 10 more minutes.

2. Combine tomato paste, Parmesan, garlic, and basil in a blender with about ¼ cup liquid from the soup. Blend until smooth. Turn blender on low speed and slowly pour in olive oil. Stir *pistou* into soup and serve.

You may also add diced carrots, celery, zucchini, and other vegetables to this chili.

Vegetarian Chili

Makes 8 cups

2 cups pinto or red kidney beans
2 Tbsp. oil
1½ cups finely chopped onion
1 tsp. finely chopped garlic
2 large green peppers, diced
1 tsp. ground cumin
4 tsp. chili powder
pinch cayenne pepper
1 tsp. oregano
4 cups chopped tomatoes, fresh or canned
2 cups water
1 bay leaf
¼ cup red wine
salt to taste
grated cheddar cheese for garnish

1. Cover beans with water and soak overnight. Drain.

2. Heat oil in a saucepan. Add onion, garlic, green pepper, cumin, chili powder, cayenne pepper, and oregano. Cook, stirring occasionally, for 5 minutes.

3. Add tomatoes, water, bay leaf, red wine, salt, and beans and bring to a boil. Reduce heat and simmer for 1½ to 2 hours, until beans are tender. Taste for seasoning and garnish with generous spoonful of grated cheddar.

Creamy White Bean Soup

Makes approx. 8 cups

2 cups dry white beans, such as navy or pea beans
2 Tbsp. butter
½ tsp. finely chopped garlic
1½ cups sliced onions
½ cup sliced leeks or scallions
2 cups chopped tomatoes, fresh or canned
4 cups water
½ tsp. thyme
1 bay leaf
salt and pepper to taste
1 cup heavy cream

1. Cover beans with water and soak overnight. Cook until tender in boiling, salted water, 1½ to 2 hours. Drain.

2. Heat butter in a saucepan. Add garlic, onions, and leeks and cook for 5 minutes. Add beans, tomatoes, water, thyme, bay leaf, salt, and pepper. Bring to a boil, reduce heat and simmer for 45 minutes.

3. Remove bay leaf and puree soup in blender until smooth. Stir in cream and reheat. Taste for seasoning. Garnish with thinly sliced green part of scallion.

Navy Bean Soup

2	cups navy beans
2	Tbsp. oil
½	tsp. finely chopped garlic
1½	cups finely chopped onion
1	cup diced carrots
1	cup diced celery
1½	cups chopped tomatoes, fresh or canned
1	tsp. basil
½	tsp. thyme
1	bay leaf
1	tsp. chopped parsley
6	cups water
	salt and pepper to taste

1. Cover beans with water and soak overnight. Drain.

2. Heat oil in a saucepan. Add garlic and onion and cook for 5 minutes. Add carrots, celery, tomatoes, basil, thyme, bay leaf, and chopped parsley and cook for 5 more minutes.

3. Add beans, water, salt, and pepper and bring to a boil. Reduce heat and simmer for 1½ to 2 hours, until beans are tender. Taste for seasoning and serve.

This is a filling stew of *pasta e fagiole:* pasta and beans.

Pasta e Fagiole

1½	cups dried navy, pea or other white beans
2	Tbsp. olive oil
1	cup finely chopped onion
½	cup diced celery
¾	cup diced carrots
1	cup chopped tomatoes, fresh or canned
2	Tbsp. tomato paste
	salt and pepper to taste
1	tsp. basil
6	cups water
¼	lb. spaghetti or other pasta, broken in small pieces
	freshly grated Parmesan cheese

1. Cover beans with water and soak overnight. Cook until tender in boiling salted water, 1½ to 2 hours. Drain.

2. Combine cooked beans in a saucepan with olive oil, onion, celery, carrots, tomatoes, tomato paste, salt, pepper, basil, and water and bring to a boil. Reduce heat and simmer for 45 minutes, until vegetables are tender.

3. Add noodles and cook for another 15 minutes. Taste for seasoning and serve with freshly grated Parmesan.

Split red lentils can be found in groceries which stock Middle Eastern or Indian foods.

Syrian Red Lentil Soup

Makes 8 cups

2   Tbsp. vegetable oil
½   tsp. finely chopped garlic
1½ cups split red lentils
6   cups water
2 · tsp. thyme
1   tsp. ground cumin
2   tsp. salt
2   Tbsp. flour
¼   cup cold water
2   or 3 pieces of toasted pita
      bread (Syrian flat
      bread)

1. Heat oil in a saucepan. Add garlic and cook one minute. Add lentils, water, thyme, cumin, and salt. Bring to a boil, reduce heat and simmer for 1 hour.

2. Mix flour with cold water until smooth and add to soup. Stir and simmer for another 5 minutes. Taste for seasoning. Serve topped with crumbled, toasted *pita* bread.

This lentil soup takes very little time to put together. It is delicious the second or third day, too.

Rudi's Lentil Soup

Makes 8 cups

2   Tbsp. oil
1   cup finely chopped
      onion
1   Tbsp. oregano
1   Tbsp. basil
½   tsp. finely chopped garlic
1   cup lentils
6   cups water
¼   cup soy sauce
1   cup carrots, cut in
      bite-size pieces

1. Heat oil in a large saucepan. Add onion, oregano, basil, and garlic and cook for 5 minutes, stirring occasionally.

2. Add lentils, water, soy sauce, and carrots and bring to a boil. Reduce heat and simmer for one hour. Serve with a sprinkle of chopped parsley.

For a richer version of this soup, puree entire soup until smooth in a blender and reheat with one cup cream.

Split Pea Soup

Makes 8 cups

1   cup split peas
6   cups vegetable stock or
      water
½   tsp. finely chopped garlic
1   cup finely chopped
      onions
1   cup diced carrots
1   cup diced celery
1   tsp. marjoram
      salt and pepper to taste
1   bay leaf

1. Combine all ingredients in a saucepan and bring to a boil. Reduce heat and simmer for one hour, until split peas are soft.

2. Remove bay leaf and puree 4 cups soup in a blender until smooth. Return to saucepan, reheat, and taste for seasoning.

Here is a creamy and very tasty version of the humble split pea.

Split Pea and Potato Soup

Makes 7 to 8 cups

2   Tbsp. olive oil
½   cup finely chopped
      onion
1   cup split peas
5   cups water
1   Tbsp. salt
2   large potatoes, peeled
      and diced
½   cup freshly grated
      Parmesan cheese

1. Heat oil in a large saucepan. Add onions and cook 3 minutes. Add split peas, water, salt, and diced potatoes. Bring to a boil, reduce heat, and simmer for 45 minutes.

2. Puree soup in blender with grated Parmesan until very smooth. Taste for seasoning.

Entrees:
Vegetable Dishes

Asparagus in March, corn in May, kiwi fruit, papayas, mangoes, and strawberries all year around—the markets of today abound with produce from all corners of the earth. Shoppers of twenty years ago would be astonished at the choices available to the modern consumer as a result of rapid transportation methods and increasing demands for quality and selection of goods.

In fact, the demands of both ethnic groups and gourmet consumers have brought a host of foreign ingredients to the American supermarket. Masa harina, corn husks, fresh tortillas, Chinese sesame oil, imported soy sauce, rice wine vinegar, vine leaves, sesame paste, and dried mushrooms are a few of the items now found in the gourmet section of large supermarkets. Produce sections stock fresh bean sprouts, fresh ginger, snow peas, and other "exotic" foods that were recently only available, if at all, in a few gourmet shops. Today, few towns are without a health or gourmet food store, which provide whatever the larger markets lack. With such a wide and exciting selection of ingredients to choose from, today's cooks have only to look to their imagination for interesting menu ideas.

The wise cook, however, will first look to the produce in season when planning a menu. Not only are they of the best quality, but vegetables in their peak season are also available at excellent prices. With this theory as the basis, the smart shopper can then invest in the more "exotic" items. Pignoli nuts in Moussaka, Italian dried mushrooms in tomato sauce, and Spanish saffron in a vegetable stew are a few of the indulgences that the budget will allow if you follow this plan.

This cheese pie has a rich strudel crust. Serve with rice and a green vegetable or salad.

Artichoke Ricotta Pie

Serves 6

1 Tbsp. olive oil
¾ cup finely chopped scallions
1 14-ounce can artichoke hearts
1½ cups ricotta cheese
1 cup grated Swiss cheese
½ cup freshly grated Parmesan cheese
3 eggs
½ tsp. dill weed
1 Tbsp. finely chopped parsley
   salt and pepper to taste
½ cup melted butter
6 sheets phyllo dough

1. Heat olive oil in a skillet. Sauté scallions until tender, but do not brown.

2. Drain artichokes and cut in quarters.

3. Combine ricotta, Swiss cheese, Parmesan, eggs, dill weed, parsley, salt, and pepper and mix until smooth. Stir in sautéed scallions and taste for seasoning.

4. Lay a sheet of phyllo on work surface and brush with melted butter. Place two more sheets on top of the first one, brushing each with more melted butter. With a sharp knife, cut sheet in half horizontally. Line a buttered 10-inch pie pan with the two halves, placing one horizontally and the other vertically. Let excess hang over the edge.

5. Spread half the filling on the bottom of the phyllo-lined pan. Cover with drained and quartered artichoke hearts and spread remaining filling on top. Fold overlapping edges of phyllo in toward the center.

6. Brush three more sheets of phyllo with melted butter layering them as you did for the bottom crust. This time, cut the sheet in quarters and place on top of the pie, offsetting the squares of phyllo to cover. Tuck overlapping edges under.

7. Bake in a preheated 375 degree oven for 25 to 30 minutes, until golden brown. Cut in wedges with a serrated knife.

Here is a *"pizza rustica"* filled with artichokes, cheese and hard-boiled eggs. The tomato sauce is poured over the pie after baking.

Deep Dish Pizza

Serves 6 to 8

1 recipe Basic Italian
    Bread
   olive oil
   few pinches dried basil
   few pinches dried mint
6 large artichoke hearts,
    sliced
2 hard-boiled eggs, sliced
4 ounces mozzarella
    cheese, thinly sliced
4 cups tomato sauce
   freshly grated Parmesan
    cheese

1. Make bread dough according to recipe and let rise in a warm place for 1½ hours. Punch down and divide in half.

2. Roll half the dough into a circle large enough to line a 10-inch pie pan or round shallow dish. Lightly oil the pan and line with dough.

3. Brush dough with olive oil and sprinkle with basil and mint. Layer with half the artichokes, half the hard-boiled eggs, and half the sliced cheese. Layer remaining artichokes, egg and cheese in the same order. Sprinkle with more olive oil, salt, pepper, mint, and basil.

4. Roll the rest of the dough into a circle large enough to cover the top. Place it over the pie and pinch the edges together. Trim excess dough and brush with olive oil. Bake in a preheated 450 degree oven for 20 to 25 minutes, until nicely browned.

5. Cut pie in serving pieces and spoon on the hot tomato sauce. Sprinkle with Parmesan cheese and serve.

Tomato Sauce

Makes 4 cups

2 Tbsp. olive oil
1 cup chopped onion
1 tsp. finely chopped garlic
1 tsp. oregano
1 tsp. basil
1 cup thinly sliced
    mushrooms
4 cups canned tomatoes,
    coarsely chopped
   small pinch sugar
1 bay leaf
2 Tbsp. capers
   salt and pepper to taste

1. Heat oil in a saucepan. Add chopped onion and garlic and cook 5 minutes, until tender. Add oregano, basil, and mushrooms and cook 3 more minutes. Add tomatoes, sugar, bay leaf, capers, salt, and pepper and simmer for 20 to 25 minutes. Taste again for seasoning.

Here, layers of seasoned vegetables, mushrooms, and chopped hard-boiled egg are baked in a delicious brioche crust.

Cabbage Brioche Loaf

Serves 8 to 10

1	*small head green cabbage, about 1 lb.*
1½	*cups carrots, cut in medium dice*
½	*lb. potatoes, peeled and cut in medium dice*
4	*Tbsp. butter*
1	*cup thinly sliced onion*
1	*tsp. dill weed*
	salt and white pepper to taste
¼	*lb. mushrooms, sliced*
2	*lbs. brioche dough*
2	*hard-boiled eggs, coarsely chopped*
1	*beaten egg*
1	*cup sour cream for garnish*

1. Cut cabbage in ½-inch thick slices and blanch 3 minutes in boiling, salted water. Drain well.

2. Blanch carrots and potatoes separately in boiling, salted water until tender. Drain.

3. Heat 3 tablespoons butter in a large skillet and add onions. Cook 3 minutes and add blanched cabbage, carrots, potatoes, dill weed, salt, and pepper. Taste for seasoning.

4. Heat remaining 1 tablespoon butter in a small skillet, add mushrooms and cook until wilted, about 5 minutes.

5. On a lightly floured board, roll brioche dough into a rectangle 18 inches long and 15 inches wide, about ⅜ thick. Mark off a smaller rectangle in the center of the dough, 12 inches long and 5 inches wide. This is where you will place the filling.

6. Spread half the cabbage mixture over the dough in the marked-off section. Cover with sliced mushrooms and spread the chopped egg over them. Top with remaining cabbage mixture.

7. Brush beaten egg along the edges of the dough. Fold one long edge over the filling, then the other, and press together to seal. Bring the side flaps in toward the center and again press gently to seal.

8. Carefully turn the loaf upside-down so that the seam is on the bottom, and place on a buttered baking sheet. Make two ¼-inch round holes for vents in the top of the loaf.

9. Preheat oven to 400 degrees. Brush loaf with beaten egg and let rest 20 minutes before baking.

10. Brush loaf again with beaten egg and bake for 15 minutes. Reduce heat to 350 degrees and bake for another 30 minutes. Check to make sure top does not brown too quickly. If so, cover loosely with aluminum foil while the loaf finishes baking. Remove from oven and let rest for 5 to 10 minutes before slicing and serving. Serve garnished with sour cream.

These cabbage rolls are filled with kasha, vegetables and nuts and baked in a tomato sauce.

Stuffed Cabbage Rolls

Serves 6

2 Tbsp. butter
½ cup chopped onion
½ cup diced celery
½ cup diced carrots
1 cup thinly sliced
   mushrooms
½ cup chopped apples
¼ cup chopped walnuts
1 tsp. dill weed
1 egg
⅔ cup kasha
1 tsp. salt
1⅓ cups boiling vegetable
   stock
1 large head green
   cabbage
   Tomato Sauce (see
   recipe below)

1. Heat butter in a saucepan. Add onions, celery, carrots, and mushrooms and cook for 8 to 10 minutes. Add apples, walnuts, and dill weed.

2. Beat egg in a bowl and mix with kasha. Add kasha to saucepan with vegetables and cook, stirring constantly for 2 minutes, until egg is set and grains of kasha are separate. Add salt and boiling stock, cover tightly, and simmer for 10 to 15 minutes, until kasha is tender. Taste for seasoning.

To Assemble:

1. Cut stem from cabbage and immerse in a large pot of boiling water. This is not to cook the cabbage, but to loosen the leaves from the core. After a few minutes, remove the cabbage from the water and pull off the loose leaves. Continue to dip the head in boiling water for a few minutes at a time and remove the loose leaves, until you have 12 to 14 leaves. You may need to cut some of the leaves free at the core, but otherwise, they should pull away from the head easily. Blanch leaves again in boiling water for 2 to 3 minutes, until pliable.

2. Place ⅓ cup filling on each leaf. Fold the sides in toward the center and roll up to form a neat package. Place the rolls close together with the seam side down in a shallow baking dish and cover with tomato sauce. Bake in a preheated 400 degree oven until hot all the way through, 15 to 20 minutes.

Tomato Sauce

2 Tbsp. olive oil
1 cup chopped onion
½ tsp. finely chopped garlic
½ tsp. thyme
½ tsp. basil
4 cups canned tomatoes,
   coarsely chopped
1 tsp. sugar
   salt and pepper to taste

1. Heat oil in a saucepan. Add onion and garlic and cook for 5 minutes. Add thyme, basil, tomatoes, sugar, salt, and pepper. Simmer for 25 minutes and taste for seasoning.

These delicious and unusual cabbage rolls are steamed and served in a cream sauce.

Chinese Cabbage Rolls

Serves 4 to 6

4   *Chinese dried
      mushrooms*
1   *potato, peeled, and cut
      in 1-inch julienne*
1   *turnip, peeled, and cut in
      1-inch julienne*
1   *carrot, peeled, and cut in
      1-inch julienne*
2   *Tbsp. cooking oil*
½   *cup finely sliced scallions*
1   *cup finely chopped
      mushrooms*
¼   *cup green peas*
¼   *cup sliced bamboo shoots*
½   *cup vegetable stock*
1   *tsp. salt*
1   *Tbsp. soy sauce*
2   *tsp. cornstarch dissolved
      in 1 tsp. cold water*
1   *tsp. Chinese sesame oil*
1   *head green cabbage
      Cream Sauce (see
      recipe below)*

1. Soak dried mushrooms in ½ cup boiling water until soft, 20 to 30 minutes. Drain, reserve stock, and slice in thin julienne.

2. Blanch potato, turnip, and carrot until tender in boiling salted water. Drain and set aside.

3. Heat oil in a wok or skillet. Add scallions and both kinds of mushrooms and cook one or two minutes, until they begin to wilt. Add blanched vegetables, green peas, bamboo shoots, stock, salt and soy sauce. Stir in cornstarch paste and cook for 3 more minutes, until liquid in the bottom of the pan comes to a full boil. Remove from heat and stir in sesame oil.

4. Cut stem from cabbage and immerse in a large pot of boiling water. This is not to cook the cabbage, but to loosen the leaves from the core. After a few minutes, remove the cabbage from the water and pull off the loose leaves. Continue to dip the head in boiling water for a few minutes at a time and remove the loose leaves, until you have 12 to 14 leaves. You may need to cut some of the leaves free at the core, but otherwise, they should pull away from the head easily. Blanch the leaves again in boiling water for 2 to 3 minutes, until pliable.

5. Place ¼ cup filling on each leaf. Fold the sides in toward the center and roll up to form a neat package. Place the rolls close together on a heatproof plate or Chinese steamer with the seam side down. Place the plate on a rack in a large skillet with about ½ inch water in the bottom. Bring water to a boil, cover pan and steam for 15 minutes. Remove the cabbage rolls to a serving platter and serve covered with cream sauce.

Cream Sauce

1½ *cups vegetable stock
      salt to taste*
1   *Tbsp. cornstarch
      dissolved in 2 tsp.
      cold water*
⅓   *cup milk*

1. Bring stock to a rolling boil and add salt. Stir in cornstarch paste and milk. Stir with a whisk until sauce returns to a boil. Pour over cabbage rolls.

The French adapted this idea from the Turks. Crepes are filled and rolled like egg rolls, then breaded and deep fried. If you wish to forego the deep frying (and miss out on a unique treat), you may also bake these in a casserole. Other fillings, such as asparagus in a mornay sauce, or curried vegetables, could also be used in beurrecks.

One beurreck makes a crispy, light appetizer. Two or more with a salad make a meal.

Beurrecks a la Turque

Makes 8 beurrecks

8 *crepes*
1 *cup milk*
1½ *Tbsp. butter*
1½ *Tbsp. flour*
1 *cup cauliflower florets, in small pieces*
1 *cup broccoli florets, in small pieces*
⅓ *cup Swiss cheese, cut in ¼-inch dice, about 2 ounces*
 salt and freshly ground pepper to taste
 flour
2 *to 3 beaten eggs*
 bread crumbs
 oil for frying

1. Make crepes. (See following recipe).

2. Bring milk to a boil in a small saucepan.

3. Melt butter and stir in flour. Cook for 2 or 3 minutes, stirring to keep the flour from browning. Add boiling milk, ¼ cup at a time, and stir with a whisk until the sauce comes to a boil. Simmer, stirring occasionally, until thick.

4. Blanch cauliflower and broccoli in boiling, salted water until tender. Drain and add to sauce with cheese. Add salt and pepper to taste. Chill in refrigerator.

5. When filling is cool, place about 2 tablespoons across the lower middle part of a crepe. Fold bottom flap up over the filling and fold the sides in towards the center. Roll away from you into a snug roll, holding the side flaps in place with your fingers. Brush a little beaten egg on the top flap to seal securely. Continue with the remaining crepes, until all the filling is used.

6. Put flour, beaten egg, and breadcrumbs in three separate pans. Lightly coat the beurrecks with flour, dip them in the beaten egg, and roll in breadcrumbs. Place the breaded crepes on a tray to dry for 15 to 20 minutes.

7. Heat 1½ to 2 inches oil in a heavy iron skillet or frying pan. Fry beurrecks until brown and crispy on both sides. Drain on absorbent paper and sprinkle with salt.

8. If you wish to bake them, arrange the filled and breaded crepes in a buttered baking dish, sprinkle with a little melted butter, and bake in a preheated 450 degree oven for 10 to 15 minutes, until crepes are hot all the way through.

Although much better if used when freshly made, crepes may be stacked, wrapped in a damp towel, and refrigerated for several days. They may also be wrapped securely in plastic and frozen.

*Makes 16 to 18
7-inch crepes*

3	*eggs*
1¾	*cups milk*
1	*cup flour*
½	*tsp. salt*
1	*Tbsp. oil*

Crepes

1. Combine all ingredients in a blender and blend until smooth.

2. If you do not have a blender, beat eggs, milk, oil and salt together in a bowl. Work one third liquid ingredients into the flour until you have a smooth paste. Gradually add remaining liquid until you have a smooth batter about the consistency of heavy cream. Strain.

3. Lightly coat a 7-inch crepe pan with oil and heat until quite hot. Pour about 2 tablespoons batter into the pan and tilt back and forth until the batter coats the bottom of the pan evenly. Cook until browned on one side, about 30 seconds. Turn and cook briefly on the other side. Turn crepe out onto a clean kitchen towel by tipping the pan upside-down over the towel. Continue until all the batter is used.

Serve Shahi Cauliflower with rice, curried beans, yogurt raita, and chutney for a complete Indian meal.

Shahi Cauliflower

Serves 6

5 Tbsp. oil
1 head cauliflower, broken in bite-sized florets
3 potatoes, peeled and cut in large dice
¾ cup water
¾ cup finely chopped onion
3 Tbsp. chopped canned, green chiles
1 tsp. grated fresh ginger
1 tsp. turmeric
1 Tbsp. Indian curry spice mix (recipe follows)
1 tsp. salt
1 cup green peas
10 cherry tomatoes
1 Tbsp. poppy seeds
1 cup plain yogurt

1. Heat 3 Tbsp. oil in a large skillet. Add cauliflower and potatoes and stir one minute. Add ½ cup water, cover and simmer for 8 to 10 minutes, until vegetables are tender.

2. Combine remaining ¼ cup water, chopped onion, chiles, ginger, spices, and salt in a blender and puree until smooth. Heat 2 Tbsp. oil in a small skillet, add curry paste and cook, stirring, for 5 minutes.

3. Add cooked curry paste, green peas, cherry tomatoes, and poppy seeds to skillet with cauliflower. Stir and simmer for 5 more minutes.

4. Stir yogurt into vegetables, taste for seasoning and serve.

I prefer this curry powder to the store-bought variety. You may adjust the degree of hotness by the amount of cayenne pepper that you use. This one is fairly mild.

Makes ¾ cup

4 Tbsp. ground cumin
4 Tbsp. ground coriander
2 Tbsp. black pepper
1 Tbsp. ground ginger
1½ tsp. ground cloves
½ tsp. cayenne pepper

Indian Curry Spice Mix

Mix all ingredients together until well blended.

A raita is a yogurt-based condiment that is usually served as a refreshing accompaniment to an Indian meal. Substitute grated zucchini or chopped, fresh tomato for the cucumber for another variation.

Makes 2 cups

½ tsp. whole cumin seed
1½ cups yogurt
½ cup cucumber, peeled, seeded and diced small
1 tsp. Indian curry spice mix
¼ tsp. salt

Cucumber Raita

Roast cumin seed under broiler or in a frying pan without oil until dark and crush with a rolling pin. Add to yogurt with remaining ingredients and mix well. Serve cold.

In this dish, the dark, shiny, purple eggplant skin surrounded by the brilliant red tomato sauce makes a most dramatic presentation. It may be made in individual souffle molds or in one large dish. Pignoli nuts, though exorbitant in price, are a special addition. However, walnuts will do in a pinch.

Moussaka

Serves 6

3 eggplants, each weighing
   2 or 3 lbs.
3 Tbsp. olive oil
1 cup chopped onion
1½ tsp. finely chopped garlic
2 cups zucchini, cut in
   ¼-inch dice
1 tomato, peeled, seeded
   and chopped, about
   ¾ cup
¾ cup cooked chick peas
2 Tbsp. capers
3 Tbsp. pignoli nuts or
   coarsely chopped
   walnuts
2 Tbsp. chopped parsley
1½ tsp. basil
1 Tbsp. lemon juice
1 cup breadcrumbs
1 egg
   salt and pepper to taste
3 artichoke hearts, halved

1. Cut eggplants in half lengthwise and score deeply with point of a sharp knife, being careful not to pierce the outer skin. Sprinkle generously with salt and set aside to drain for 30 minutes. Place eggplant halves, cut side up, in a baking pan and bake at 375 degrees for 45 minutes to an hour, until tender.

2. Heat olive oil in a skillet. Add onions and garlic and cook 3 minutes. Add zucchini, chopped tomatoes, chick peas, capers, nuts, parsley, and basil and cook 15 to 20 minutes, until zucchini is tender.

3. Remove eggplant from oven and scrape the pulp away from the skin, taking care to leave the skin intact. Chop pulp coarsely and add to zucchini mixture along with lemon juice, breadcrumbs, and beaten egg. Season with plenty of salt and pepper.

4. Oil a 6-cup souffle dish or ovenproof bowl and line it with eggplant skin, the shiny side against the sides of the mold. Fill with half the eggplant mixture and distribute the halved artichoke hearts evenly over the top. Cover with the remaining filling. Cover the mold tightly with aluminum foil.

5. Place the souffle dish in a baking pan with one inch of water on the bottom. Bake in a preheated 375 degree oven for one hour. Invert on a serving platter and serve hot, surrounded with tomato sauce. Pass extra sauce separately. Note: For individual molds, follow the same procedure, placing one artichoke half in the center of each mold.

Tomato Sauce for Moussaka

2 Tbsp. olive oil
1 cup chopped onion
1 tsp. finely chopped garlic
¾ cup finely diced carrots
¾ cup finely diced celery
1 tsp. basil
5 cups canned tomatoes,
   with juice
   small pinch sugar
1 bay leaf
   salt and pepper to taste

1. Heat oil in a saucepan. Add chopped onion and garlic and cook 3 minutes. Add carrots and celery and cook until vegetables are tender. Add basil, tomatoes, sugar, bay leaf, salt, and pepper. Simmer for 25 minutes and taste for seasoning.

2. Remove bay leaf and puree sauce in blender. Taste again for seasoning.

A versatile dish, ratatouille may be eaten plain, topped with poached eggs and grated cheese, or wrapped inside an omelet for a satisfying brunch or Sunday supper dish. Many contend ratatouille is even better a day or two after it is made. Here is a main course recipe for ratatouille baked in a cheesy pie crust.

Ratatouille Pie

One 9-inch pie

Crust:

3 cups flour
½ tsp. salt
4½ Tbsp. butter, cut in pieces
¾ cup shortening
1 tsp. dried basil
½ tsp. thyme
¼ cup freshly grated
    Parmesan cheese
7 to 8 Tbsp. water

1. Combine flour and salt in a bowl. With a hand mixer or a food processor, cut butter and shortening into flour until well blended. When it is thoroughly blended, the mixture will look crumbly and turn a shade darker in color.

2. Mix in the basil, thyme, and grated Parmesan.

3. Sprinkle water over pastry mix and toss with your hands until the dough starts to hold together in a mass.

4. Roll out half the dough and line a nine-inch pie pan. Fill with one-third of the ratatouille and sprinkle with one-third of the grated cheese. Continue to layer until all the filling is used, ending with a layer of cheese on top.

Filling:

6 cups cold ratatouille
⅓ cup freshly grated
    Parmesan cheese
2 cups grated Swiss cheese
    (about ¼ lb.)

5. Roll out remaining dough and cover the top of the pie. Seal, crimp the edges, and brush with beaten egg. Make a small cross in the center of the pie with the tip of a knife for a vent. Bake in a preheated 375 degree oven for 40 to 45 minutes, until crust is golden brown.

Ratatouille

Makes 6 cups

1 small eggplant, about
    1 lb.
¼ cup olive oil
1 large onion, about ½ lb.,
    cut in large dice
1 tsp. finely chopped garlic
1 lb. zucchini, cut in
    ½-inch pieces
2 green peppers, seeded
    and cut in ½-inch dice
1 lb. tomatoes, peeled and
    cut in ½-inch dice
1 bay leaf
    salt and pepper to taste
⅓ cup finely chopped
    parsley

1. Peel eggplant and cut in ½-inch cubes. Sprinkle with salt and let drain on paper towels for 30 minutes.

2. Heat olive oil in a skillet. Add eggplant and cook, stirring, for 5 minutes.

3. Add onion, garlic, zucchini, and green peppers and cook for 5 more minutes.

4. Add tomatoes, bay leaf, salt, pepper, and chopped parsley. Cover and cook over medium heat for 15 minutes, stirring occasionally. Remove cover and cook for 15 to 20 minutes. Taste for seasoning.

Use a full-bodied tomato sauce for this simple yet satisfying dish.

Eggplant Parmesan

Serves 4 to 6

1 medium-sized eggplant,
   about 1¼ lbs.
flour for breading
beaten egg
breadcrumbs for
   breading
oil for frying
4 cups tomato sauce
¾ cup freshly grated
   Parmesan cheese
¼ lb. sliced mozzarella
   cheese

1. Slice eggplant lengthwise in ½-inch thick slices. With the point of a sharp knife, score the slices and sprinkle them with salt. Drain on paper towels for 30 minutes.

2. Pat slices dry and coat lightly with flour. Dip in beaten egg and coat with breadcrumbs. Fry in ¼ inch hot oil until golden brown on both sides. Drain on absorbent paper.

3. Spoon one cup tomato sauce in the bottom of a shallow baking dish. Arrange half the eggplant slices over the sauce and cover with more sauce. Layer with half the Parmesan cheese and half the sliced mozzarella. Repeat with remaining eggplant, Parmesan, and mozzarella, reserving a little cheese for the top. Cover with remaining sauce and sprinkle with more cheese. Bake in a preheated 400 degree oven until cheese starts to brown and casserole is hot all the way through.

Baked Stuffed Eggplant

Serves 4

2 small eggplants, about
   1 lb. each
6 Tbsp. olive oil
1 tsp. finely chopped garlic
1 cup chopped tomatoes,
   fresh or canned
¾ cup finely chopped
   onion
¼ cup finely chopped
   parsley
1 tsp. basil
salt and pepper to taste
1 cup breadcrumbs
¾ cup freshly grated
   Parmesan cheese
¼ lb. thinly sliced
   mozzarella

1. Trim tops and cut eggplants in half lengthwise. Scoop out flesh, leaving a shell that is thick enough to hold its shape when baked. Sprinkle salt over eggplant shells and let drain in a colander for 30 minutes.

2. Coarsely chop eggplant pulp. Heat 4 tablespoons olive oil in a skillet. Add garlic, tomatoes, and onion and cook 3 minutes. Add eggplant, parsley, basil, salt, and pepper and cook for 20 to 30 minutes, stirring occasionally, until tender.

3. Remove from heat and add breadcrumbs and grated Parmesan. Taste for seasoning.

4. Wipe insides of eggplant shells dry with a paper towel and fill with stuffing. Sprinkle with remaining 2 tablespoons olive oil. Place in a baking pan and pour ½ inch boiling water on bottom of pan.

5. Cover loosely with aluminum foil and bake in a preheated 375 degree oven for 50 minutes. Remove from oven, remove foil, and cover eggplant halves with sliced mozzarella. Return pan to oven and bake 10 more minutes. Sprinkle with chopped parsley and serve.

While the crispy phyllo crust is optional, it does add a special touch to this Greek style macaroni and cheese casserole. A layer of eggplant, zucchini and tomatoes is an added bonus.

Pastitso

Serves 6

2	*Tbsp. olive oil*
1	*tsp. finely chopped garlic*
1	*cup chopped onion*
1½	*cups diced zucchini*
1½	*cups diced eggplant*
½	*tsp. cinnamon*
1	*tsp. oregano*
	salt and pepper to taste
1	*Tbsp. finely chopped parsley*
1	*cup peeled and chopped tomatoes, fresh or canned*
6	*Tbsp. butter*
6	*Tbsp. flour*
4	*cups milk, heated to the boiling point*
1	*lb. elbow macaroni*
1½	*cups freshly grated Parmesan cheese*
2	*eggs*
2	*sheets phyllo dough*
4	*Tbsp. melted butter*

1. Heat olive oil in a large skillet. Add garlic and onion and sauté 3 to 4 minutes, until tender. Add zucchini, eggplant, cinnamon, oregano, salt, pepper, parsley, and tomatoes and simmer for 15 to 20 minutes. Taste for seasoning.

2. Make a béchamel sauce: Melt butter in a small saucepan. Add flour and cook, stirring with a wire whisk, for 3 minutes. Do not let flour brown. Whisk in boiling milk, ¼ cup at a time, and cook, stirring, until thick. Season well with salt and pepper. Stir 2 tablespoons béchamel into cooked vegetables and set the remaining sauce aside.

3. Cook macaroni in plenty of boiling, salted water until tender. Drain.

4. Spread one half of the cooked macaroni on the bottom of a buttered baking dish. Sprinkle with one third of the grated cheese. Spread cooked vegetables over the top and sprinkle with one third more cheese. Cover with remaining macaroni and top with remaining cheese.

5. Beat the eggs into the béchamel sauce and pour it over the macaroni. (If the sauce is still hot, beat it into the eggs a little at a time.)

6. Brush the sheets of phyllo with melted butter and layer them over the top of the baking dish. With a sharp knife, cut into portions before baking. Bake in a preheated 375 degree oven for 20 to 25 minutes, until top is golden brown.

These pies can be made in advance and baked just before serving time.

Greek Spinach Pies

Six individual pies

1   *10-ounce package fresh spinach*
1   *Tbsp. butter*
¼ *cup thinly sliced scallions*
1   *cup crumbled feta cheese, about 5 ounces*
1   *cup cottage cheese*
2   *eggs*
1   *Tbsp. farina (cream of wheat)*
1   *tsp. dill weed*
2   *Tbsp. finely chopped parsley*
    salt and pepper to taste
12 *sheets phyllo dough*
1   *cup melted butter*

1. Clean and stem spinach and cook in a small amount of boiling water until tender. Drain, cool, and squeeze out excess water in a towel.

2. Heat butter in a small skillet and add scallions. Cook, stirring, for 2 minutes. Do not brown.

3. Mix crumbled feta, cottage cheese, eggs, farina, dill weed, and parsley together until blended. Add scallions and spinach and mix again. Season with salt and pepper to taste.

4. Brush one sheet of phyllo with melted butter. Place another sheet on top and brush it with butter. Fold the two sheets in half lengthwise and brush again with butter.

5. Place a scant ½ cup spinach filling on the lower right hand corner of the strip. With the bottom right-hand corner as your starting point, fold the strip of dough as you would a flag until you end up with a neat triangle encasing the filling. Brush with butter and place on a greased baking sheet. Repeat until all the filling is used.

6. Bake in a preheated 400 degree oven for 25 to 30 minutes, until golden brown and crispy. Serve hot.

Spinach Crepes

Serves 4 to 6

12 *crepes (See page 106.)*
2   *10-ounce packages fresh spinach*
3   *Tbsp. butter*
2   *Tbsp. finely chopped shallots*
½ *lb. thinly sliced mushrooms*
1   *Tbsp. Pernod*
½ *cup cream*
    salt and pepper to taste

1. Clean and stem spinach and cook in a small amount of boiling water until tender. Drain and squeeze out excess liquid in a towel. Chop.

2. Heat butter in a skillet. Add shallots and mushrooms and cook 4 to 5 minutes, until mushrooms start to brown. Add chopped spinach, Pernod, cream, salt, and pepper. Cook rapidly for a few minutes to reduce cream. Taste for seasoning.

3. Place one-fourth cup filling in the center of each crepe. Roll up and place in a buttered baking dish with the seam side down. Cover with cream sauce and bake in a preheated 375 degree oven, until crepes are hot all the way through and sauce bubbles.

Cream Sauce

1 cup milk
1 Tbsp. butter
1 Tbsp. flour
  salt and pepper to taste
1 egg yolk
¼ cup heavy cream,
  whipped

1. Bring milk to a boil in a small saucepan.

2. Melt butter and stir in flour. Cook, stirring, for 2 to 3 minutes. Do not let flour brown.

3. With a wire whisk, stir in boiling milk ¼ cup at a time. Cook, stirring, until thick. Season with salt and pepper.

4. Beat hot sauce into egg yolk a little at a time. Fold in whipped cream and taste for seasoning.

This potato pie is peasant fare, made with a pasta crust, potatoes, and fresh spinach. For variety, Swiss chard may be substituted for the spinach. The potato torta may also be baked in a large, flat pan, cut in squares, and served as an appetizer or accompaniment to drinks.

Makes one 9-inch pie

Pasta Crust:

1 cup all-purpose flour
6 Tbsp. semolina
½ tsp. salt
1 egg yolk
1 whole egg
3 to 4 Tbsp. milk

Filling:

2 Tbsp. butter
1 cup finely sliced leeks
1 10-ounce package fresh
  spinach
3 lbs. potatoes
1 cup freshly grated
  Parmesan cheese
  salt and pepper to taste

Potato Torta

1. Place the flour, semolina, and salt directly on the countertop in a mound. Make a deep well in the center and break the eggs into it. Scramble eggs with a fork and stir in milk. Little by little, draw the flour from the inside wall of the well into the center, continuing to scramble until the mixture starts to thicken. When the dough is stiff enough to handle, push the remaining flour over the eggs and mix together with your hands. Knead until smooth, about 5 minutes. Let dough rest while you make the filling.

1. Heat butter in a small skillet. Add leeks and sauté until tender, about 5 minutes.

2. Cook spinach in a small amount of boiling water until tender. Drain and press out excess moisture. Chop coarsely and mix with one-fourth of the sauteed leeks. Season well with salt and pepper.

3. Peel potatoes and cook until tender in boiling, salted water. Mash as you would for mashed potatoes and mix with remaining sauteed leeks, Parmesan, and plenty of salt and pepper.

4. Divide pasta dough in two slightly unequal pieces. Roll the larger piece into a circle large enough to fit a nine-inch pie pan. Lightly oil the pie pan and line it with the circle of dough, leaving a little overlap at the edge. (See following page.)

5. Spread one-half of the mashed potato mixture over the bottom of the pie pan and cover with the seasoned spinach and leeks. Top with the rest of the mashed potatoes.

6. Roll the remaining dough into a circle large enough to fit the top of the pie pan. Brush the rim of the pie with water, place the circle of dough on top, and press together with a fork. Trim excess dough and brush the top of the pie with beaten egg. Bake in a preheated 375 degree oven for 25 to 30 minutes, until golden brown.

When cooked, the flesh of this large, yellow summer squash miraculously separates into long, spaghetti-like strands. Unlike its pasta counterpart, spaghetti squash is low in calories, yet bland enough in taste to adapt to a number of treatments—simply tossed with butter and Parmesan cheese, or elaborately sauced with vegetables and tomatoes. In this recipe, a combination of Italian dried mushrooms and fresh mushrooms adds a unique dimension to the tomato sauce.

Spaghetti Squash with a Mushroom Tomato Sauce

Serves 4

¼   cup Italian dried
       mushrooms
2   Tbsp. olive oil
½· cup finely chopped
       onion
½   tsp. finely chopped garlic
1   cup thinly sliced
       mushrooms
2   cups chopped, canned
       tomatoes, with juice
1   cup tomato puree
     salt and pepper to taste
2   Tbsp. finely chopped
       parsley
1   large spaghetti squash,
       about 3 lbs.
     freshly grated Parmesan
       cheese

1. Cover dried mushrooms with boiling water and soak until soft, about 30 minutes. Drain and slice. Reserve liquid.

2. Heat olive oil in a skillet. Add onion, garlic, and fresh mushrooms and cook 5 minutes, until mushrooms start to brown. Add tomatoes, tomato puree, salt, pepper, parsley, and soaked, dried mushrooms. Bring to a boil, reduce heat and simmer for 45 minutes, stirring occasionally. Thin with reserved mushroom stock if necessary. Taste for seasoning.

3. Pour two inches of water in the bottom of a pot large enough to hold the squash easily. Place a steamer rack or heatproof plate in the bottom of the pot. Place the whole squash on the rack, cover the pot, and steam for 30 to 40 minutes, until the surface of the squash gives when pressed with a finger.

4. Cut the squash in half lengthwise and scoop out the seeds in the very center. Scoop remaining pulp onto a flat serving dish and break up the spaghetti strands with a fork. Sprinkle generously with salt and pepper and cover with tomato sauce. Top with plenty of grated Parmesan and serve immediately.

Like Greek Spinach Pies, Zucchini Pie may be made in individual portions, refrigerated, and baked just before serving.

Serves 6

2 Tbsp. butter
¼ cup finely chopped onion
½ tsp. finely chopped garlic
1 tsp. oregano
4 cups coarsely grated zucchini
1 cup grated carrot
1 Tbsp. finely chopped parsley
2 eggs
1 cup crumbled feta cheese, about 5 ounces
1 Tbsp. farina (cream of wheat)
salt and pepper to taste
½ cup melted butter
6 sheets phyllo dough

Zucchini Pie

1. Heat butter in a large skillet. Add onion, garlic, and oregano. Cook 2 minutes and add grated zucchini. Cook 5 minutes, stirring occasionally. Add grated carrot and chopped parsley. Remove from heat.

2. Beat eggs in a bowl and stir in feta cheese and farina. Add zucchini, mix well, and season with salt and pepper. Taste for seasoning.

3. Brush a sheet of phyllo with melted butter. Place two more sheets on top, brushing each with more melted butter. Cut sheet in half horizontally with a sharp knife. Line a buttered 10-inch pie pan with the two halves, placing one horizontally and the other vertically. Let the excess hang over the edge.

4. Pour the filling into the phyllo-lined pan and fold the overlapping edges in toward the center.

5. Brush three more sheets of phyllo with melted butter and place them on top of each other as you did for the bottom crust. This time, cut in quarters and place on top of the pie, off-setting the squares of phyllo to cover. Tuck the overlapping edges under.

6. Bake in a preheated 375 degree oven for 25 to 30 minutes, until golden brown. Cut in wedges with a serrated knife.

This supremely simple casserole dish takes advantage of some of summer's best produce. In preparing the peppers, do not skip the roasting and peeling step. The skinned peppers have an extraordinarily sweet and delicious flavor that differs markedly from peppers with the skins left on.

Casserole of Zucchini, Peppers, and Tomatoes

Serves 4

2 Tbsp. olive oil
1 clove garlic
¼ cup chopped onion
a few parsley stems
1 bay leaf
½ tsp. basil
3½ cups coarsely chopped, canned tomatoes with juice, or peeled, fresh tomatoes
salt and pepper to taste
3 small zucchini, each about 6 inches long
2 sweet peppers, red or green
¼ lb. sliced mozzarella cheese

1. Heat olive oil in a saucepan. Add whole garlic clove, chopped onion, parsley stems, bay leaf, and basil and cook for 3 or 4 minutes. Add tomatoes, salt, and pepper and simmer for 30 to 35 minutes. Remove garlic clove, parsley stems, and bay leaf. Taste for seasoning.

2. Trim zucchini ends and blanch whole in boiling, salted water until tender but on the firm side, 8 to 10 minutes. Remove and cut in half lengthwise.

3. Roast peppers over an open gas flame or under a broiler, until skins are blistered. Scrape off skins and rinse under cold water. Cut off tops, remove seeds and slice peppers in wide strips.

4. Spread a few spoonfuls of tomato stew in the bottom of a baking dish. Arrange the zucchini halves in the dish cut side up, and cover them with strips of pepper. Spoon on more tomato stew and top with slices of mozzarella cheese. Bake in a preheated 375 degree oven for 15 minutes, until cheese is melted and zucchini is hot all the way through.

Serve these zucchini croquettes with a tomato salad, or topped with a tomato sauce and a slice of cheese.

Zucchini Croquettes

Serves 4 to 6

1 large potato
2 cups grated zucchini
¼ cup finely chopped onion
¼ cup breadcrumbs
1 cup freshly grated Parmesan cheese
1 egg
1 Tbsp. finely chopped parsley
salt and pepper to taste
flour for dredging

1. Cook potato until tender in boiling water. Cool. Peel and coarsely grate.

2. Mix grated zucchini, potato, onion, breadcrumbs, cheese, egg and parsley together in a bowl. Add salt and pepper to taste.

3. Form mixture into oval patties and dust with flour. Fry in a heavy skillet in ⅛ inch hot oil until brown and crispy on both sides. Serve hot.

In Italy, pizza can mean almost any kind of pie made with almost any kind of filling. Here is a pizza rustica, "country pie," filled with Swiss chard, olives, capers, hard-boiled eggs and cheese. Note the omission of tomato sauce.

Pizza Rustica with Swiss Chard

One 9 inch pie

1 recipe Basic Italian
   Bread
¼ cup olive oil
4 cups sliced yellow onions
1 lb. Swiss chard
½ tsp. finely chopped garlic
   salt and pepper to taste
2 Tbsp. capers
6 to 8 Greek olives, pitted
   and coarsely chopped
1 hard-boiled egg, coarsely
   chopped
¼ lb. thinly sliced
   mozzarella cheese

1. Make bread according to recipe and let rise 45 minutes to one hour. Punch down and let rest while you prepare the filling.

2. Heat 2 tablespoons olive oil in a skillet. Add onions and cook until soft, 5 to 8 minutes. Set aside.

3. Trim stems from Swiss chard. Rinse under cold water and cut leaves crosswise in one-inch strips. Place leaves in a pot with ½ inch water on the bottom, cover, and steam until leaves are tender, about 5 minutes. Drain well.

4. Heat remaining olive oil in a skillet. Add garlic and Swiss chard and cook 5 minutes, until excess liquid evaporates. Add salt and pepper to taste.

5. Roll half of the bread dough into a large circle. Oil a 9-inch pie pan and line it with the dough. Brush dough with olive oil and cover with half the cooked onions. Sprinkle with half the capers, olives, hard-boiled egg, and sliced cheese. Spread the Swiss chard over this. Sprinkle with the remaining capers, olives, egg, and cheese and cover with remaining onions.

6. Roll remaining dough into a circle and place it over the top of the pie. Press edges together to seal, brush with olive oil, and prick all over with a fork. Bake in a preheated 450 degree oven for 20 to 25 minutes, until crust starts to brown. Serve hot.

Here is another example of how phyllo dough, that wonderful Greek invention, can spruce up a meal.

The paper-thin sheets of dough come packaged in one pound boxes and can be found in most gourmet food shops or groceries that carry Middle Eastern foods. Much like strudel dough, phyllo "leaves" are brushed with melted butter, built up in layers, and used to encase both sweet and savory fillings. The baked result is a crisp and buttery crust that transforms an everyday dish into something special.

Greek Vegetable Pies

Serves 8

1 Tbsp. butter
½ tsp. finely chopped garlic
½ cup chopped onion
½ cup chopped scallions
1 cup diced celery
1 cup diced zucchini
½ tsp. dill weed
¼ tsp. oregano
¼ tsp. basil
1 medium potato, boiled, peeled, and diced
1 cup diced carrots, blanched until tender
salt and pepper to taste
1 egg yolk
2 cups béchamel sauce (see following page)
1½ cups freshly grated Parmesan cheese
16 leaves phyllo dough
¾ cup melted butter

1. Heat butter in a large skillet. Add garlic, onions, and scallions. Cook gently for five minutes and add celery, zucchini, dill weed, oregano, and basil. Cook until vegetables are tender. Add cooked potato and carrots and season well with salt and pepper.

2. Break egg yolk into a bowl and beat in hot béchamel sauce a little at a time. Stir in grated Parmesan cheese.

3. Mix cheese sauce with vegetables. Season with salt and pepper and cool to room temperature, or set aside in refrigerator until ready to use.

4. Brush one sheet of phyllo with melted butter. Place another sheet directly on top and brush again with butter. Fold in half lengthwise and brush the top with butter. You now have four layers of phyllo in a narrow strip.

5. Place ½ cup filling in the lower right-hand corner of the strip with the bottom right-hand corner as your starting point, fold the strip of dough as you would a flag, until you end up with a neat triangle of dough encasing the filling.

6. Brush the top of the "pie" with a little more butter and place on a greased baking sheet. Repeat with remaining filling. Bake in a preheated 375 degree oven for 20 to 25 minutes, until crust is golden brown.

Note: Pies may be made in advance, refrigerated and baked just before serving time.

Béchamel Sauce

2 cups milk
3 Tbsp. butter
3 Tbsp. flour
  salt and white pepper to
  taste

1. Bring milk to a boil in a small saucepan.

2. Melt butter, stir in flour, and cook for 2 to 3 minutes, stirring to keep the flour from browning. Add boiling milk, ¼ cup at a time, and stir with a whisk until the sauce comes to a boil. Simmer, stirring occasionally, until thick. Season with salt and pepper.

Serves 6

6 green peppers
6 tomatoes
¼ cup olive oil
2 cups chopped onion
¼ cup chopped parsley
1 Tbsp. dry mint
1 cup uncooked rice
½ tsp. cinnamon
1 tsp. salt
  pinch pepper
¼ cup raisins
1 cup cooked chick peas
½ cup tomato juice or
  water

Greek Stuffed Tomatoes and Peppers

1. Cut a thin sliver from the bottom of each green pepper so that it will stand upright in the baking dish. Cut off the tops and remove the seeds and pith from the inside of the peppers.

2. Cut a thick slice from the bottom of each tomato. This will be the cap of the stuffed tomato. Remove and discard the seeds. Remove the pulp and chop.

3. Heat olive oil in a skillet. Add onions, parsley, and mint and cook 5 minutes, until onion is tender. Add rice, cinnamon, salt, pepper, raisins, chick peas, chopped tomato pulp, and tomato juice. Cook, covered, for 10 minutes over low heat.

4. Place tomatoes and peppers in an oiled baking dish with their cavities facing up. Fill three-fourths full with rice mixture, leaving room for rice to expand during baking.

5. Cover stuffed vegetables with their "caps" and pour ¼ inch water in the bottom of the baking dish. Bake in a preheated 375 degree oven for 35 to 40 minutes, until peppers and tomatoes are tender.

Here is a vegetarian "stew in a pie," reminiscent of Shepherd's Pie.

Brown Gravy Pie

Serves 8

pastry for a 10-inch pie
¼ lb. pearl onions, about 12 to 15 small onions
4 Tbsp. butter
2 potatoes, peeled and cut in one-inch pieces
2 carrots, peeled and cut in one-inch pieces
1 turnip, peeled and cut in one-inch pieces
3 cups vegetable stock
⅓ cup red wine
2 Tbsp. soy sauce
1 bay leaf
½ tsp. thyme
salt and pepper to taste
2 Tbsp. flour
few drops of caramel color (optional)
8 to 10 mushrooms, quartered
2 stalks celery, sliced in ½-inch pieces

1. Line a 10-inch deep-dish pie pan with pastry.

2. Blanch pearl onions in boiling water for one minute. Drain and peel.

3. Melt 2 Tbsp. butter in a stockpot. Add onions and brown lightly.

4. Add potatoes, carrots, turnip, vegetable stock, red wine, soy sauce, bay leaf, thyme, salt, and pepper. Bring to a boil.

5. Blend remaining 2 Tbsp. butter with flour and add it to boiling stock. Stir until dissolved. Simmer vegetables for 10 minutes. You may add a few drops of caramel color if you like a darker brown gravy.

6. Add mushrooms and celery to stew and simmer for 10 more minutes. Taste for seasoning.

7. Pour vegetables into pastry lined pie pan. Cover with a top crust and make a vent in the top for steam to escape. Bake in a preheated 425 degree oven for 30 to 35 minutes, until crust is lightly browned.

My friend Anna Pardini claims that this is a traditional Hobbit "homecoming" meal.

Hobbit Pie

Serves 6 to 8

pastry for a two-crust pie
3 Tbsp. oil
1½ lbs. sliced mushrooms
2 cups sliced onions
⅓ cup flour
½ cup dry, white wine
¼ cup finely chopped parsley
salt and pepper to taste
1 cup cottage cheese
1½ cups grated cheddar cheese
2 beaten eggs

1. Line a 10-inch deep-dish pie pan with pastry.

2. Heat oil in a large skillet. Add mushrooms and cook until they start to brown, about 5 minutes. Add onions and cook for 5 more minutes.

3. Turn off heat and stir in flour. When well blended, add white wine and mix again. Stir in remaining ingredients and taste for seasoning.

4. Pour filling into pastry lined pan and cover with a lattice top. Bake in a preheated 375 degree oven for 40 to 45 minutes.

A pumpkin shell provides a festive presentation for this slightly spicy stew.

Vegetable Stew in a Pumpkin Shell

Serves 6

1   8 to 10-lb. pumpkin
6   Tbsp. butter
1   large onion, cut in
      large dice
1   tsp. finely chopped garlic
2   Tbsp. flour
2   green peppers, seeded
      and cut in large dice
2   medium tomatoes,
      peeled and diced
3   cups vegetable stock
1   tsp. oregano
1   bay leaf
1   small piece hot, red
      pepper
1   lb. sweet potatoes, peeled
      and cut in 1-inch
      cubes
1   lb. white potatoes, peeled
      and cut in 1-inch
      cubes
1   cup corn, off the cob
1   medium sized zucchini,
      cut in ½-inch pieces
¼   lb. chestnuts, peeled
      salt and pepper to taste

1. Cut a 4-inch lid from the top of the pumpkin, leaving the stem intact for a handle. Scoop out seeds and pulp and rub the inside of the pumpkin with 2 Tbsp. butter. Place lid back on pumpkin and place it in a roasting pan. Bake in a pre-heated 400 degree oven for 45 to 50 minutes, until pumpkin is tender but on the firm side. The sides must support themselves to hold the filling.

2. Heat remaining butter in a stock pot. Add onions and garlic and cook for 5 minutes, until tender. Sprinkle with flour and cook 3 more minutes, stirring often.

3. Add diced green peppers, tomatoes, vegetable stock, oregano, bay leaf, and red pepper and bring to a boil. Add both kinds of potatoes and simmer for 10 minutes.

4. Add zucchini, corn, and peeled chestnuts and simmer 15 to 20 minutes longer, until vegetables are tender. Add salt and pepper to taste. Ladle into pumpkin shell and serve.

Note: To peel chestnuts: With the point of a sharp knife, make a small cross on the flat side of each chestnut. Cover with cold water, bring to a boil, and boil 2 minutes. Turn off heat. Remove 3 or 4 chestnuts at a time with a slotted spoon and peel inner and outer skins. The chestnuts will peel easily while still hot.

Cous-Cous is a North African dish that is usually prepared in a specially invented steamer called a couscousière. The fine grain, which looks a little like semolina, is steamed over a gently simmering stew. To steam the cous-cous without a couscousière, you may substitute a strainer or colander lined with a cloth. In this dish, the contrast of the hot and spicy vegetables with the delicate grain and sweet onion garnish is especially appealing.

Cous-Cous with a Vegetable Stew

Serves 6

Vegetable Stew:

2	Tbsp. oil
2½	cups sliced onion
1	tsp. ginger
1	tsp. chili powder
1	tsp. curry powder
¼	tsp. cayenne pepper
¼	tsp. cinnamon
⅛	tsp. nutmeg
1½	cups chopped canned tomatoes, with juice
1	cup vegetable stock
1¼	cups sliced carrots
2	small acorn squash, about 1 lb. each
1	medium-sized zucchini
1	medium-sized turnip
1	cup cooked chick peas
⅓	cup raisins
	salt and pepper to taste

1. Heat oil in a large casserole or stock pot. Add onions and cook until tender, about 5 minutes. Stir in spices, chopped tomatoes, and stock and bring to a boil. Add carrots, cover, and simmer over low heat for 10 minutes.

2. Peel squash and cut into ¾-inch cubes. Cut zucchini in pieces of the same size, but do not peel. Peel turnip and cut the same as the other vegetables. Add these to the pot with chick peas and raisins. Season well with salt and pepper. Simmer, covered, for 25 to 30 minutes, until vegetables are tender. Serve with cous-cous grain and onion garnish.

Cous-Cous

1	lb. cous-cous
¾	cup water
3	Tbsp. olive oil
	salt to taste

1. Mix cous-cous with water and let stand 10 minutes. Place in a large strainer that has been lined with a kitchen towel. Place the strainer over a pot of simmering water and steam, covered, for 7 to 10 minutes.

2. Spread cous-cous out on a tray. As soon as it is cool enough to handle, rub in the olive oil to separate the grains. Add salt to taste. Return to your "steamer" and steam for 5 more minutes, until hot. Serve with vegetable stew.

Onion Garnish:

2	Tbsp. butter
1	large onion, sliced, about 2 cups
¼	cup sliced almonds
¼	cup raisins
½	tsp. cinnamon

1. Heat butter in a skillet. Add onions and cook until tender, about 5 minutes. Add remaining ingredients and cook, stirring occasionally, for 8 to 10 minutes. Serve warm with cous-cous and vegetables.

If you cannot obtain sweet red peppers for this recipe, do not omit them but substitute canned, red pimientos.

Vegetables with Saffron Rice

Serves 6 to 8

2   *Tbsp. olive oil*
1¼ *cup finely chopped onion*
1   *tsp. finely chopped garlic*
1   *tsp. ground coriander*
1   *tsp. oregano*
1   *tsp. ground cumin*
1½ *cups chopped, canned tomatoes, with juice*
2   *green peppers, cut in ½-inch dice*
2   *sweet red peppers, cut in ½-inch dice*
1   *Tbsp. capers*
½   *cup halved green olives*
1   *cup cooked chick peas*
2   *cups rice*
2½ *cups boiling water*
¼   *tsp. crushed Spanish saffron*
1½ *tsp. salt*
6   *artichoke hearts, halved or quartered*
1   *cup green peas*

1. Heat oil in the bottom of a six-quart pot. Add onion and garlic and sauté for 3 minutes. Add coriander, oregano, and cumin and cook 3 more minutes.

2. Add tomatoes, red and green peppers, capers, olives, and chick peas and cook 5 minutes. Add rice and cook, stirring occasionally for 5 more minutes.

3. Add boiling water, saffron, and salt. Cover and simmer gently without stirring for 10 minutes.

4. Remove cover, add artichoke hearts and peas to the pot but do not stir. Cover and simmer 5 to 7 minutes longer, until most of the liquid has been absorbed. Stir and taste for seasoning.

A pleasant departure from traditional Indian curry.

Vegetables in a Creamy Curry Sauce

Serves 4

½   bunch broccoli
3   Tbsp. oil
⅔   cup finely chopped
     onion
4   tsp. Indian curry spice
     mix (curry powder)
¼   tsp. turmeric
2   cups carrots, peeled and
     sliced
1   Tbsp. soy sauce
1   cup water
¼   lb. sliced mushrooms
10 cherry tomatoes
1   Tbsp. butter
1   Tbsp. flour
1   cup heavy cream or
     half-and-half
    salt to taste
    cayenne pepper

1. Trim broccoli and cut in bite-size pieces. Blanch in boiling, salted water until tender but on the firm side. Drain.

2. Heat oil in a large skillet. Add onions and cook 2 to 3 minutes. Add curry powder and turmeric and stir. Add carrots, soy sauce, water, and ¼ teaspoon salt. Cover and cook over medium heat until carrots are tender, 4 to 6 minutes.

3. Add mushrooms and cherry tomatoes. Cover again and cook over medium heat until vegetables are tender.

4. Mix butter and flour together until smooth. Stir into vegetables until dissolved. Add cream and broccoli and bring to a boil. Stir in salt and cayenne pepper and taste for seasoning. Serve over yellow rice.

Yellow Rice

1½ cups water or vegetable
     stock
¼   tsp. turmeric
1   tsp. salt
1   tsp. butter
1   cup extra long grain rice

1. Bring stock to a boil with turmeric, salt, and butter. Add rice and reduce heat. Simmer, covered, for 15 minutes, until all the water has been absorbed. Turn off heat and let rice steam with the cover on for 5 minutes.

One of the secrets of good tempura is an icy cold batter.

Vegetable Tempura

Vegetables:

asparagus, whole,
    trimmed
eggplant, sliced
sweet potato, peeled and
    sliced
turnip, peeled and sliced
parsley sprigs, whole
broccoli florets, blanched
    if large
cauliflower florets,
    blanched if large
green beans, whole,
    trimmed
carrots, peeled and
    sliced; or grated
onions, sliced in rounds
scallions, whole, trimmed

Batter for 4 servings:

1   egg
½   cup cold water
½   tsp. salt
1   cup flour
2   tsp. baking powder

1½   cups vegetable stock
2   Tbsp. soy sauce
1   tsp. sugar
2   Tbsp. finely grated turnip
1   Tbsp. finely chopped
       scallion

Choose three or four vegetables from the above suggestions, or try your own. Remember that they will be dipped in batter and fried only briefly in hot oil, so be sure they are sliced thin enough to cook in a short time. Large pieces of cauliflower or broccoli should be blanched first. Allow approximately one cup prepared vegetables per serving.

1. Beat egg with water. Add salt, flour, and baking powder and mix just until blended. Do not overmix. Chill in refrigerator until ready to use. You may thin with ice cubes or ice water. The batter should be the consistency of thin pancake batter and coat the vegetables evenly, not thickly.

Procedure:

1. Make batter and chill.

2. Prepare vegetables.

3. Heat 3 to 4 cups oil in a deep frying pan or French fryer to a temperature of 365 degrees. This temperature should be maintained throughout the frying. Use a vegetable oil such as soybean, safflower, or peanut oil, either alone or in combination.

4. Dip the vegetables in the batter until well coated. Drop into hot oil and fry until crisp. Fry in small batches, allowing enough room in the pan for vegetables to move about freely. Drain on absorbent paper and serve with dipping sauce.

Dipping Sauce for Tempura

1. Mix all ingredients together and serve in small bowls with tempura.

The essence of the Chinese cooking method stir-frying is quick cooking over very high heat. The hot oil seals in the flavor and juices of the vegetables. A wok is the ideal utensil for this technique, since it retains heat well and its high, sloping sides allow for easy stirring. However, a large frying pan may also be used.

Hot and Spicy Stir-Fried Vegetables

Serves 4

4   Tbsp. oil
1   tsp. finely chopped garlic
1   Tbsp. chili paste
1   Tbsp. grated fresh ginger
1½   cups carrots, peeled and
       sliced on the diagonal
1½   cups turnips, peeled and
       sliced
2   cups broccoli, cut in bite-
       size pieces
1   cup vegetable stock
2   Tbsp. soy sauce
       pinch sugar
2   cups thinly sliced Chinese
       cabbage
1   cup sliced mushrooms
1   Tbsp. cornstarch
       dissolved in 1 Tbsp.
       cold water
1.   Tbsp. cider vinegar
1   cup green peas
2   tsp. Chinese sesame oil
½   cup finely sliced scallions
       salt to taste

1. Heat oil in a wok or skillet. Add garlic, chili paste, and ginger and stir-fry one minute. Add carrots, turnips, and broccoli and stir-fry 2 minutes. Add vegetable stock, soy sauce, and sugar to the pan and bring to a boil. Cover and simmer for 5 minutes, until vegetables are nearly tender.

2. Add cabbage and mushrooms and stir over high heat for 3 minutes. Stir in cornstarch paste, vinegar, and peas. Cook one minute, or until liquid in pan comes to a rapid boil. Stir in sesame oil and scallions and taste for seasoning. Serve immediately.

While we are accustomed to taking our sugar in the form of dessert, the Japanese tend to use it in small quantities in many different dishes and pay less attention to satisfying the sweet tooth in a separate course. The combination of sugar and salt in this vegetable marinade seems typically Japanese.

Vegetable Brochettes a la Japonnaise

Serves 6

Miso Marinade:

1   cup light miso
⅓   cup sugar
2   Tbsp. rice wine or
      sherry
½   tsp. grated fresh
      ginger
½   cup sesame seeds
½   cup water

Vegetables:

2   or 3 carrots
½   bunch broccoli
12   mushrooms
1   bunch scallions
1   block tofu
12   long bamboo skewers

1. Mix ingredients for miso sauce together in a bowl.

2. Peel carrots and slice on the diagonal in thick slices.

3. Break broccoli in bite-sized florets.

4. Trim the tips of the mushroom stems.

5. Cut scallions in 1-inch lengths.

6. Cut tofu in 1-inch cubes.

7. Blanch broccoli, carrots and mushrooms in boiling, salted water until tender. Marinate blanched vegetables, scallions, and tofu in miso sauce for one half hour or more.

8. Thread ingredients on bamboo skewers alternately, so that each skewer has a variety of vegetables. Place on a broiling pan, spoon over any extra sauce, and broil for 7 to 10 minutes, until vegetables start to brown. Serve hot over rice.

This tofu dish is high in protein—a good accompaniment to steamed vegetables and brown rice.

Japanese Style Fried Tofu

Serves 4

1   block tofu
      flour for dredging
      oil for frying

¼   cup light miso
¼   cup rice wine vinegar
1   tsp. grated fresh ginger
1   Tbsp. sugar

1. Cut tofu in one-inch cubes and dredge lightly in flour.

2. Heat ¼ inch oil in a heavy skillet. Add floured tofu cubes and fry until golden brown on all sides. Drain on absorbent paper and serve with miso sauce.

Miso Sauce:

Mix ingredients together until well blended.

The beauty of this dish is its simplicity. The vegetables should be cooked to perfection and arranged on a platter with artistic effort. With brown rice, this makes a nice, light supper.

Platter of Winter Vegetables with Tofu

Serves 4 to 6

1 or 2 carrots
2 sweet potatoes
1 turnip
½ head cauliflower
½ lb. Brussels sprouts
1 block tofu
  oil for frying
  shallot herb butter
    (see recipe below)

1. Make shallot herb butter.

2. Peel carrots and cut in half lengthwise. If carrots are very thick, cut in quarters. Cut in three-inch lengths.

3. Peel sweet potatoes and cut in thick slices.

4. Peel turnip and cut in wedges, about the same size as the carrot pieces.

5. Break cauliflower in large pieces (branches).

6. Trim Brussels sprouts.

7. Cut tofu in 1-inch cubes.

8. Place a vegetable steamer in the bottom of a large pot. Pour in 1 inch water. Bring water to a boil, add carrots, cover, and steam for 5 minutes. Add sweet potatoes and turnips and steam 5 more minutes. Finally, add cauliflower and Brussels sprouts and steam for 3 to 5 minutes, until all the vegetables are tender.

9. While vegetables are steaming, heat ¼ inch oil in skillet. Add cubed tofu and fry until lightly browned. Drain on paper towels. If tofu is ready before vegetables have finished steaming, you may keep it warm in the oven for a few minutes.

10. Arrange steamed vegetables and fried tofu on a serving platter and dot with shallot herb butter.

Shallot Herb Butter

1½ Tbsp. finely chopped
    shallots
1 Tbsp. lemon juice
1 tsp. tarragon
½ tsp. coarsely crushed
    peppercorns
2 tsp. finely chopped
    parsley
½ cup butter

1. Mix all ingredients together until well blended.

Subtle, light, and delicate, these egg rolls are wrapped in paper thin sheets of omelet and gently steamed. Serve with soy sauce for dipping.

Japanese Egg Rolls

Serves 4 to 6

½ 10-ounce package fresh
    spinach
1 package kampyo
    (Japanese dried gourd)
1 block tofu
1 cup grated carrots
⅓ cup finely sliced scallions
1 cup green peas
2 Tbsp. toasted sesame
    seeds
1 tsp. sugar
1 tsp. salt
1 Tbsp. soy sauce
1 egg
8 egg sheets (see recipe
    below)

1. Clean and stem spinach and cook until tender in a small amount of boiling water. Squeeze dry in a towel. Chop coarsely.

2. Soak kampyo in hot water until soft, about 20 minutes. Cut in 8-inch strips.

3. Squeeze excess moisture from tofu and mash with a fork. Mix with carrots, scallions, peas, sesame seeds, sugar, salt, soy sauce, egg, and chopped spinach. Taste for seasoning.

4. Make egg sheets. Spread ⅓ cup filling on each egg sheet, leaving a 1-inch gap at the edges. Roll jelly-roll fashion. Tie ends with kampyo strips. Steam for 20 minutes and serve hot with small dishes of soy sauce for dipping.

Note: You may improvise a steamer with a large skillet and a heatproof plate. Place the eggrolls on the plate and put the plate in the skillet. Pour water in the bottom of the pan, making sure that it does not exceed the level of the plate (you want to steam, not boil, the egg rolls). Bring the water to a boil, cover the pan and steam. Check the water level from time to time to be sure it doesn't evaporate during cooking.

Egg Sheets:

5 eggs
2 Tbsp. cornstarch
1 Tbsp. cold water
1 tsp. salt

1. Dissolve cornstarch in cold water and add to eggs. Add salt and beat until smooth.

2. Lightly coat a 7-inch crepe pan with oil and heat until a drop of water sizzles in the bottom of the pan. Pour 2 or 3 tablespoons beaten egg into the pan and quickly tilt it back and forth to coat in a thin layer. Cook for a few seconds, until egg is set. Turn out of pan. Repeat with remaining beaten egg. Trim edges of pancakes to make them square.

This delicious vegetable burger is made with tofu and peanuts.

Tofu Burgers

Serves 4

½ 10-ounce package fresh
    spinach
1 cup grated carrots
½ cup grated turnip
2 Tbsp. finely sliced
    scallions
1 tsp. salt
2 Tbsp. soy sauce
2 tsp. sugar
⅓ cup chopped, roasted
    peanuts
1 block tofu
2 beaten eggs

1. Clean and stem spinach. Cook until tender in a small amount of boiling water. Drain and squeeze out excess liquid in a towel. Chop coarsely.

2. Mix spinach with carrots, turnip, scallions, salt, soy sauce, sugar, and peanuts.

3. Squeeze out excess liquid from tofu and mash well with a fork. Mix with vegetables and beaten eggs. Taste for seasoning.

4. Form mixture into patties, about ⅓ cup each. Fry in a little hot oil until golden brown on both sides. Serve hot. Makes 8 to 10 patties.

Toasted sesame seeds and light miso disguise the blandness of tofu in this interesting combination of cold, cooked vegetables.

Vegetables with Tofu Sauce

Serves 4 to 6

1 cup vegetable stock
2 Tbsp. soy sauce
1 Tbsp. sugar
½ tsp. salt
1 cup carrots, peeled and
    cut in thin julienne
1 cup turnips, peeled and
    cut in thin julienne
½ bunch broccoli, cut in
    bite-sized pieces
½ 10-ounce package fresh
    spinach, cleaned and
    stemmed
½ cup sliced bamboo shoots
1½ cups sliced mushrooms

1. Bring stock, soy sauce, sugar, and salt to a boil in a large saucepan. Add carrots and turnips and cook 3 minutes. Add remaining vegetables, cover, and cook for 3 to 5 minutes, until tender. Drain and cool. Reserve stock for soup.

2. Mix vegetables with tofu sauce and taste for seasoning. Serve cold or at room temperature.

Tofu Sauce

½ block tofu
3 Tbsp. light miso
1 Tbsp. sugar
2 Tbsp. toasted sesame
    seeds

1. Press out excess water from tofu. Mash and mix with remaining ingredients. Toss with vegetables.

Entrees:
Mexican Dishes

 The basis of Mexican cuisine—beans, cheese, and masa—make it ideal fare for vegetarians, since many of the nutritional requirements of the vegetarian diet are met in these foods. Masa, the specially treated corn meal used in tortillas and tamales, can be purchased in many large supermarkets under the Quaker brand (instant masa harina). Although tortillas made with instant masa may be a little tougher than those made with fresh masa, they are far superior to the ready-made, store-bought varieties. Developing a passion for fresh, hot tortillas is easy since you can make them fairly quickly with practice and the help of a tortilla press.

One element of Mexican cookery that bewilders most newcomers is the use of chiles. To minimize confusion, familiarize yourself with the chiles one at a time. The names of the different varieties and their characteristics will begin to sort themselves out as you use them. Wear rubber gloves when handling hot chiles, or wash your hands very thoroughly afterwards. The oil from the seeds and stems—once on the skin—can burn for several hours, especially if you inadvertently rub your eyes or face with peppery hands.

Although generally simple, Mexican cooking is not necessarily easy or quick. One dish may consist of many individual components, in and of themselves simple, but which must be prepared separately—often a time consuming task. I am convinced, however, that the time and patience required are more than justly rewarded.

If you cannot obtain Anaheim peppers for this dish, you may substitute green peppers.

Chiles Rellenos (Mexican Stuffed Peppers)

Serves 4 to 6

6 Anaheim peppers (mild, green, chili peppers)
1 4-ounce package cream cheese
¼ lb. grated mild cheddar cheese, about 1¾ cups
oil for frying
3 eggs, separated
flour for dredging
tomato sauce (see recipe below)

1. Roast peppers over an open gas flame or under a broiler, until skins are blistered. Scrape off skins and rinse under cold water. Cut off tops and remove seeds. Blanch whole peppers one minute in boiling water. Drain.

2. Stuff the peppers with cream cheese and grated cheddar, reserving a little cheddar to sprinkle over the top of the finished dish.

3. Heat 1½ to 2 inches oil in a heavy iron skillet or frying pan.

4. Beat egg yolks until thick. Beat egg whites until stiff and gently fold into yolks.

5. Lightly coat the stuffed peppers with flour and dip in egg batter. Fry in hot oil until golden brown on both sides. Drain on absorbent paper. Arrange peppers on a platter and cover with tomato sauce. Sprinkle with a little more grated cheese.

Tomato Sauce

½ cup chopped onion
1 clove garlic
2 cups canned tomatoes, with juice
2 Tbsp. oil
1 tsp. oregano
salt and pepper to taste
1 tsp. wine vinegar

1. Puree onion, garlic, and canned tomatoes in a blender.

2. Heat oil in a skillet. Add tomato puree, oregano, salt, and pepper and simmer for 5 minutes. Stir in vinegar and taste for seasoning. Serve hot over stuffed peppers.

All the components for this casserole may be made in advance, reheated, and assembled at the last minute.

Chilequile

12 stale corn tortillas
2   cups tomato sauce (see recipe below)
4   cups refried beans (see recipe, p. 173)
½   lb. grated Monterey jack cheese
1   avocado
    sliced radishes
    red onion rings

1. Heat ¾ inch oil in a heavy skillet. Cut tortillas in eighths and fry briefly in hot oil (to wilt, not to crisp). Drain on paper towels.

2. Reheat sauce and beans if you have made them in advance.

3. Oil a casserole and layer the ingredients in the following order: tomato sauce, tortilla chips, tomato sauce, beans, and grated cheese. Continue to layer until all the ingredients are used, ending with sauce and cheese on the top.

4. Bake in a preheated 350 degree oven for 15 to 20 minutes, until cheese is melted and casserole is heated through. Serve garnished with sliced avocado, radishes, and red onion rings.

Tomato Sauce

Makes 2 cups

4   or 5 ancho chiles
    approx. 1 cup boiling water
2   cups canned tomatoes, with juice
1   cup chopped onion
1   clove garlic, peeled
½   tsp. oregano
2   Tbsp. vegetable oil
    salt and pepper to taste
    small pinch of sugar

1. Wash chiles in cold water and remove seeds and veins. Wash hands well with soap and water after handling chiles. Cover chiles with boiling water and soak for 25 to 30 minutes, until soft.

2. Combine soaked chiles and their liquid in a blender with tomatoes, onion, garlic, and oregano. Puree until smooth.

3. Heat oil in a skillet and add sauce. Cook, stirring often, for 5 minutes. Season with salt, pepper, and sugar.

Tamales are steamed "cakes" made with masa, a specially treated cornmeal, and filled with a spicy filling. Be sure that the masa dough is well salted, or the tamales will be bland. You may adjust the hotness of the cheese filling by adding more or less chopped jalapeno pepper. The corn filling is milder, yet also delicious. Leftover, cooked tamales may be refrigerated and reheated by steaming.

Makes 2 dozen

2   dozen dried corn husks
¾   cup shortening
2   cups masa harina
1½   tsp. salt
1   cup water
     cheese or corn filling

Tamales

1. Soak dried corn husks in water for ¾ hour to soften.

2. Beat shortening until fluffy. Mix masa with salt and beat into shortening one third at a time. Add water and beat again.

3. Spread 1 to 2 tablespoons masa dough over the wide part of each corn husk. It should be about ⅜ inch thick. Place a tablespoon of filling in the center of the dough and fold the long sides of the corn husk in towards the center. Fold the top flap over to make a neat package. Continue spreading and filling until all the dough and filling are used.

4. Fit a large saucepan with a rack or vegetable steamer. Pour one inch water in the bottom of the pan. Stand the tamales in the steamer so that the folded part is on the bottom. Cover and steam for 45 minutes, until the dough separates from the husk. Serve hot.

Makes enough for 2 dozen tamales

2 Tbsp. oil
¼ cup chopped onion
½ tsp. finely chopped garlic
½ cup chopped green
　　pepper
1 cup chopped tomato
2 tsp. chili powder
½ tsp. oregano
¼ tsp. salt
4 tsp. finely chopped
　　jalapeno pepper
8 ounces mild cheese, such
　　as Monterey jack, brick
　　and Muenster

Cheese Filling for Tamales

1. Heat oil in a skillet. Add onion, garlic, green pepper, tomato, chili powder, oregano and salt. Simmer over medium heat until mixture reduces to a thick sauce, 10 to 15 minutes.

2. Grate cheese and mix with chopped jalapeno pepper until evenly blended.

3. Place a spoonful of tomato sauce in the center of each tamale and cover with grated cheese. Fold and steam according to directions above.

Makes enough for 2 dozen tamales

1 Tbsp. oil
⅓ cup chopped onion
½ cup chopped green
　　pepper
1 tsp. paprika
3 cups corn, off the cob
2 Tbsp. milk
1 beaten egg
½ cup freshly grated
　　Parmesan cheese
　　salt and pepper to taste

Corn Filling for Tamales

1. Heat oil in a skillet. Add onion, green pepper, and paprika and cook until vegetables are soft, about 5 minutes.

2. Combine corn in a blender with milk and blend until creamy. Add to skillet and cook 3 minutes.

3. Stir in beaten egg, grated cheese, salt, and pepper. Taste for seasoning and cool. Fill and steam tamales according to directions above.

Masa harina is a specially treated corn meal used for making tortillas and tamales and is readily available in many large supermarkets or groceries that carry Mexican and Latin American foods. In this recipe, it provides a pleasant complement to the vegetable stew.

Serves 8

Dough:

¾ cup shortening
2 cups masa harina
1½ tsp. salt
1 tsp. baking powder
1 cup milk

Filling:

4 ancho chiles
1 cup boiling water
    (approx.)
2 Tbsp. oil
1¼ cup chopped onion
1 tsp. finely chopped garlic
1 tsp. oregano
1 tsp. ground cumin
2 diced green peppers
1 cup corn kernels
1 small zucchini, diced,
    about 1¼ cups
1 cup chopped tomatoes,
    fresh or canned
3 Tbsp. sliced almonds
3 Tbsp. raisins
    salt and pepper
1 cup grated cheddar
    cheese

Vegetable Tamal Pie

1. Beat shortening until light and fluffy. Mix in masa, salt, and baking powder. Beat in milk a little at a time.

1. Wash chiles under cold, running water and remove seeds and veins. Place in a small bowl and cover with boiling water. Soak until soft, 45 minutes to an hour, and puree chiles and their liquid in a blender.

2. Heat oil in a skillet and add onion and garlic. Cook 3 minutes and add oregano, cumin, green pepper, corn, and zucchini. Cook for 5 more minutes. Stir in tomatoes, chili puree, almonds, and raisins and cook 5 minutes. Season with salt and pepper to taste.

To Assemble:

1. Grease a 10-inch deep-dish pie pan and line it with half the masa dough.

2. Pour in the filling and top with grated cheese. Cover the pie with the remaining dough and bake in a preheated 350 degree oven for 45 minutes to an hour, until golden brown on top.

These enchiladas have a spicy vegetable filling.

Squash Enchiladas

Serves 6

1 butternut squash, about
   2½ lbs.
2 Tbsp. oil
1 cup chopped onion
2 tsp. chili powder
1 tsp. ground coriander
1 tsp. ground cumin
1 tsp. oregano
¼ tsp. cinnamon
1 cup green peas, blanched
2 ounces cream cheese
   salt and pepper to taste
12 flour tortillas
   oil for frying
4 cups red enchilada sauce
   (see recipe below)
¼ lb. grated Monterey
   jack cheese

1. Peel squash and remove seeds and pulp. Cut in one-inch cubes and cook until tender in a small amount of boiling water, 15 to 20 minutes. Drain.

2. Heat oil in a skillet. Add onions and cook until tender, about 5 minutes. Add chili powder, coriander, cumin, oregano, and cinnamon.

3. Stir in green peas and cooked squash and season well with salt and pepper. Add more chili powder if you like a spicier filling. Break cream cheese in small pieces and stir into filling.

4. Heat ¾ inch oil in a heavy skillet. Fry tortillas briefly (to wilt, not to crisp). Drain on paper towels.

5. Dip fried tortillas in warm enchilada sauce, coating well on both sides. Spread ¼ cup filling over the face of the tortilla. Roll and place with the seam side down in a baking dish. When all the tortillas have been filled, pour the remaining sauce over them and sprinkle with grated cheese.

6. Bake in a preheated 350 degree oven for 15 minutes, until cheese is melted and enchiladas are hot all the way through.

Red Enchilada Sauce

Makes 4 cups

4 or 5 ancho chiles
   approximately 1 cup
   boiling water
2 cups canned tomatoes,
   with juice
1 cup chopped onion
1 clove garlic
½ tsp. oregano
2 Tbsp. oil
   salt and pepper to taste
   pinch sugar
2 eggs
1 cup heavy cream

1. Wash chiles in cold water and remove seeds and veins. Wash hands well with soap and water after handling chiles. Cover chiles with boiling water and let soak for 25 to 30 minutes, until soft.

2. Combine soaked chiles and their liquid in a blender with tomatoes, onion, garlic, and oregano. Puree until smooth.

3. Heat oil in a skillet and add sauce. Cook, stirring often, for 5 minutes. Season with salt, pepper, and sugar and remove from heat.

4. Beat eggs and mix with cream. Stir into sauce and taste for seasoning. Keep warm until ready to use.

Farmer's cheese is the most readily available substitute for *queso anejo*, the dry, salty, crumbly cheese most often used in enchiladas. It needs plenty of salting, and could also be used in combination with Romano cheese to give it the extra bite that farmer's cheese lacks.

Black Bean Enchiladas

Serves 6

1 recipe Mexican style black beans (see recipe below)
4 cups red enchilada sauce (see preceding recipe)
12 corn tortillas
oil for frying
8 ounces crumbled farmer's cheese
salt to taste
½ cup chopped onion
1 cup sour cream
3 cups shredded lettuce (Romaine or Iceberg)
1 sliced avocado

1. Prepare black beans and red enchilada sauce.

2. Heat ¾ inch oil in a heavy skillet and fry tortillas briefly (to wilt, not to crisp). Drain on paper towels.

3. Dip fried tortillas in warm enchilada sauce, coating well on both sides. Place a spoonful of beans on the face of each tortilla. Sprinkle with a tablespoon of well salted farmer's cheese and roll up. Reserve some cheese for garnish. Place the filled tortillas with the seam side down in a baking dish and pour the remaining sauce over them.

4. Sprinkle the top with remaining farmer's cheese and bake in a preheated 350 degree oven for 15 minutes, until enchiladas are heated all the way through. Garnish with chopped onion, sour cream, avocado and shredded lettuce.

Mexican Style Black Beans

Makes 5 cups

2 cups black beans
1½ cups chopped onion
1 bay leaf
2 tsp. salt
3 Tbsp. vegetable oil
1 tsp. finely chopped garlic
½ tsp. oregano
1 tsp. chopped serrano pepper, or 1 crumbled red, hot pepper, such as pequin

1. Combine black beans, ¾ cup onion, bay leaf, salt, and 1 Tbsp. oil in a saucepan and cover with water. Bring to a boil, reduce heat and simmer, covered, until beans are soft, about 1½ hours. Check every 30 minutes or so and add more water if necessary.

2. When beans are soft, taste for salt and add more if necessary. Continue to cook for another 30 minutes, but do not add any more water.

3. Heat remaining 2 tablespoons oil in a skillet. Add the rest of the chopped onion, the garlic, oregano, and hot pepper. Cook 4 to 5 minutes and add 1½ cups cooked black beans. Mash beans with a fork or the back of a wooden spoon until almost a puree. Return the mashed beans to the sauce pan, stir, and taste for seasoning.

Mexican green tomatoes and cream give these enchiladas a subtle yet distinctively spicy flavor.

Cheese Enchiladas with a Green Tomato Sauce

Serves 6

½ cup finely chopped
   onion
½ lb. crumbled farmer's
   cheese
½ lb. grated colby cheese
   salt and pepper to taste
   oil for frying
12 corn tortillas
4 cups green enchilada
   sauce (see recipe
   below)
1½ cups (approx.)
   guacamole
   sliced radishes for
   garnish
   shredded lettuce for
   garnish

1. Mix chopped onion, farmer's cheese, and grated colby together and season well with salt and pepper.

2. Heat ¾ inch oil in a heavy skillet and fry tortillas briefly (to wilt, not to crisp). Drain on paper towels.

3. Dip fried tortillas in warm enchilada sauce, coating well on both sides. Spread about ¼ cup cheese mixture on the face of each tortilla and roll. Arrange in a baking dish with the seam side down.

4. When all the tortillas have been filled and rolled, pour the remaining sauce over them and bake in a preheated 350 degree oven for 15 minutes, until hot all the way through. Serve garnished with guacamole, radishes, and lettuce.

Green Tomato Sauce

1 13-ounce can Mexican
   green tomatoes
   (tomatillos)
3 or 4 poblano chiles, or
   canned, green chiles
   leaves from 4 sprigs
   fresh coriander
½ cup finely chopped
   onion
1 or 2 serrano chiles, for
   extra hotness
   (optional)
1 cup water
2 Tbsp. oil
   salt and pepper
   small pinch sugar
2 eggs
1 cup heavy cream

1. Drain tomatoes and combine in a blender with chiles, coriander, onion, serrano chiles, and water. Puree until smooth.

2. Heat oil in a skillet and add blended sauce. Cook, stirring often, for 5 minutes. Season with salt, pepper, and sugar. Remove from heat.

3. Beat eggs and mix with cream. Stir into sauce. Keep warm until ready to use.

Entrees: Pasta, Gnocchi And Noodles

 Freshly made pasta is so far superior to store-bought that it hardly bears comparison. Mixing and rolling the dough by hand is time consuming, but it can become a labor of love resulting in one of the great pleasures of dining. If pasta becomes a passion in your household, then, by all means, invest in a pasta machine. With the aid of this machine and a food processor or table mixer, you can complete the whole operation in less than an hour.

Pasta making methods vary from cook to cook. Whether to use whole eggs or egg yolks, milk or water, oil or no oil, or simply flour and eggs is a question decided by the individual pasta maker. Through experimentation and practice you can discover your own particular preferences. Following are instructions for mixing, rolling, and cutting pasta by machine as well as by hand, and a few basic recipes.

Pasta—rolled, cut, filled, and sauced in innumerable ways—makes a versatile component of vegetarian menus. Italian pasta, most familiar and popular with Americans, can be dressed with tomatoes, cream, and many vegetable sauces. However, the Japanese and Chinese also have ingenious ways with pasta which are gaining in popularity. I have included two cold noodle dishes in this chapter as a sampling.

Gnocchi (loosely defined as dumplings but hardly resembling the heavy fare encountered under that name) are a less widely known Italian contribution to cuisine. More the pity. Made with potatoes and smothered in a luscious tomato sauce, Gnocchi alla Francese is supremely light. Other gnocchi dishes that deserve attention as entrees are the rich and cheesy Spinach Gnocchi and Semolina Gnocchi.

MAKING PASTA BY HAND

Mixing

1. Place flour directly on countertop in a mound. (You may use a wooden, marble, or formica surface.) Make a deep well in the center and break the eggs into it. Scramble the eggs with a fork and slowly add the milk or other liquid ingredients. Little by little, draw the flour from the inside wall of the well into the center, stirring with the fork until the mixture begins to thicken.

2. When the dough in the center is fairly stiff, push the remaining flour over it and mix with your hands until most of the flour has been absorbed into the dough. Knead until smooth, about 5 minutes. Cover and set aside to rest for at least 20 minutes, so that the dough may relax before being rolled out.

Rolling

1. Lightly dust the countertop with flour. Roll the dough away from you, turning it slightly clockwise every few turns of the rolling pin, so that you end up with a round sheet of dough. The sheet should be about the thickness of a quarter for fettucine, slightly thinner for ravioli and lasagne. Let the dough dry for 15 to 20 minutes before cutting, so that it will still be flexible, but not sticky.

Cutting Fettucine

1. When the dough has dried for a few minutes, sprinkle it lightly with cornmeal and fold in thirds. Using a rolling pin or a ruler as a straight edge, cut the dough in ⅛-inch strips with a pastry wheel. Spread the noodles on a tea towel, or a tray lightly dusted with cornmeal. Let dry in the open air for 15 to 20 minutes more before cooking. If the noodles are not going to be cooked immediately, cover them loosely with a tea towel. If you plan to use the noodles much later (a day or two, or a week), place them directly in the freezer.

MAKING PASTA BY MACHINE

Mixing

1. Fit a food processor with the cutting blade and combine all ingredients in the bowl. Turn the machine on and off rapidly until dough is thoroughly mixed and smooth. Form into a ball, cover, and let dough relax for at least 20 minutes before rolling. If you are using a table mixer, follow the same procedure with a dough hook and mix until the dough is smooth.

Rolling

1. Most pasta machines include operating instructions. To ensure a thorough kneading of the dough, it is a good practice to run it through the machine two or three times on the widest setting before sheeting it to the desired thickness.

Cutting the Dough for Fettucine

1. Divide the dough in four pieces and sheet to the desired thickness (about the thickness of a quarter for fettucine, slightly thinner for ravioli and lasagne). Set aside for about 10 minutes to dry partially (keeps the noodles from sticking to one another when cut). Be careful not to let the dough dry completely, or it will crack when cut. Run the sheets of pasta through the machine on the fettucine setting. Spread the noodles on a tea towel or a tray lightly coated with cornmeal. Let dry for 15 to 20 minutes before cooking. If you plan to use the noodles much later (a day or two, or a week), place them in the freezer at this point.

FREEZING FRESH PASTA

As soon as they are cut, spread the noodles or filled pasta on a tray lightly coated with cornmeal. Place the tray directly in the freezer. When the pasta is "frozen stiff," remove and wrap in plastic storage bags. Return to freezer until ready to use. Do not defrost frozen pasta, but place it directly in boiling, salted water.

COOKING FRESH PASTA

Freshly made pasta takes much less time to cook than dried, store-bought pasta. Use a large pot with at least 2 quarts water. When the water comes to a rolling boil, add a generous pinch of salt and a few drops of oil. Drop the noodles into the boiling water and stir once with a wooden spoon. Cook for three minutes and begin tasting every minute or so thereafter to test for doneness. Never let the pasta become mushy from overcooking. It should be slightly chewy, *al dente*. Drain and toss with olive oil, butter, or desired sauce.

This is a firm pasta, excellent for ravioli or other filled pasta.

Egg Pasta

Makes one lb. dough
Serves 4 to 6

2   cups flour
2   whole eggs
3   to 4 Tbsp. water

1. Follow directions outlined above.

Semolina (called *semolino* in Italy) is ground durum wheat with a texture of fine sand. It should not be confused with the white breakfast cereal we call cream of wheat, for semolina is a light golden color similar to our yellow cornmeal. It can be found in grocery stores where Italian specialty foods are sold.

Semolina makes this pasta tender and the dough easy to work with. It comes from Anna Pardini, an artist and wonderful vegetarian cook who lives in the New York Catskills.

Semolina Pasta

Makes 1¼ lbs. dough
Serves 4 to 6

2   cups flour
¾   cup semolina
2   whole eggs
2   egg yolks
6   to 7 Tbsp. milk

1. Mix flour and semolina together and follow the procedure outlined above.

This pasta makes delicious fettucine or green lasagne.

Spinach Pasta

Serves 4

½   10-ounce package fresh
      spinach
2   whole eggs
1¾ cups flour

1. Cook spinach until tender in a small amount of boiling water. Squeeze dry in a towel.

2. Puree cooked spinach and eggs in a blender until smooth.

3. Follow procedure outlined above, pouring the spinach puree into the center of the "well."

The broccoli in this rich pasta dish is complemented by Fontina cheese, walnuts and cream.

Fettucine with Broccoli in a Cream Sauce

Serves 4

1   recipe semolina or
     spinach pasta, made
     into fettucine noodles
4   cups broccoli buds,
     about 1 bunch
     broccoli
1   Tbsp. butter
¼   cup finely chopped
     shallots
2   cups heavy cream
¼   cup finely chopped
     parsley
     salt and pepper to taste
¼   lb. grated Fontina cheese
1   Tbsp. finely chopped
     walnuts
     grated Romano cheese

1. Cut broccoli in bite-sized pieces. Blanch until tender in boiling, salted water. Drain and set aside.

2. Heat butter in a skillet. Add shallots and cook 2 to 3 minutes. Add cream, bring to a boil, and simmer 5 to 8 minutes to reduce cream slightly.

3. Cook fettucine in a large amount of boiling, salted water.

4. Stir parsley and broccoli into cream sauce and cook only long enough to heat all the way through. Stir in salt, pepper and grated cheese. Taste for seasoning.

5. Toss hot fettucine with sauce and pour into a buttered serving dish. Sprinkle with Romano and chopped walnuts.

Red bits of pimiento fleck this sauce of cauliflower, cream, and Bel Paese.

Fettucine with Cauliflower in a Cream Sauce

Serves 4

1   recipe semolina or
       spinach pasta, made
       into fettucine
       noodles
4   cups cauliflower, about
       1 small head
1   Tbsp. butter
¼   cup finely chopped
       shallots
2   cups heavy cream
¼   cup finely chopped
       parsley
¼   cup diced pimiento
¼   lb. Bel Paese, cut in
       small cubes
     salt and white pepper
       to taste
     freshly grated Parmesan
       cheese, for garnish
     finely chopped parsley,
       for garnish

1. Cut cauliflower in bite-size pieces. Blanch until tender in boiling, salted water. Drain and set aside.

2. Heat butter in a skillet. Add shallots and cook 2 to 3 minutes. Add the cream, bring to a boil, and simmer for 5 to 8 minutes to reduce the cream slightly.

3. Cook fettucine in a large amount of boiling, salted water.

4. Stir parsley, pimiento, and cauliflower into cream sauce and cook only long enough to heat all the way through. Add cheese, salt and pepper and taste for seasoning.

5. Toss hot fettucine with sauce and pour into a buttered serving dish. Sprinkle with grated Parmesan and chopped parsley.

The assortment of vegetables in this pasta dish make it as fresh and springlike as its name implies.

Pasta Primavera

1. Heat 1 Tbsp. butter in a large skillet and add garlic. Cook and stir for 1 minute and add cream. Reduce until thick over medium heat.

2. Heat remaining butter in a separate skillet, add mushrooms and cook until mushrooms start to brown. Add zucchini and cook for 3 to 4 minutes longer.

3. Add chopped tomatoes to reduced cream and simmer for 5 minutes. Add mushrooms, zucchini, and artichoke hearts and season with salt and pepper. Cook just until vegetables are heated through.

4. Cook fettucine and arrange on individual serving plates. Pour sauce over noodles, sprinkle with Parmesan and plenty of chopped parsley, and serve.

For best results, puree the tomato sauce for the ravioli until silky smooth before adding the cream.

Spinach Ravioli in a Tomato Cream Sauce

1. Wash and stem spinach. Cook until tender in a small amount of boiling water. Drain, squeeze out excess liquid in a kitchen towel, and finely chop.

2. Combine chopped spinach with ricotta, Parmesan, egg, salt, pepper, and nutmeg. Taste for seasoning.

To Assemble:

1. Working with ¼ of the dough at a time, roll it out as thin as possible into a rectangular sheet.

2. Mark off the sheet in 1½ inch squares with the edge of a ruler or yardstick by gently pressing it into the dough at regular intervals. These will be the cutting lines for the finished ravioli. With a pastry brush, very lightly brush the lines with water to ensure a tight seal of the finished squares.

3. Fit a pastry bag with a large tip and place the spinach filling in the bag. Pipe out about ¼ teaspoon in the center of each marked-off square of pasta. You may use a spoon for this, but a pastry bag will move things along much faster.

4. Roll out another piece of dough slightly larger than the first, but close to the same size and shape. Lay this piece of dough over the top of the first one and gently press to fit over the filling. With the edge of the ruler, press along the lines of demarcation to seal the squares. Cut with a pastry wheel and transfer the filled ravioli to a cookie sheet lightly coated with cornmeal to prevent sticking. Repeat until all the dough and filling are used.

5. Bring a large pot of water to a rolling boil. Add plenty of salt and one teaspoon of olive oil. Add ravioli and cook until tender, 4 or 5 minutes. Drain and serve with tomato cream sauce and plenty of freshly grated Parmesan cheese.

Makes about 4 cups

2   *Tbsp. butter*
½   *cup chopped onion*
½   *cup finely diced carrots*
½   *cup finely diced celery*
4   *cups canned tomatoes,*
       with juice
     salt and white pepper
       to taste
1   *cup cream*

Tomato Cream Sauce

1. Heat butter in a saucepan. Add onions and cook 4 to 5 minutes, without browning. Add carrots and celery and cook 3 minutes. Add tomatoes and salt and simmer, uncovered, for 45 minutes.

2. Puree tomato sauce in a blender until very smooth. Add cream, salt, and pepper and taste for seasoning. Reheat and serve over spinach ravioli.

Spaghetti with Eggplant

Serves 4 to 6

1 small eggplant, about
   1¼ lbs.
2 sweet, red or green
   peppers
5 Tbsp. olive oil
1 tsp. finely chopped garlic
3 cups chopped canned
   tomatoes, with juice
1 tsp. basil
½ tsp. oregano
   salt and pepper to taste
   small pinch sugar
½ cup halved black olives
2 Tbsp. capers
1 1-lb. box spaghetti
   freshly grated Parmesan
   cheese

1. Cut eggplant in ½-inch cubes. Sprinkle with salt and let drain in a colander 25 to 30 minutes.

2. Roast peppers over an open gas flame or under a broiler until skins are blistered. Run under cold water and scrape off skins. Remove seeds and cut peppers in ½-inch squares.

3. Heat oil in a large skillet. Add garlic and eggplant and cook 5 minutes. Add tomatoes, basil, oregano, peppers, salt, pepper, sugar, olives, and capers. Cover and simmer for 40 to 45 minutes. Thin with a little water if necessary and taste for seasoning.

4. Cook spaghetti in plenty of boiling, salted water. Serve with eggplant sauce and plenty of freshly grated Parmesan cheese.

You may assemble this lasagne dish in advance and bake just before serving.

Spinach Lasagne

Serves 8

1 recipe egg pasta, or
 about ½ lb. dry
 lasagne noodles
4 cups tomato sauce (see
 recipe below)
1 10-ounce package fresh
 spinach
1 4-ounce package cream
 cheese
1½ cups (¾ lb.) ricotta
 cheese
¾ cup freshly grated
 Parmesan cheese
1 egg
 plenty of salt and pepper
8 ounces thinly sliced
 mozzarella cheese

1. Prepare tomato sauce.

2. Clean and stem spinach. Cook until tender in a small amount of boiling water, 3 to 5 minutes. Drain, cool, and squeeze out excess moisture in towel.

3. Beat cream cheese until smooth. Mix with ricotta, ½ cup grated Parmesan, and egg until well blended. Season with plenty of salt and pepper.

4. Roll pasta dough paper-thin and cut in strips 3 inches wide and 12 inches long. Lay on a kitchen towel and let dry for 10 to 15 minutes while you bring a large pot of water to a boil. Salt the water and add 1 tablespoon oil. When water comes to a rolling boil, add lasagne noodles and cook until tender, from 3 to 5 minutes. Drain and immerse noodles in cold water until ready to assemble. Pat the noodles dry with a kitchen towel as you use them.

5. To assemble, spread a little tomato sauce on the bottom of a 9×13 inch baking pan. Cover with a layer of noodles, arranging them so that the edges overlap a little. Spread with more sauce and dot with cheese mix, cooked spinach and sliced mozzarella. Repeat once more with a layer of noodles, sauce, cheese mix, spinach, and mozzarella. Finally, top with more noodles, sauce, remaining ¼ cup Parmesan, and the rest of the sliced mozzarella.

5. Bake in a preheated 425 degree oven for 10 to 15 minutes, until sauce bubbles and cheese melts. Let rest for 5 minutes, slice in squares, and serve from the pan.

Tomato Sauce for Spinach Lasagne

Makes 4 cups

2 Tbsp. olive oil
1 cup finely chopped
 onion
1 tsp. finely chopped garlic
½ tsp. basil
4 cups coarsely chopped,
 canned tomatoes
 pinch sugar
 salt and pepper to taste

1. Heat oil in a saucepan. Add onions and garlic and cook 3 minutes. Add basil, chopped tomatoes, sugar, salt, and pepper. Bring to a boil, reduce heat and simmer for 20 to 25 minutes. Taste for seasoning.

The combination of red and white sauces in this recipe brings out the subtle and delicate flavor of paper thin spinach noodles.

Lasagne Verdi

Serves 8

½ recipe spinach pasta
4 cups mushroom tomato sauce (see below)
2 cups bechamel sauce (see below)
2 cups grated Swiss cheese

1. Make spinach pasta and roll dough as thin as possible. Cut in 2½-inch wide strips. Lay on a kitchen towel and let dry for 10 to 15 minutes while you bring a large pot of water to a boil. Salt the water and add 1 tablespoon oil. When water comes to a rolling boil, add lasagne noodles and cook until barely tender, 20 to 30 seconds. Drain and immerse the noodles in cold water until ready to assemble. Pat the noodles dry with a kitchen towel as you use them.

2. Spoon a little tomato sauce on the bottom of a 9 × 13 inch baking pan. Cover with a layer of noodles, arranging them so that the edges overlap a little. Spread with more tomato sauce, bechamel, and Swiss cheese. Continue to layer in the same order, ending with a layer of bechamel and Swiss cheese.

3. Bake in a preheated 400 degree oven for 15 minutes, until hot all the way through. Let lasagne settle for 5 minutes before cutting and serving.

Mushroom Tomato Sauce

Makes 4 cups

3 Tbsp. butter
1 Tbsp. olive oil
1 cup finely chopped onions
½ lb. sliced mushrooms
3 cups chopped, canned tomatoes
 salt and pepper to taste
 small pinch sugar

1. Heat butter and oil in a saucepan. Add onions and mushrooms and cook 5 minutes, until vegetables are tender. Add tomatoes, salt, pepper, and sugar and simmer for 35 to 40 minutes. Taste for seasoning.

Bechamel Sauce

Makes 2 cups

2 cups milk
4 Tbsp. butter
3 Tbsp. flour
 salt and white pepper to taste

1. Bring milk to a boil in a small saucepan.

2. In a separate saucepan, melt butter and add flour. Cook, stirring with a wire whisk for three minutes, without browning the flour. Whisk in the boiling milk, ¼ cup at a time, and cook, stirring, until thick. Season well with salt and pepper.

Serve these cheesy gnocchi with a green vegetable and a salad.

Semolina Gnocchi

Serves 4 to 6

4   *cups milk*
1   *cup Italian semolina*
2   *tsp. salt*
5   *Tbsp. butter*
1¼ *cups freshly grated*
     Parmesan cheese
2   *eggs*

1. Bring milk to a boil in a large saucepan. Stir in semolina in a thin stream and add salt. Cook, stirring constantly, until mixture is very thick. Patience, this takes about twenty minutes. When a wooden spoon will stand up in the semolina, it is ready. Stir in 2 tablespoons butter and 1 cup Parmesan cheese. Beat in eggs.

2. Pour semolina onto a buttered baking sheet and spread to a thickness of ⅜ inch. Use a wet spatula, or wet your hands with cold water and pat out until smooth. Chill in refrigerator until hard.

3. With a 1½-inch round cookie cutter, cut semolina into rounds and arrange in an overlapping pattern in a buttered ovenproof serving dish. Dot with butter and sprinkle with remaining ¼ cup of Parmesan cheese.

4. Bake in a preheated 425 degree oven for 15 to 20 minutes, until top starts to brown. Serve hot.

Gnocchi Casserole

Make gnocchi according to steps one and two above. When cold, cut in triangles. Arrange half the triangles in a buttered baking dish. Spread with hot tomato sauce and grated Swiss or Gruyere cheese. Cover with another layer of gnocchi, sauce and cheese and bake as directed above, until cheese melts and top starts to brown.

When you simmer gnocchi, be sure to allow plenty of room in the pan. They may be cooked in batches, arranged in the serving dish, and reheated for a few minutes in the oven just before serving.

Spinach Gnocchi with Butter and Cheese

Serves 4 to 6

2 10-ounce packages fresh
    spinach
1 cup ricotta cheese
2 eggs
6 Tbsp. flour
½ cup freshly grated
    Parmesan cheese
    salt and pepper to taste
    small pinch nutmeg
¼ cup melted butter
    freshly grated Parmesan
    cheese for garnish

1. Clean and stem spinach. Cook until tender in a small amount of boiling water. Squeeze out excess liquid in a kitchen towel and chop.

2. Mix ricotta, eggs, flour, and grated cheese together in a bowl. Add chopped spinach, salt, pepper, and nutmeg. Taste for seasoning. Chill several hours in refrigerator, until firm.

3. Divide spinach mixture in 6 portions. On a well floured board, roll each portion into a coil ¾ inch thick. Cut the coil in one-inch pieces and shape each piece into a small oval.

4. Heat two inches of water in a large, flat pan. When the water is just simmering, add a generous pinch of salt and drop in the gnocchi. Do not overcrowd them, but cook them in batches if they do not all fit comfortably in the pan. As soon as they rise to the top, the gnocchi are done. If they start to fall apart, they have cooked too long.

5. Remove the gnocchi from the simmering water with a slotted spoon and transfer to a buttered baking dish. Drizzle with melted butter and sprinkle with more grated Parmesan. Serve immediately.

These potato gnocchi are miles apart from the heavy fare you would expect of a potato dumpling. The secret of their lightness is the eggy dough known as *pate à chou* (cream puff dough), which is mixed with the mashed potatoes.

Gnocchi all Francese

Serves 4 to 6

4 *Tbsp. butter*
½ *cup milk*
¾ *cup all-purpose flour*
2 *large eggs*
2 *lbs. potatoes, preferably baking potatoes*
    plenty of salt and white pepper
    tomato sauce (see recipe below)
1 *cup grated Swiss or Gruyere cheese*

1. Combine butter and milk in a saucepan and bring to a rolling boil. Stir in ½ cup flour all at once, remove from heat, and beat vigorously with a wooden spoon until well mixed. Return pan to heat for 1 more minute and cook, stirring with the wooden spoon, until dough pulls away from the sides of the pan.

2. Remove from heat and beat a few minutes to cool the dough slightly. Beat in eggs one at a time. The dough will separate and seem slippery, then it will come back together. It will be quite stiff and sticky.

3. Cut potatoes in half if they are large and boil them with their jackets still on, until tender. Drain and peel while still hot. Spread the peeled potatoes on a pie tin and place in a 350 degree oven for 4 to 5 minutes to dry out a little. This is especially important if you are not using baking potatoes, which are drier than standard boiling potatoes. The dryness is what keeps the gnocchi light.

4. Remove the potatoes from the oven and mash them as you would for mashed potatoes. Do not overmix or potatoes will become gummy, the major cause of heavy dumplings. As soon as they are fairly smooth, stir in the remaining ¼ cup flour and mix well. Combine the mashed potatoes with the eggy dough and season well with salt and pepper.

5. Heat about 2 inches water in a large flat pan. When water is just simmering, add a pinch of salt and begin dropping the potato mixture into the water by small teaspoons. The dumplings are done as soon as they rise to the top, from 1 to 2 minutes. Remove with a slotted spoon and place in a buttered ovenproof dish. Continue to drop the dumplings into the simmering water until all the potato mixture is used.

6. Heat the tomato sauce and pour it over the dumplings. Top with grated cheese and place under a hot broiler, or in a preheated 400 degree oven, just until cheese melts. Serve immediately. (See following page.)

Note: If you are handy with a pastry bag, there is a quick and simple way to cook these gnocchi. Fit your bag with a large, round tip, about ½-inch in diameter. Fill with potato mixture and rest the edge of the tip on the side of the pan of simmering water. Squeeze with one hand and, holding a small paring knife in the other, cut through the "snake" of dough as it comes out of the bag at one inch intervals. The gnocchi will drop into the water continuously as you squeeze and cut.

Tomato Sauce for Gnocchi

2 Tbsp. olive oil
1 cup finely chopped onion
½ tsp. finely chopped garlic
½ tsp. oregano
½ tsp. basil
½ tsp. thyme
4 cups canned tomatoes pinch sugar salt and pepper to taste
1 bay leaf

1. Heat olive oil in a saucepan. Add onion and garlic and cook until onions are tender. Add oregano, basil, and thyme.

2. Chop tomatoes roughly in a food processor, or drain and press out excess juice and chop on a board. Add tomatoes and juice to saucepan, stir in sugar, salt, pepper, and bay leaf and simmer for 25 to 30 minutes. Taste again for seasoning.

Note: If you wish to make the gnocchi in advance, cook them and place them in the buttered serving dish. When ready to serve, pour the hot tomato sauce over them and heat them in the oven for about 20 minutes. When the gnocchi are hot all the way through, sprinkle on the cheese and return to the oven until the cheese melts.

Although these noodles are served cold, they are spicy hot.

Chinese Cold, Spicy Noodles

Serves 6 to 8

½ lb. Chinese noodles, about the thickness of spaghetti
2 tsp. chili paste
½ cup finely sliced scallions
1 Tbsp. grated fresh ginger
2 tsp. finely chopped garlic
2 Tbsp. Chinese sesame oil
3 Tbsp. tahini
2 Tbsp. soy sauce
1½ tsp. sugar salt to taste

1. Cook noodles in plenty of boiling, salted water until tender, about 5 minutes. Drain and run under cold water until cool.

2. Mix remaining ingredients together until well blended. Toss with noodles and season with salt. Chill until ready to serve.

As an appetizer or part of a Japanese meal, these cold noodles are delightful in hot weather.

Serves 6 to 8

1   12-ounce package saimin (Japanese noodles)
½   cup rice wine vinegar
½   cup soy sauce
¼   cup sugar
½   tsp. Chinese sesame oil
3   cups vegetable stock

Garnishes:

finely sliced scallions
seeded and diced
    cucumber
toasted sesame seeds
thinly sliced mushrooms
egg strips
bean sprouts

Japanese Style Cold Noodles in Broth

1. Bring a large pot of water to a boil. Add noodles and cook for 5 to 7 minutes after the water returns to a boil, until tender. Drain and run under cold water for about 5 minutes. Immerse in cold water until ready to use.

2. Mix remaining ingredients together and chill until ready to serve.

3. Drain noodles and arrange in individual serving bowls. Pour broth over noodles and garnish with one or a combination of the suggested garnishes.

1. Serve in small condiment bowls to accompany noodles.

Fried or Blanched

Vegetables and Side Dishes

 The advent of commercial canning and frozen foods has, in past decades, almost eclipsed the American consumer's awareness of the wonderful produce available on a seasonal basis. Luckily, the delicious and often more economical alternative of fresh produce has gained more notice recently in light of a renewed interest in health food and organic gardening. In response to this trend, large supermarkets carry a wide variety of fresh vegetables for the shopper wishing to avoid convenience foods.

One method of cooking that brings out the best in fresh vegetables is stir-frying. In this Chinese technique, vegetables are cooked briefly in very hot oil and then steamed in a small amount of water until barely tender. This quick cooking method retains both the flavor and color of the vegetables.

Whether your method is stir-frying or simply blanching, vegetables should be cooked quickly in a small amount of water. "Drowning" vegetables in a pot of water only serves to dissipate their precious minerals. You can reserve this liquid for later use in soups and sauces. Finally, if you wish to preserve fresh color and flavor, you may add a little lemon juice to the cooking water.

Here is a delicious way to serve artichokes, hot or cold. To serve as part of an antipasto platter, quarter whole, cooked artichokes and serve with a dot of sauce on top.

Artichokes Dijonnais

Serves 4

4   artichokes
1   cup freshly made
      mayonnaise or
      Hollandaise sauce
1   Tbsp. or more Dijon
      mustard

1. Cut stems from the bottoms of the artichokes. With a sharp knife, trim about ½ inch from the tops. Trim the pointed ends of the leaves with a kitchen scissors.

2. Bring a large pot of water to a boil. Add artichokes and cook until tender, 20 to 30 minutes for medium-sized artichokes, longer for larger ones. To test for doneness, remove artichoke from water and pierce the bottom with a sharp knife. It should be of the same consistency as a cooked carrot.

3. Mix mustard with mayonnaise or Hollandaise sauce to taste.

4. Serve artichokes hot or cold with sauce on the side.

The striking simplicity characteristic of Japanese cooking is illustrated by their use of kampyo. Kampyo, Japanese dried gourd strips, has little distinctive flavor of its own but serves as a convenient and pleasing method of tying bundles or rolls together. The long dried strands must be soaked in boiling water to soften.

Asparagus à la Japonnaise

Serves 4

3 18-inch strands of kampyo (Japanese dried gourd)
1 lb. fresh asparagus
3 Tbsp. lemon juice
3 Tbsp. soy sauce
2 tsp. mirin or sherry
1 Tbsp. toasted sesame seeds

1. Simmer kampyo in boiling water for 10 minutes, drain, and run under cold water. Cut in 6-inch lengths.

2. Tie asparagus in bundles of 3 or 4 stalks with kampyo strips. Steam until tender and arrange on a plate.

3. Make a dressing with lemon juice, soy sauce, and mirin and pour over asparagus. Sprinkle with sesame seeds. Serve hot or cold.

Serve these beans as a side dish for a Chinese meal.

Dry-Cooked String Beans

Serves 4 to 6

2 lbs. green beans
2 cups oil for frying
¼ cup finely sliced scallions
2 Tbsp. minced fresh ginger
1 4-ounce can Chinese pickled cucumber, finely chopped
2 tsp. finely chopped garlic
4 tsp. vinegar
2 Tbsp. soy sauce
½ cup water
2 tsp. Chinese sesame oil

1. Trim ends from green beans, but leave them whole.

2. Heat oil in a wok or skillet. When oil is smoking hot, add green beans and cook, turning often, until skins are wrinkled and beans start to brown. Drain on paper towels.

3. Pour all but 2 tablespoons oil out of the frying pan. Return beans to pan and cook until brown on all sides. Add scallions, ginger, pickled cucumber, garlic, vinegar, soy sauce, and water. Cook until most of the liquid evaporates. Stir in sesame oil and taste for seasoning.

Broccoli Italian Style

Serves 4 to 6

1   large bunch broccoli
¼   cup olive oil
     juice of ½ large lemon
½   cup coarsely chopped
        black olives,
        preferably Greek
     salt and pepper to taste

1. Trim stems and cut broccoli in medium-sized serving pieces. Blanch until tender in boiling, salted water. Drain and toss with olive oil, lemon juice, olives, salt, and pepper. Taste for seasoning and serve hot.

Broccoli with Almonds

Serves 4 to 6

1   bunch broccoli
2   Tbsp. soy sauce
2   tsp. Chinese sesame oil
     pinch salt
½   cup toasted, sliced
        almonds

1. Trim broccoli stems and cut in medium-sized serving pieces. Blanch in boiling, salted water until tender. Drain.

2. Toss broccoli with soy sauce, sesame oil, and salt. Taste for seasoning. Sprinkle with toasted almonds. Serve hot.

A nice 'wintery' side dish.

Red Cabbage with Apples

Serves 4

2   Tbsp. butter
½   cup chopped onion
2   tsp. sugar
1   small head red cabbage,
        about 1¼ lbs.
2   apples, peeled and diced
½   cup vegetable stock
        or water
     salt and pepper to taste
2   Tbsp. cider vinegar
3   Tbsp. red wine

1. Heat butter in a large skillet. Add onions and sugar and cook 2 minutes.

2. Slice cabbage in ¼-inch thick slices. Add to skillet with apples, stock, and salt. Cover and simmer for 20 minutes.

3. Add vinegar, red wine, and pepper and simmer for 5 more minutes with cover off. Taste for seasoning.

These beautiful, golden, brown fritters are appealingly speckled with green bits of fresh parsley—a tempting and unusual way to serve carrots. The mustard sauce is a perfect complement.

Carrot Fritters

Serves 4 to 6

2½ cups *finely diced carrots*
2 *Tbsp. finely chopped onion*
2 *Tbsp. finely chopped parsley*
2 *egg yolks*
3 *Tbsp. milk*
¼ *cup flour*
¼ *tsp. salt*
    pinch pepper
2 *egg whites, stiffly beaten oil for frying*

1. Blanch carrots in boiling, salted water for two minutes and drain well. Mix with chopped onion and parsley.

2. Mix egg yolks and milk together and stir in flour, salt and pepper. When well blended, fold in egg whites. Mix with carrots.

3. Heat ⅛ inch oil in the bottom of a heavy skillet. Using about ⅓ cup per pancake, drop batter in hot oil and fry 2 to 3 minutes on each side, until golden brown. Drain on absorbent paper and serve with mustard sauce. Makes about 10 fritters.

Tangy Mustard Sauce

2 *Tbsp. Dijon mustard*
1 *Tbsp. red wine vinegar*
1 *Tbsp. finely chopped parsley*
1 *tsp. finely chopped onion*
¼ *cup olive oil*
    salt and pepper

1. Mix mustard, vinegar, parsley, and onion together in a small bowl. With a wire whisk, beat in olive oil a little at a time. Add salt and pepper and taste for seasoning.

Turnips are also delicious cooked this way.

Glazed Carrots

Serves 4

1½ *lbs. carrots*
2 *Tbsp. butter*
1 *Tbsp. oil*
1 *Tbsp. sugar*
1 *cup water or stock*
    pinch salt

1. Peel carrots. Halve or quarter them lengthwise if they are more than ½-inch in diameter. Cut in two-inch lengths.

2. Heat butter and oil in a large skillet. Add carrots and cook until golden brown, turning often. Add sugar, water, and salt and cook, uncovered, until carrots are tender and liquid has reduced to a thick syrup. Serve hot.

This dish may be made well in advance and reheated just before serving.

Cauliflower Gratinata

Serves 4

1 head cauliflower
  béchamel sauce
  (see recipe below)
½ cup freshly grated
  Parmesan cheese
¼ cup breadcrumbs
1 Tbsp. butter

1. Break cauliflower in large florets. Blanch in boiling, salted water until tender. Drain.

2. Mix béchamel sauce with half the Parmesan cheese. Arrange cooked cauliflower in a buttered baking dish and cover with sauce.

3. Mix remaining Parmesan with breadcrumbs and sprinkle over top. Dot with butter and bake in a preheated 400 degree oven for 10 to 15 minutes.

Béchamel Sauce

2 cups milk
4 Tbsp. butter
4 Tbsp. flour
  plenty of salt and pepper

1. Bring milk to a boil in a small saucepan.

2. In a separate saucepan, melt butter and add flour. Cook, stirring with a wire whisk, for 3 minutes. Do not let flour brown. Whisk in boiling milk ¼ cup at a time and cook, stirring, until thick. Season well with salt and pepper.

A good side dish for a Mexican meal.

Sweet Corn Pudding

Serves 6

4 cups corn, off the cob
  or frozen
2 cups milk
⅓ cup sugar
½ tsp. salt
2 Tbsp. butter
¼ cup raisins
4 well beaten eggs
  cinnamon sugar

1. Simmer corn with milk, sugar, and salt until tender, about 5 minutes. Chop coarsely in a food processor, or partially blend in a blender.

2. Mix corn with butter, raisins and beaten eggs. Pour into a buttered 6-cup casserole and bake in a preheated 325 degree oven for 35 to 40 minutes. Serve hot sprinkled with cinnamon sugar.

A fine component of an Indian meal, this eggplant dish may be spiced according to taste by adjusting the amount of cayenne pepper. I like it hot served with plenty of raita, curried beans, rice pilaf, and chutney. Be sure that the eggplant is completely cooked or the dish will have a bitter taste.

Curried Eggplant

Serves 6

2 *small eggplants, about
      1 lb. each*
6 *Tbsp. oil*
2 *tsp. whole cumin seed*
1 *cup chopped onion*
2 *Tbsp. Indian curry spice
      mix (curry powder)
      cayenne pepper to taste*
1 *cup chopped tomatoes,
      fresh or canned*
¼ *cup chopped canned
      green chiles*
1 *cup yogurt*
1 *Tbsp. chopped fresh
      coriander*

1. Slice eggplant in ¼-inch rounds and spread on a baking sheet. Sprinkle with 4 Tablespoons oil and bake in a preheated 425 degree oven for 25 to 30 minutes, until tender.

2. Heat remaining 2 Tablespoons oil in a large skillet, add cumin seeds, and cook briefly, until seeds start to brown. Add onion, curry powder, and cayenne pepper and cook 3 to 4 minutes. Add tomatoes and chiles and cook 3 more minutes. Stir in yogurt and coriander and taste for seasoning. Mix with cooked eggplant and reheat. Taste again for seasoning and serve.

Eggplant Provencal

Serves 4 to 6

1 *large eggplant (about
      1½ lbs.)*
2 *Tbsp. olive oil*
1 *tsp. finely chopped garlic*
3 *cups coarsely chopped,
      canned tomatoes,
      with juice*
6 *to 8 parsley stems
      salt and pepper to taste*
2 *bay leaves
      small pinch sugar
      oil for frying*
½ *lb. sliced mozzarella or
      Swiss cheese*

1. Slice eggplant in ½-inch thick rounds. Sprinkle with salt and let drain on paper towels for 30 minutes.

2. Heat olive oil in a saucepan. Add garlic, tomatoes, parsley stems, salt, pepper, bay leaves, and sugar. Simmer gently for 30 minutes. Remove parsley stems and bay leaves and taste for seasoning.

3. Heat about ½ inch oil in a heavy iron skillet or frying pan. Gently pat eggplant slices dry and fry a few minutes on each side, until tender. Drain on paper towels.

4. For individual servings, place two slices of eggplant on small, heatproof plates. Cover with a spoonful of tomato sauce and top with sliced cheese. Run under a hot broiler for a few minutes just before serving, until eggplant is hot and cheese is melted.

For best results, the batter for these pancakes must be made just before you are ready to cook them.

Potato Pancakes

Makes about 12 pancakes

1½ lbs. potatoes
¼ cup flour
2 Tbsp. finely chopped onion
1 egg
1 tsp. salt
pinch pepper
1 Tbsp. finely chopped parsley
oil for frying

1. Peel potatoes and coarsely grate them. Mix with remaining ingredients until well blended.

2. Heat a thin coating of oil in the bottom of a large frying pan. Drop potato mixture in pan, about ¼ cup for each pancake. Flatten "batter" with a spatula and cook 3 to 4 minutes on each side, until golden brown. Drain on absorbent paper. Serve hot garnished with sour cream if you like.

Encased in a crunchy almond crust, these potatoes are ideal for a special, fancy occasion.

Potato Croquettes

Serves 4 to 6

4 medium-sized potatoes
salt and pepper
¾ cup grated Swiss cheese
1 Tbsp. finely chopped parsley
approximately 1 cup flour
¾ cup finely chopped almonds
⅓ cup breadcrumbs
oil for frying
2 beaten eggs

1. Peel potatoes and boil until tender. Press through a ricer or a coarse sieve and season well with salt and pepper. Stir in cheese and parsley and let stand until cool.

2. With floured hands, form potatoes into cigar-shaped cylinders about 3 inches long. Mix chopped almonds and breadcrumbs together until combined. Dredge croquettes lightly in flour, coat with beaten egg, and roll in mixture of chopped almonds and breadcrumbs. Set aside until ready to fry.

3. Heat one inch oil in a heavy iron skillet or frying pan. When oil is hot but not quite smoking, add the croquettes a few at a time and fry until golden brown on all sides. Drain on absorbent paper and sprinkle generously with salt. Serve immediately.

A treat for Thanksgiving Day or any other!

Maple Candied Sweet Potatoes

Serves 6 to 8

2   lbs. sweet potatoes
¼   cup melted butter
¼   cup pure maple syrup
    salt to taste

1. Peel and halve or quarter potatoes lengthwise. Arrange them with the flat sides down in a buttered baking dish.

2. Mix melted butter with maple syrup and brush on potatoes. Drizzle the rest over the top. Sprinkle lightly with salt and bake in a preheated 400 degree oven for 45 minutes. Baste two or three times during baking. Serve hot.

This is a 'fancy' dish for turnip lovers, and may be prepared in advance and reheated.

Stuffed Turnips

Serves 4

4   turnips
1   potato
½   10-ounce package fresh
    spinach
¼   cup freshly grated
    Parmesan cheese
1   Tbsp. butter
    salt and pepper to taste

1. Choose uniform turnips that are each a good serving size. Peel and trim off ends. With a small round cutter or a sharp paring knife, make a deep circular incision in the top of each turnip. Cook in boiling, salted water until tender but still on the firm side.

2. Peel potato and cook in boiling, salted water until tender.

3. Clean and stem spinach and cook in a small amount of boiling water. Drain, cool, and squeeze out excess moisture. Chop coarsely.

4. When turnips are done, remove from boiling water and carefully scoop out centers, leaving a shell to hold the filling. Mash the scooped out turnip with the cooked potato and butter. Stir in spinach, cheese, salt, and pepper and taste for seasoning.

5. Stuff turnip shells, piling the filling high, and place them in a baking pan. Pour a little water in the bottom of the pan and place in a preheated 400 degree oven. Bake 10 to 15 minutes, until turnips are heated through.

Creamed Spinach

Serves 4

1   10-ounce package fresh
      spinach
1   Tbsp. butter
1   Tbsp. finely chopped
      onion
⅛   tsp. finely chopped garlic
2   Tbsp. flour
1   cup reserved spinach
      stock
      salt and pepper to taste

1. Clean and stem spinach and cook in boiling water until tender. Drain and reserve 1 cup stock for sauce.

2. Melt butter in a saucepan. Add onion and garlic and cook 2 minutes. Stir in flour and cook for 1 minute. Bring spinach stock to a boil and stir into flour with a whisk, until smooth. Continue stirring until sauce comes to a boil. Boil one minute.

3. Add cooked spinach to sauce and season with salt and pepper. Taste for seasoning.

Butternut Squash with Apples

Serves 6

1   large butternut squash,
      about 3 lbs.
3   Tbsp. butter
¼   cup brown sugar
¼   cup heavy cream
¼   tsp. ginger
      salt and pepper to taste
2   apples, peeled and diced

1. Peel squash and remove seeds and pulp. Cut in large pieces and cook until tender in a small amount of boiling water, about 20 minutes. Drain well.

2. Mash cooked squash with 2 Tbsp. butter, brown sugar, cream, and ginger. Season with salt and pepper to taste. Stir in diced apples and pour into a buttered baking dish. Dot with remaining one tablespoon butter and bake in a preheated 375 degree oven for 20 minutes, until apples are tender.

Baked Tomato Halves

Serves 4

4   medium-sized tomatoes
¾   cup breadcrumbs
1   tsp. finely chopped garlic
¼   tsp. thyme
2   Tbsp. finely chopped
      parsley
2   Tbsp. olive oil
      salt and pepper to taste

1. Halve the tomatoes and remove the seeds. (Gently squeeze and shake tomato half upside-down over a bowl. The seeds should fall right out.)

2. Mix remaining ingredients together and season well with salt and pepper. Gently press mixture over tomatoes in a mound. Place in a lightly oiled baking pan and bake in a preheated 375 degree oven for 20 minutes, until tender. If you like, you may also brown these tomato halves under the broiler.

Zucchini with Garlic and Tomatoes

Serves 4

2   Tbsp. olive oil
1   tsp. or more finely
      chopped garlic
2   Tbsp. finely chopped
      onion
1   tomato, peeled and
      chopped
1½ lbs. zucchini, sliced in
      ¼-inch thick rounds
2   Tbsp. finely chopped
      parsley
    salt and pepper to taste
2   Tbsp. breadcrumbs
2   to 3 Tbsp. freshly grated
      Parmesan cheese

1. Heat oil in a skillet. Add garlic and onion and cook 3 minutes. Add chopped tomato and cook, stirring often, for 5 minutes.

2. Blanch zucchini 3 minutes in boiling, salted water. Drain well.

3. Add cooked zucchini to skillet with chopped parsley and season with salt and pepper. When heated all the way through, transfer to a serving dish and sprinkle with breadcrumbs and grated cheese. Serve immediately.

You may keep the first 'batches' of French fried zucchini warm in the oven while you finish frying them.

French Fried Zucchini

Serves 4

1   lb. zucchini
      approximately 1 cup
      flour
      approximately 1½ cups
      fine, dry breadcrumbs
2   beaten eggs
      oil for frying

1. Wash zucchini but do not peel. Cut in 3-inch julienne, about the same size as skinny French-fried potatoes.

2. Dredge zucchini lightly in flour, coat with beaten egg, and roll in breadcrumbs. Spread breaded zucchini sticks on a tray until you are ready to fry them.

3. Heat one inch oil in a heavy iron skillet or frying pan. When the oil is hot but not yet smoking, add breaded zucchini in batches and fry until golden brown. Drain on absorbent paper and sprinkle generously with salt. Serve immediately.

In this 'Western' version of tempura, the batter is light and flavorful. Serve plain or with a tangy mustard sauce.

Vegetables in Beer Batter

Vegetables:

> *whole asparagus spears*
> *sliced eggplant*
> *blanched broccoli florets*
> *blanched cauliflower*
>   *florets*
> *onions, sliced in rounds*
> *whole mushrooms*

1. Choose one or several vegetables from the above suggestions, or try your own. Since they will be dipped in batter and then fried only briefly in hot oil, the vegetables must be sliced thin enough to cook in a short time. Large pieces of broccoli or cauliflower should be blanched first. I especially like cauliflower and eggplant for this. Here are two recipes for the batter.

Makes enough batter for vegetables for 4 people

Beer Batter:

> 1   *cup flour*
> 1   *cup beer, at room*
>   *temperature*
> ¼ *tsp. salt*
> 1   *Tbsp. oil*
> 1   *egg, separated*

1. Mix flour with beer until smooth. Add salt, oil, and egg yolk and mix well. Set aside in a warm place to ferment for two to three hours.

2. Beat egg white until stiff and fold into batter.

3. Heat three inches oil in a heavy saucepan or deep fryer.

4. Dredge prepared vegetables lightly in flour. This will help the batter adhere to the vegetables. Dip floured vegetables in batter and drop in hot oil. Fry until golden brown. Fry in small batches so that the vegetables can move about freely when frying. Drain on absorbent paper and serve immediately. Serve plain sprinkled with salt, or with a tangy mustard sauce.

Not quite as flavorful, but great for spur of the moment onion rings.

Quick Beer Batter:

> 1   *cup beer*
> 1   *cup flour*
> ½ *tsp. salt*

1. Mix all ingredients together to make a smooth batter. Follow the same procedure as above for frying.

In addition to its merit as a supplier of protein and vitamins to the vegetarian diet, brown rice has a lovely, nutty taste and crunchy texture. Serve this whole grain plain, or as in this recipe, cooked with chopped vegetables.

Brown Rice Pilaf

Serves 6

3   Tbsp. butter
½   cup finely sliced scallions
½   tsp. finely chopped garlic
½   cup finely chopped
        mushrooms
1½ cups brown rice
3   cups boiling vegetable
        stock or water
2   Tbsp. finely chopped
        parsley
    salt to taste

1. Heat butter in a 2-quart saucepan. Add scallions, garlic, and mushrooms and cook, stirring, for 5 minutes. Add rice and cook 3 more minutes, stirring constantly.

2. Taste stock for salt and add more if needed. Pour boiling stock over rice, add parsley, and stir. Reduce heat and cover tightly with a lid. Simmer 45 minutes to an hour, until all the water has been absorbed and rice is tender.

Prepared this way, fried rice can be quite a delicate dish, unlike the fried rice found in many Chinese-American restaurants. Here is a basic recipe. Other vegetables, such as chopped mushrooms, carrots, peas, green pepper, etc., may be added to make a more substantial dish. Vegetable oil and leftover rice will do just fine, but for a superb treat, use peanut oil and freshly cooked white rice. Don't forget the salt!

Fried Rice

Serves 4 to 6

¼   cup vegetable oil
4   cups cooked rice (white
        or brown)
2   beaten eggs
½   cup finely sliced scallions
    salt to taste

1. Heat oil in a wok or skillet. Add rice and stir-fry until rice is hot all the way through. Stir in scallions and beaten egg and continue to cook and stir until egg is set. Season with salt and serve hot. Pass the soy sauce on the side.

This rice and vegetable dish is good served with tempura or as part of a Japanese meal.

Japanese Mixed Rice

Serves 6

2 cups Japanese rice
3½ cups water
1 small carrot
3 Japanese dried
   mushrooms (shitake)
¼ cup finely sliced scallion
¾ cup green peas
1 Tbsp. sugar
¼ cup soy sauce
1 tsp. salt

1. Wash rice in cold water until water runs clear. Drain.

2. Bring rice and 2 cups water to a boil in a saucepan. Reduce heat, cover and simmer for 10 minutes, until all the water has been absorbed. Turn off heat and let rice steam with the cover on for 15 minutes.

3. Peel carrot and cut in ½-inch slivers. Soak mushrooms in ½ cup boiling water until soft. Cut in slivers.

4. Bring remaining 1 cup water to a boil in a small saucepan. Add carrots and cook for 3 minutes. Add scallions, mushrooms, peas, sugar, soy sauce and salt. Bring to a boil again and boil 30 seconds. Remove from heat and drain. Reserve stock for soup.

5. Mix vegetables with hot rice and serve. Garnish with egg strips if you like.

Egg Strips

1 egg
2 tsp. oil

1. Beat egg thoroughly with a fork. Heat half the oil in an omelet pan. Pour in half the beaten egg and quickly tilt the pan back and forth so that the egg coats the bottom of the pan in a thin sheet. As soon as the egg is set, remove from pan. Repeat with the remaining egg. Cut in narrow strips.

Spanish Rice

Serves 6 to 8

3 Tbsp. oil
1 cup finely chopped
   onion
1 tsp. finely chopped garlic
2 cups rice
1½ cups chopped, canned
   tomatoes, with juice
1½ cups vegetable stock or
   water
1 tsp. salt

1. Heat oil in a 2-quart saucepan. Add onions and garlic and cook, stirring occasionally, for 5 minutes. Add rice and cook, stirring constantly, for 3 more minutes, until golden brown.

2. Stir in chopped tomatoes, stock, and salt and bring to a boil. Reduce heat and cover tightly with a lid. Simmer for 15 to 20 minutes, until all the liquid has been absorbed and rice is tender.

Serves 6 to 8

2 cups water
1½ cups rice
1 tsp. butter
1 tsp. salt
¼ tsp. turmeric
¼ cup oil
1 Tbsp. whole cumin seed
1 cup sliced onion
1 small green pepper, diced
½ cup sliced mushrooms
⅛ tsp. cinnamon
2 whole cloves, coarsely
   crushed
1 cardamon pod, split
   open and coarsely
   crushed
¼ cup raisins
1 cup finely chopped
   tomato, fresh
   or canned
½ cup grated carrots
¼ toasted, sliced almonds
½ cup green peas, fresh
   or frozen

Here is a super deluxe version of an Indian rice pilaf.

Byriani

1. Combine water, rice, butter, salt, and turmeric in a saucepan and bring to a boil. Reduce heat, cover tightly, and simmer for 10 minutes, until water has evaporated and rice is tender.

2. Heat oil in a skillet, add cumin seeds, and cook briefly, until seeds start to brown. Add onion, green pepper, and mushrooms and cook 3 minutes.

3. Stir in cinnamon, crushed cloves and cardamon, raisins, and tomatoes. Cook 3 more minutes. Add grated carrots, almonds, and peas. Heat mixture through and mix with hot, cooked rice. Season with salt to taste and serve.

Serves 6

2 cups dry chick peas
1 tsp. salt
1 tsp. tamarind
   concentrate
2 Tbsp. butter
1 tsp. whole cumin seed
1 Tbsp. grated fresh ginger
1 large tomato, peeled and
   finely chopped
4 tsp. Indian curry spice
   mix (curry powder)
3 Tbsp. chopped, canned,
   green chiles
1 Tbsp. finely chopped fresh
   coriander

Curried Chick Peas

1. Cover chick peas with water and soak overnight. If necessary, add more water to cover and bring to a boil. Add salt and tamarind concentrate and simmer until tender, about 1½ hours.

2. Heat butter in a skillet. Add cumin seeds and cook until they start to brown. Add ginger, chopped tomato, curry powder, and green chiles. Cook 5 minutes. Add to chick peas with chopped coriander and simmer for 20 to 25 minutes. Taste for seasoning.

An excellent accompaniment to an Indian meal.

Split Red Lentils

Serves 4 to 6

1½   cups split red lentils
1   tsp. salt
¼   tsp. turmeric
3   Tbsp. butter
½   tsp. whole cumin seed
1   tsp. finely chopped garlic
1   cup finely chopped
        onion
        pinch sugar
2   tsp. grated fresh ginger
3   Tbsp. chopped, canned,
        green chiles
2   tsp. Indian curry spice
        mix (curry powder)
2   Tbsp. lemon juice

1. Cover lentils with water. Add salt and turmeric and bring to a boil. Simmer until tender, about 15 minutes, adding more water as needed.

2. Heat butter in a skillet. Add cumin seeds and garlic and cook until they start to brown. Add onions and sugar and cook until onions are soft. Add ginger, green chiles, curry powder, and lemon juice. Cook 3 to 4 minutes and add to lentils. Stir and taste for seasoning.

The pods of the tamarind tree produce an acid, juicy pulp that is often used in Indian cooking. Tamarind concentrate, a pure extract of natural tamarind, can be found in Oriental or Indian groceries under the name of *tamcon*.

Curried Red Beans

Serves 6 to 8

2   cups small red beans
2   tsp. salt
3   Tbsp. chopped, canned,
        green chiles
1   tsp. tamarind
        concentrate
3   Tbsp. oil
¾   tsp. whole cumin seed
½   cup finely chopped
        onion
½   tsp. grated fresh ginger
2   tsp. Indian curry spice
        mix (curry powder)
        pinch cayenne pepper
½   cup chopped, canned
        tomatoes

1. Combine red beans, salt, and water to cover in a saucepan. Bring to a boil, reduce heat, and simmer, covered, until beans are soft, about 1½ hours. Check beans every 30 minutes or so and add more water if necessary.

2. When beans are soft, add chopped chiles and tamarind concentrate (dissolved in a small amount of hot water).

3. Heat oil in a small skillet. Add cumin seed, onion, ginger, curry powder, cayenne, and tomatoes. Cook, stirring, for five minutes. Add to red beans and cook for another 20 minutes. Taste for seasoning.

Indian Black Beans

Makes 5 cups

1½ cups dry black beans
1 tsp. salt
1 Tbsp. butter
1 cup chopped onion
1 tsp. grated fresh ginger
½ tsp. paprika
½ cup chopped tomatoes, fresh or canned
½ cup chopped, canned, green chiles
1 Tbsp. chopped, fresh coriander
½ cup yogurt

1. Combine beans, salt, and water to cover in a saucepan. Bring to a boil and reduce heat. Simmer, covered, until tender, about 1½ hours.

2. Heat butter in a small skillet. Add onion, ginger, and paprika and cook 3 minutes. Stir in tomatoes, chiles, and coriander and cook 3 to 4 more minutes. Add to beans when they are tender and cook for another 20 minutes. Stir in yogurt and taste for seasoning.

Like those found at many a New England church supper, these sweet baked beans far surpass their canned imitations in flavor. For a large gathering, make them a day ahead.

Boston Baked Beans

Serves 8 to 12

1½ lbs. dry pea beans or small navy beans
½ cup molasses
¾ cup brown sugar
½ small onion
1½ tsp. dry mustard
1½ tsp. salt
½ tsp. ginger

1. Combine beans with water to cover in a large, ovenproof casserole and bring to a boil on the top of the stove. Mix in remaining ingredients. Cover the casserole and bake in a preheated 250 degree oven for 6 to 8 hours, until beans are tender. Check every hour or so and add more water as necessary to keep beans from drying out.

These beans are good cooked with a small piece of hot, red pepper. Be sure that they are sufficiently mashed or they will lack the true character of this staple of Mexican cooking.

Refried Beans

Makes 4 cups

1½ cups dry pinto, kidney or
    black beans
1 tsp. salt
    small piece of dried, hot,
    red pepper, such as
    pequin (optional)
5 Tbsp. vegetable oil
1 cup finely chopped
    onion
1 tsp. finely chopped garlic
1 medium tomato, finely
    chopped

1. Combine beans, salt, red pepper, 1 tablespoon oil, and ½ cup chopped onion in a saucepan and cover with water. Bring to a boil and reduce heat. Cover and simmer until tender, about 1½ hours. Check beans every 30 minutes or so and add more water if necessary.

2. When beans are soft, taste and add more salt if needed. Cook for another 30 minutes, but do not add any more water.

3. Heat remaining 4 tablespoons oil in a skillet. Add the remaining chopped onion and the garlic and cook for 3 minutes. Add chopped tomato and cook, stirring, for 5 more minutes.

4. Add beans to skillet in batches of about one cup. Mash to a paste with a fork or the back of a wooden spoon as you add them. Continue to mash and cook the beans until thick. Taste for seasoning.

Salads

Thanks to a recent trend of diet and health consciousness in today's eating habits, salads play a more and more prominent role in the overall scheme of dining. Green, leafy salads—tossed at the table with oil and vinegar—provide a pleasant accompaniment to any meal, from a light lunch to an elaborate supper. You may prepare more substantial salads in advance and serve as a main course with soup and fresh bread for an entirely satisfying meal, especially when light eating is called for.

A combination of greens makes a lovely salad, but be sure to consider their effect on each other, since one may overpower all the others. Iceberg and romaine are among the crisper greens, while bibb, Boston, and leaf lettuce, along with spinach and watercress, are soft and tender. Chicory, escarole, endive, and arugula, somewhat bitter but spicy, are delicious eaten in combination with other greens. Do not neglect fresh herbs, such as basil, dill, coriander, chervil, parsley, sorrel, and tarragon;—these herbs, added in generous quantities, enhance a salad immensely.

Pure olive oil and red wine vinegar are the classic components of a green salad tossed to perfection. However, many other exciting choices are now available to the more adventuresome diner, and though on the expensive side, these add even more variety. Walnut oil, hazelnut oil, almond oil, Chinese sesame oil (just a drop), rice wine vinegar, and herbed, flavored vinegars such as raspberry, tarragon, and mixed "herbes de Provence" are among the possible exotic fixings.

To prepare greens for a salad, wash carefully and pat or shake as dry as possible. Excess water on the leaves will only serve to dilute the dressing. If you have time, enclose the greens in a plastic bag and crisp them in the refrigerator. Season and toss the greens with dressing just a few moments before serving.

For the most part, this chapter deals with hearty salads made up of a combination of vegetables. Fresh vegetables are shown off to their best advantage in this area. If vegetables need blanching, such as broccoli, green beans, beets, or cauliflower, you may preserve their fresh, bright color by plunging them in ice water as soon as they reach the point of tenderness. This also cools the vegetables quickly if you need to serve the salad immediately.

Creamy and delicious, this pretty, pale green dressing merits the enthusiasm it has received from countless Tao customers through the years. It suits a plain green salad as well as an elaborate vegetable or chef's salad.

Tao Dressing

Makes 1⅓ cups

- ⅓ cup mayonnaise
- ⅓ cup yogurt
- 1½ Tbsp. cider vinegar
- ½ tsp. honey
- ⅛ tsp. salt
  pinch black pepper
- ½ tsp. finely chopped parsley
- ⅛ tsp. basil
- ⅛ tsp. dill weed
- 3 or 4 spinach leaves
- ⅔ cup salad oil

1. Combine all ingredients except salad oil in a blender and puree until smooth. Turn blender on low speed. While motor is still running, slowly pour in oil in a thin stream. When all the oil has been absorbed, turn blender on high speed and blend for a few more seconds to thicken.

Creamy Parmesan Dressing

Makes 1 cup

- ¼ cup yogurt
- ½ tsp. sugar
- ½ tsp. oregano
- ½ tsp. basil
- ¼ tsp. finely chopped garlic
- ⅛ tsp. salt
  pinch pepper
- 4 tsp. white vinegar
- 2 Tbsp. freshly grated Parmesan cheese
- ⅔ cup salad oil

1. Combine yogurt, sugar, oregano, basil, garlic, salt, pepper, vinegar, and Parmesan cheese in a blender and puree until smooth.

2. Turn blender on low speed. While motor is running, pour in oil in a thin stream. When all the oil has been absorbed, turn blender on high speed and blend for a few more seconds to thicken.

Serve this delicate, creamy dressing over a salad of mixed greens, tender lettuce, or cold, cooked vegetables.

Creamy Mustard Dressing

3   Tbsp. Dijon mustard
¾   cup heavy cream
1   Tbsp. lemon juice
    salt to taste
    pinch white pepper

1. Combine mustard, cream, lemon juice, salt, and pepper together in a bowl. Beat with a wire whisk until frothy. Taste for seasoning.

Coriander and cumin distinguish this tangy lemon vinaigrette from the traditional French style dressing. It is especially nice on a salad of soft lettuce such as bibb, Boston, or leaf lettuce. Serve with a Mexican or Middle Eastern meal.

Lemon Garlic Dressing

Makes ½ cup

1½ Tbsp. lemon juice
½   tsp. ground coriander
½   tsp. ground cumin
½   tsp. or more finely
        chopped garlic
        pinch paprika
        salt and coarsely ground
        black pepper to taste
⅓   cup olive oil

1. Combine lemon juice, coriander, cumin, garlic, paprika, salt, and pepper together in a bowl. With a wire whisk, beat in olive oil a few tablespoons at a time. Taste for seasoning.

Makes ⅔ cup

1   Tbsp. Dijon mustard
2   Tbsp. red wine vinegar
1   Tbsp. finely chopped
        shallots or scallions
2   Tbsp. finely chopped
        parsley
        salt and freshly ground
        pepper to taste
½   cup olive oil, salad oil,
        or a mixture of both

This is a fine all-purpose vinaigrette dressing.

Vinaigrette Dressing

1. Combine mustard, red wine vinegar, shallots, parsley, salt, and pepper together in a bowl. With a wire whisk, beat in oil a few tablespoons at a time. Taste for seasoning.

Homemade mayonnaise has a decidedly fresh, gentle taste that makes store-bought mayonnaise seem harsh and vinegary in comparison. Since it will only keep its fresh taste for 4 or 5 days, it should be made in small batches, a factor which minimizes the time required to make it.

Like hollandaise sauce, mayonnaise is made by slowly beating oil (or melted butter in the case of hollandaise) into egg yolks. The lemon juice or vinegar "cooks" the egg yolks slightly and helps them absorb the oil, which is added little by little. The trick here is not to add the oil too quickly, so that the yolks can absorb it smoothly. If a minimum amount of care is taken, there is little danger of separation when making the small quantity given below.

If you wish, you may thin the mayonnaise with a few drops of water or lemon juice.

Mayonnaise

Makes 1 cup

2   egg yolks
1   Tbsp. lemon juice or
        white vinegar
¼   tsp. salt
        pinch white pepper
¼   tsp. prepared mustard
1   cup olive oil, salad oil,
        or a mixture of both

1. With a wire whisk, beat egg yolks with lemon juice, salt, pepper, and mustard until thick and lemon colored. Start adding oil a few drops at a time. As soon as some of the oil has been absorbed, add the rest in a thin stream, beating constantly with the wire whisk. Do not add more oil than the yolks can "take" at one time. Taste for seasoning.

Serve this mustard mayonnaise over cooked, chilled vegetables, or use to make devilled eggs.

Mustard Mayonnaise

1   cup homemade
        mayonnaise
2   tsp. Dijon mustard
1   tsp. white vinegar
        dash Tabasco sauce
        dash Worcestershire sauce

1. Combine all ingredients together in a small bowl. Mix until well blended.

Here is a simple addition to any fresh fruit salad. If you wish to add some color, stir in a little strawberry or raspberry puree.

Makes 1 cup

1 cup plain yogurt
1 to 2 tsp. honey
¼ tsp. cinnamon
⅛ tsp. nutmeg
¼ tsp. vanilla

Garden of Eden Dressing for Fruit Salad

1. Mix all ingredients together and serve over fresh fruit.

Makes 6 servings

1 cup peeled and diced carrots
1 cup peeled and diced potatoes
1 cup broccoli florets, cut in bite-size pieces
½ cup diced celery
½ cup Russian dressing*
1 Tbsp. lemon juice (approx.)
   salt and pepper to taste
3 avocados
1 hard boiled egg, finely chopped
1 Tbsp. finely chopped parsley
   lettuce leaves for garnish

Stuffed Avocado a la Russe

1. Blanch carrots, potatoes, and broccoli separately in boiling salted water until tender. Drain and cool.

2. Mix blanched vegetables with celery, Russian dressing, lemon juice, salt, and pepper. Taste for seasoning.

3. Halve avocados and place each half on a bed of lettuce on an individual serving plate. Mound about ½ cup filling over each avocado and sprinkle with hard boiled egg and chopped parsley.

*Mayonnaise and ketchup mixed together to taste

New Mexican Bean Salad

Serves 4

1 cup dried kidney beans,
 about 3 cups cooked
1 cup green beans,
 cut in 1-inch pieces,
 about ¼ lb.
2 Tbsp. olive oil
½ tsp. salt
½ tsp. ground cumin
½ tsp. ground coriander
1 Tbsp. chopped fresh
 coriander or parsley
pinch black pepper
2 Tbsp. white vinegar
¼ cup finely sliced scallions

1. Soak beans overnight. Cover with water, add salt to taste, and cook until tender, about 1½ hours. Drain.

2. Blanch green beans in boiling, salted water until tender. Drain.

3. While beans are still warm, toss with olive oil, salt, cumin, coriander, fresh coriander, and pepper. Add vinegar and scallions and taste for seasoning. Serve cold or at room temperature.

The mild quality of rice wine vinegar brings out the natural sweetness of fresh beets.

Beet Salad

Serves 4

1 lb. beets, weighed without
 the greens
1 Tbsp. finely minced
 scallions
2 Tbsp. rice wine vinegar
pinch sugar
salt and pepper to taste
hard-boiled egg

1. Steam beets in their skins. Cool, peel, and slice.

2. Mix scallions, vinegar, sugar, salt, and pepper together. Toss with beets and taste for seasoning. Serve on a lettuce leaf, topped with a sprinkle of sieved hard-boiled egg.

You may make this salad ahead and allow the broccoli to marinate in the dressing. If this is the case, however, do not add the toasted almonds until moments before serving or they will lose their crispness.

Oriental Broccoli Salad

Serves 4 to 6

½ cup sliced almonds
1 bunch broccoli
½ cup thinly sliced water chestnuts
¼ tsp. finely chopped garlic
½ tsp. finely grated fresh ginger
3 Tbsp. soy sauce
1 Tbsp. Chinese sesame oil
2 tsp. vinegar
pinch sugar

1. Preheat oven to 375 degrees. Spread almonds on a pie plate and toast in the oven until golden brown, 7 to 10 minutes.

2. Trim stems and blanch broccoli in boiling, salted water until tender but on the firm side. Do not drain in a colander, but remove broccoli with tongs to prevent it from falling apart. To ensure a bright green color, plunge cooked broccoli in ice water. When cool, slice in bite-sized pieces.

3. Mix garlic, ginger, soy sauce, sesame oil, vinegar, and sugar together in a small bowl.

4. Gently toss broccoli, toasted almonds, and water chestnuts with dressing. Serve cold.

Serve this carrot salad with Artichoke Ricotta Pie or Greek Spinach Pie.

Greek Carrot and Caper Salad

Serves 4 to 6

4 cups grated carrots, about 1 lb.
4 Tbsp. rinsed capers
1½ tsp. prepared mustard
4 tsp. white vinegar
¼ cup olive oil
plenty of freshly ground black pepper

1. Combine grated carrots and rinsed capers in a bowl.

2. Beat mustard, vinegar, and oil together until well mixed. Toss with carrots and capers. Season with black pepper.

A delicious salad to take along on a summer picnic.

Scandinavian Cucumber Salad

Serves 4

2 or 3 cucumbers
½ cup sour cream
¼ tsp. dill weed
⅛ tsp. finely chopped garlic
2 tsp. finely chopped red
    onion
   pinch salt
   pinch black pepper
   pinch sugar
1 tsp. vinegar
1 Tbsp. olive oil

1. Peel cucumbers and cut them in half lengthwise. Scoop out seeds with a spoon and discard. Cut the cucumbers in ½-inch dice and sprinkle with salt. Let stand for 20 minutes and drain.

2. Combine sour cream with dill weed, garlic, red onion, salt, pepper, sugar, and vinegar. Stir in olive oil.

3. Mix drained cucumbers with dressing and taste for seasoning.

This salad has the nutty taste of Chinese sesame oil. Serve with a Chinese or Japanese meal.

Cucumber and Bean Sprout Salad

Serves 4 to 6

2 or 3 cucumbers
4 cups mung bean sprouts
3 Tbsp. rice wine vinegar
   pinch sugar
2 Tbsp. soy sauce
   pinch salt
   pinch hot pepper flakes
1 Tbsp. Chinese sesame oil

1. Peel cucumbers and cut in half lengthwise. Scoop out seeds with a spoon and discard. Cut in ¼-inch thick slices. You should have about 3 cups.

2. Blanch mung bean sprouts in boiling water for 2 minutes. Drain and set aside to cool.

3. Combine vinegar, sugar, soy sauce, salt, hot pepper flakes, and sesame oil together in a bowl.

4. Toss cucumbers and bean sprouts with dressing. Marinate in the refrigerator for one or two hours before serving.

Serve this eggplant salad as an appetizer "spread" with pita bread, as an accompaniment to a Syrian meal, or as a component of an antipasto.

Syrian Eggplant Salad

Makes 2 cups

1 medium eggplant, about 1 lb.
½ tsp. finely chopped garlic
3 Tbsp. finely chopped onions
1 medium tomato, coarsely chopped
1 Tbsp. finely chopped parsley
½ tsp. ground cumin
½ tsp. salt
4 tsp. lemon juice
2 Tbsp. olive oil

1. Preheat broiler.

2. Cut eggplant in half lengthwise. Deeply score the flesh with the tip of a sharp knife. Place eggplant, cut side down, under the hot broiler. Broil for 15 to 20 minutes, until tender. Remove from the oven, cool slightly and peel. Discard the skin.

3. Coarsely chop eggplant and combine with garlic, onion, tomato, parsley, cumin, salt, lemon juice, and olive oil. Taste for seasoning. Chill until ready to serve.

Syrian Tomato Salad

Serves 4 to 6

1 cucumber
2 medium tomatoes
¾ cup diced celery
1 diced green pepper
2 cups romaine or leaf lettuce, torn in bite-sized pieces
⅓ cup lemon garlic dressing (see recipe, this section)
½ tsp. crushed, dried mint
salt and pepper to taste

1. Peel cucumber and cut in half lengthwise. Scoop out seeds with a spoon and discard. Cut in ¾-inch dice.

2. Seed tomatoes and cut in dice, about the same size as the cucumber.

3. Mix diced cucumbers and tomatoes with diced celery, green pepper, and lettuce. Toss with lemon garlic dressing, crushed mint, salt, and pepper. Taste for seasoning.

Tofu, or bean curd, is made from soy beans and is a staple of Oriental cooking. Sold fresh in Oriental markets or in many health food stores, tofu will keep in the refrigerator for 3 to 4 days. It is mild in flavor, high in protein and relatively inexpensive. It can be served hot in soup and in stir fried vegetables, or cold, as in this recipe, complemented by a soy sauce and rice vinegar dressing.

Japanese Spinach Salad with Sesame and Tofu

Serves 4

2 *lbs. fresh spinach*
2 *Tbsp. soy sauce*
4 *tsp. rice wine vinegar*
2 *Tbsp. toasted sesame seeds*
½ *block tofu*

1. Clean and stem spinach. Steam just until wilted, drain, and cool. Toss with 1 Tbsp. soy sauce, 2 tsp. rice wine vinegar, and sesame seeds. Chill until ready to serve.

2. Cut tofu in ½-inch cubes and gently mix with remaining soy sauce and vinegar. Marinate in refrigerator for 10 minutes, or until serving time.

3. When ready to serve, spread spinach on a flat serving dish and arrange tofu on top.

To toast sesame seeds: In a small skillet, heat sesame seeds over a high flame, shaking the pan back and forth. When seeds start to brown and pop, remove from heat and shake for a few more seconds as pan cools.

A time honored vegetarian chef's salad at the Tao.

Tao Salad

Serves one

3 *cups lettuce, torn in bite-sized pieces*
3 *sliced raw mushrooms*
3 *tomato wedges*
3 *cucumber slices*
½ *cup grated colby cheese*
toasted whole wheat croutons
alfalfa sprouts
Tao dressing (see recipe, this section)

1. Arrange lettuce on a large plate and top with remaining ingredients. Use plenty of croutons, sprouts, and Tao dressing.

An unusual salad that goes well with a Middle Eastern meal.

Arabian Salad

Serves 4 to 6

1   small head romaine or
      leaf lettuce
3   oranges
8   to 10 black olives
3   thin slices Bermuda
      onion
2   Tbsp. olive oil
      salt and pepper to taste
2   tsp. red wine vinegar

1. Wash lettuce and tear in bite-sized pieces.

2. Peel oranges and slice in ¼-inch thick rounds. Halve or quarter the rounds if the oranges are large.

3. In a salad bowl, combine lettuce, oranges, black olives, and red onion rings. Toss with olive oil. Add salt, pepper, and vinegar and toss again. Taste for seasoning.

These pickles are delicious as part of an hors d'oeuvres plate with hard-boiled eggs and slices of mild cheese, such as brick or Monterey Jack.

Chili Pickles

Makes 4 cups

½   lb. yellow summer
       squash, cut in
       1-inch pieces
1   large potato, peeled and
       cut in 1-inch pieces
1   cup green peas
¼   head cauliflower, broken
       in bite-sized florets
1   cup corn, off the cob
½   large sweet, red pepper,
       cut in ¼-inch strips
3   Tbsp. chili powder
1   tsp. ground cumin
1   tsp. ground coriander
¼   tsp. finely chopped garlic
½   cup white vinegar
½   cup water
1   Tbsp. salt
1   bay leaf

1. Blanch squash, potatoes, green peas, cauliflower, and corn separately in boiling, salted water until tender. Drain and cool. Layer in a large jar with red pepper strips.

2. Mix chili powder, cumin, coriander, garlic, vinegar, water, salt, and bay leaf together and pour over vegetables. Cover jar and let vegetables marinate at room temperature for 12 to 24 hours. Chill and serve. Vegetables will keep for several weeks in refrigerator.

Sweet yet light, these pickles are a nice, crunchy accompaniment to a sandwich or a plate of cottage cheese.

Pickled Cucumbers and Onions

Makes 1 quart

3   cups thinly sliced
      cucumbers
1   cup thinly sliced
      Bermuda onion
¾   cup white vinegar
⅓   cup sugar
¾   cup water
1   tsp. salt

1. Stripe the cucumber with a vegetable peeler by peeling it lengthwise and leaving a one-inch gap between peels. Slice as thin as possible.

2. Combine vinegar, sugar, water, and salt in a large jar. Stir until sugar is dissolved. Add cucumbers and onions to the jar in alternating layers. Refrigerate 12 hours or overnight.

Won ton wrappers (the squares of dough from which won tons are fashioned) can be bought ready-made in most Oriental grocery stores.

Chinese Salad with Crispy Fried Won Tons

Serves 4 to 6

8   won ton wrappers
      oil for frying
1   cup bite-sized cauliflower
      florets
1   cup broccoli, cut in
      bite-sized pieces
¼   cup chopped, fresh
      coriander
2   Tbsp. finely sliced
      scallions
½   cup thinly sliced water
      chestnuts
¼   cup toasted sesame seeds
1   small head romaine
      lettuce, torn in
      bite-sized pieces
2   tsp. Chinese sesame oil
3   Tbsp. rice wine vinegar
      pinch salt
      pinch sugar
1   Tbsp. soy sauce

1. Cut won ton wrappers in ¼-inch strips and deep fry until golden. Drain on absorbent paper.

2. Blanch cauliflower and broccoli in boiling, salted water until tender. Drain and cool.

3. Combine blanched vegetables, chopped coriander, scallions, water chestnuts, sesame seeds, and romaine in a salad bowl.

4. Mix sesame oil, vinegar, salt, sugar, and soy sauce together and pour over salad. Toss and garnish with crispy fried won tons.

Stuffed vine leaves, marinated mushrooms, and artichoke hearts are a few of the ingredients that could be added to a Greek salad in addition to those listed below.

Greek Salad

Serves 4 to 6

4   cups salad greens, such as leaf lettuce or romaine
8   radish roses
¼   lb. green beans
8   Greek olives
1   slice red onion
8   tomato wedges
¼   cup lemon garlic dressing (see recipe this section)
½   cup crumbled feta cheese (about ¼ lb.)
    salt and freshly ground pepper to taste

1. Wash salad greens and tear in bite-sized pieces.

2. Make radish roses and leave in ice water for one hour to open.

3. Cook green beans in boiling, salted water until tender. Drain and cool.

4. Combine salad greens, radishes, olives, red onion rings, tomatoes, and green beans in a salad bowl. Toss with dressing and season with salt and pepper. Taste for seasoning. Arrange crumbled feta cheese in the center of the salad and serve.

For the full flavor of the vegetables, serve this salad at room temperature.

Italian Marinated Vegetables

Serves 4 to 6

2   potatoes, peeled and cut in ¾-inch cubes, about 2 cups
1   cup zucchini, cut in julienne
1   cup carrots, cut in julienne
¾   cup diced celery
2   Tbsp. olive oil
½   tsp. salt
    pinch black pepper
¼   tsp. basil
¼   tsp. oregano
2   tsp. red wine vinegar
1   tomato, cut in wedges

1. Blanch potatoes, zucchini, and carrots separately in boiling, salted water until tender. Drain.

2. While still warm, combine blanched vegetables with celery in a bowl and gently toss with olive oil. Add seasonings and vinegar and mix together. Taste for seasoning.

3. When ready to serve, toss with tomato wedges and taste for seasoning.

A pretty way to serve this salad is to arrange the vegetables on lettuce leaves in groups and pass the dressing separately.

Vegetables a la Polonaise

Serves 4 to 6

1   large potato, peeled and
      cut in ¾-inch cubes
¼   head cauliflower, cut in
      bite-sized pieces
1   cup broccoli, cut in
      bite-sized pieces
¼   lb. trimmed green beans
1   cup carrots, sliced in
      ⅛-inch thick rounds
1   cup zucchini, sliced in
      ⅛-inch thick rounds
1   cup sliced beets
½   cup creamy mustard
      dressing or mustard
      mayonnaise (see
      recipes this section)
      salt and pepper to taste
      lettuce leaves for garnish

1. Blanch vegetables separately in boiling, salted water until tender. Drain and cool.

2. Combine cooled vegetables with creamy mustard dressing and season with salt and pepper. Line a large serving platter with lettuce leaves and arrange salad on top.

Red Lentil Salad

Serves 4 to 6

1½   cups split red lentils
½   tsp. salt
1½   cups diced zucchini
3   Tbsp. oil
¼   cup lemon juice
¼   cup finely chopped
      parsley
2   Tbsp. finely chopped
      onion
½   tsp. finely chopped garlic
1   tsp. ground coriander
      pinch cayenne pepper

1. Combine split red lentils in a saucepan with salt and water to cover and bring to a boil. Cook 7 to 10 minutes, until lentils are tender but not mushy. You may need to add a little more water while the lentils are cooking. Drain and cool to lukewarm.

2. Blanch zucchini in boiling, salted water 1 minute. Drain and cool to lukewarm.

3. Toss lentils and zucchini with remaining ingredients and taste for seasoning. Add enough cayenne pepper to give the salad a "bite." Serve at room temperature.

The presentation of this salad with its center of potatoes surrounded by many colored vegetables, olives, and hard-boiled eggs is what makes it so irresistible.

Salad Niçoise

Serves 4 to 6

2 or 3 potatoes
1½ cups trimmed green beans
  lettuce leaves
1 large tomato, cut in wedges
8 black olives
2 hard-boiled eggs, quartered
1 sweet, red pepper, cut in julienne
4 halved artichoke hearts
1 Tbsp. capers
½ cup vinaigrette dressing (see recipe this section)

1. Peel potatoes and cut in ½-inch cubes. Cook in boiling, salted water until tender. Drain and toss with 3 tablespoons vinaigrette while still warm. Season with salt and pepper and set aside to cool.

2. Blanch green beans in boiling, salted water until tender. Drain and cool.

3. Line a serving platter with lettuce leaves and arrange potatoes in the middle. Surround with green beans, tomato wedges, black olives, quartered hard-boiled eggs, red pepper strips, and artichoke hearts. Sprinkle capers over the center of the salad. Pour vinaigrette over salad or pass separately.

This salad is also good made with blanched asparagus instead of the green beans.

Rice Salad Macedoine

Serves 4 to 6

2 cups cooked white rice
½ cup finely diced carrots
½ cup cucumber, peeled, seeded and finely diced
¼ cup finely diced sweet, red pepper, or green pepper
1 cup cooked green peas
1 Tbsp. yogurt
3 Tbsp. mayonnaise
  salt and pepper to taste
¼ lb. green beans, trimmed
8 cherry tomatoes
  lettuce leaves

1. Combine cooked rice with carrots, cucumber, peppers, green peas, yogurt, mayonnaise, salt, and pepper. Taste for seasoning.

2. Blanch green beans in boiling, salted water until tender. Drain and cool.

3. Line a serving platter with lettuce leaves and arrange the rice mixture in the center. Surround with green beans and cherry tomatoes.

The unorthodox addition of cauliflower to this version of the Middle Eastern dish called *tabbouleh* makes it a substantial salad.

Serves 4 to 6

½ small head cauliflower
1⅓ cups cracked wheat (bulghur)
2 cups water
¼ cup finely chopped scallions, including some of the green part
¼ cup finely chopped parsley
1 cup diced celery
1 tomato, seeded and coarsely chopped

Dressing

½ cup olive oil
¼ cup lemon juice, about 1½ lemons
2 tsp. ground cumin
1 tsp. ground coriander
1 tsp. salt

Cracked Wheat Salad

1. Break cauliflower in bite-sized florets. You should have about 2½ cups. Blanch in boiling, salted water until tender. Drain and cool.

2. Soak cracked wheat in water for 5 minutes to soften. Drain in a sieve and press out excess water.

3. Combine soaked wheat with scallion, parsley, celery, tomato, and cauliflower.

4. A few minutes before serving, toss salad with dressing. Since the cracked wheat absorbs much of the flavor of the dressing, do not pour over the salad too far in advance or it will lose its zing.

Mix all ingredients together until well blended.

Plum Tart

Desserts

When it comes to dessert, Americans have the best of all worlds. For the influence of European confectionery has not overshadowed our heritage of country fruit pies and simple desserts. In fact, I have watched many a discerning customer, who could well appreciate the subtleties of a *dacquoise* or a *soufflé glacé,* head straight for peach pie *à la mode* and dive in without a second thought. Still, pastry shops in large cities do a thriving business on the sale of such delicacies as rum babas, fancy gateaux and torten, napoleons, eclairs, and elegant fruit tarts.

The desserts in this section are within the scope of the home kitchen. When planning a meal, keep in mind the time needed to prepare the dessert. Some desserts may be made a day or two ahead, a decided advantage if you are entertaining. On the other hand, elaborate meals may require little more than a simple, fresh fruit dessert for a finale. Offering dessert *and* fresh fruit to guests is a nice gesture, especially in these diet-conscious times. Chances are, even dieters will succumb to a "sliver."

PASTRY

A good, flaky pastry is an accomplishment that escapes even the best of cooks. Following is some advice to beginners and frustrated pastry-makers.

Ingredients

Use all-purpose flour, or a combination of all-purpose flour and whole wheat flour for a whole wheat crust. Cake flour is too fine, while whole wheat flour alone is too coarse. Shortening (not butter or margarine) produces the flakiest crust. You may use a little butter in combination with the shortening for flavor. Cold water also gives the best results.

Proportions

Too much flour in a pastry dough will make it tough. Too much shortening will make it crumble and break. Add just enough water to hold the dough firmly together, since too much will make it sticky and produce a tough crust, while too little will cause the dough to fall apart and crack at the edges when you are rolling it.

Blending

Although a hand pastry blender is a fine tool for cutting the shortening into the flour, I prefer an electric mixer or food processor for maximum speed and efficiency. Avoid using your fingers, since the warmth from your hands will soften the shortening and 'melt' it into the flour. When the mixture begins to turn a shade darker in color, it has been blended enough. Do not blend beyond this point or the mixture will clump together in a mass. Underblended pastry mix, on the other hand, looks floury and produces a tough crust.

Mixing and Storing

Pastry mix will keep several weeks in the refrigerator, longer in the freezer. You may mix a large batch at one time, store it, and add water to the mix as needed. There is no exact formula for the amount of water you must add to the pastry mix—it will vary according to the moisture in the flour. Add it until the dough comes together in a mass without crumbling. Never knead the dough, since overhandling will make it tough. Although many recipes recommend chilling the dough in the refrigerator before rolling, it is pliable and easy to handle immediately after mixing.

Rolling

Particularly for beginners, I recommend the use of a pastry cloth when rolling the dough. (You may use a special pastry canvas, or a clean, linen napkin or tea towel.) Rubbing the flour into the cloth prevents sticking, and the excess flour goes into the weave of the cloth, not the pastry. You may also use a formica, wooden, or marble countertop for rolling, but be sure there are no traces of garlic or onion on your surface! Flatten the ball of dough with a few taps of the rolling pin and roll from the center outward. Roll lightly and lift the pin up at the edges to maintain an even thickness.

Plain Pastry

Makes two 9-inch pastry shells or one 2-crust pie

3	cups all-purpose flour
½	tsp. salt
1	tsp. sugar
¾	cup shortening
4½	Tbsp. butter broken in pieces
7	to 8 Tbsp. cold water

1. Mix flour, salt, and sugar together in a bowl. With a hand mixer or a food processor, cut shortening and butter into dry ingredients until well blended. When it is thoroughly blended, the mixture should turn a shade darker in color and look like coarse meal.

2. Sprinkle water over pastry mix and toss with your hands until dough starts to hold together in a mass. Use immediately, or wrap in plastic and store in refrigerator until ready to use.

Note: Pastry mix, without the water, will keep several weeks in the refrigerator, longer in the freezer. Add water when ready to use.

Whole Wheat Pastry

Makes two 9-inch pastry shells or one 2-crust pie

1½	cups unbleached white flour, or all-purpose flour
1½	cups whole wheat flour
¾	tsp. salt
¾	cup shortening
4½	Tbsp. butter, broken in pieces
7	to 8 Tbsp. cold water

1. Mix white flour, whole wheat flour, and salt together in a bowl. With a hand mixer or food processor, cut shortening and butter into dry ingredients until well blended. When it is thoroughly blended, the mixture should turn a shade darker in color and look like coarse meal.

2. Sprinkle water over pastry mix and toss with your hands until the dough starts to hold together in a mass. Use immediately, or wrap in plastic and store in refrigerator until ready to use.

Note: Pastry mix, without the water, will keep several weeks in the refrigerator, longer in the freezer. Add water when ready to use.

Graham Cracker Crust

4 Tbsp. butter
1 Tbsp. honey or sugar
1½ cups graham cracker
 crumbs
1 tsp. grated orange or
 lemon rind (optional)

1. Melt butter with honey. Mix with graham cracker crumbs and orange or lemon rind until well blended. If you are using sugar instead of honey, mix it with graham cracker crumbs and add melted butter.

2. Press into the bottom and sides of a nine-inch pie pan. Bake in a preheated 350 degree oven for 7 to 10 minutes, until crust starts to brown.

The cinnamon-nut cookie crust of this tart provides a pleasing contrast to the tart plum filling.

Plum Walnut Tart

Makes one 9-inch tart

Dough:

6 Tbsp. butter
½ cup sugar
1 egg
1 egg yolk
¼ cup ground walnuts
½ tsp. cinnamon
1 tsp. grated lemon rind
1¾ cups flour
¼ tsp. baking powder

Filling:

1½ lbs. plums, cut in sixths,
 about 4 cups
2 Tbsp. flour
3 Tbsp. sugar, more for a
 sweeter filling
2 Tbsp. ground walnuts

1. Cream butter, add sugar, and mix until smooth. Add egg, egg yolk, walnuts, cinnamon, and lemon rind and mix well.

2. Sift flour and baking powder together. Add to eggs and mix to a smooth dough. Chill several hours, until firm.

3. Butter and flour a 9-inch cake pan. Roll half the dough into a circle and fit it into the bottom and sides of pan.

4. Mix plums with flour, sugar, and walnuts and pour into pastry lined pan.

5. Roll out remaining dough and cut in ½-inch strips. Lay them over the top of the tart to make a lattice top. Trim edges.

6. Bake in a preheated 350 degree oven for 40 to 45 minutes, until crust is brown. Turn out of pan when cool and sprinkle with powdered sugar. Serve with lightly sweetened whipped cream.

This is a classic formula for a fresh fruit pie: fresh peaches sweetened with brown sugar, spiced with cinnamon, and thickened with flour. In any fruit pie, the juices must visibly bubble to ensure a thick and delicious filling. For a beautiful, golden top crust, brush the pastry with beaten egg before baking.

Peach Pie

Makes one 9-inch pie

pastry for a two-crust pie
7   cups peeled and sliced
      peaches, about 3¼ lbs.
½   cup brown sugar
4   Tbsp. all-purpose flour
½   tsp. cinnamon
      pinch salt
1   Tbsp. lemon juice
1   Tbsp. butter
      beaten egg

1. Line a nine-inch pie pan with pastry. Trim edges.

2. Mix sliced peaches, brown sugar, flour, cinnamon, salt, and lemon juice together until well combined. Pour into pie shell and dot with butter.

3. Cover pie with top crust and crimp edges. Brush with beaten egg and make a cross in the center with the tip of a paring knife for a vent. Bake in a preheated 375 degree oven for 45 to 55 minutes, until crust is golden and filling bubbles.

This pie is a favorite harbinger of summer. When baking fruit pies, it is a good practice to place the pie pan on a cookie sheet in case the filling bubbles over during baking.

Strawberry Rhubarb Pie

Makes one 9-inch pie

pastry for a two-crust pie
1   pint strawberries, washed
      and halved
2   cups rhubarb sliced in
      ½-inch pieces, about
      ½ lb.
¾   cup sugar
⅓   cup flour
      pinch salt
1   Tbsp. butter

1. Mix strawberries, rhubarb, sugar, flour, and salt in a bowl and let stand 10 minutes.

2. Line a nine-inch pie pan with pastry and trim edges.

3. Pour filling into pastry lined pan and dot with butter. Roll out remaining dough and cut ½-inch wide strips. Lay strips horizontally, then vertically, over the pie to make a lattice top. Trim edges. Lay more strips around the outer rim of the pie and crimp.

4. Bake in a preheated 375 degree oven for 45 to 50 minutes, until crust starts to brown and filling bubbles. Serve with lightly sweetened whipped cream.

In this custard tart, golden, paper-thin apple slices glisten under a shiny layer of apricot jam. Serve cold.

Apple Custard Tart

Makes one 9-inch pie

pastry for a nine-inch
  pie shell
approximately 1½ lbs.
  apples
⅓ cup plus 1 Tbsp. sugar
½ tsp. vanilla extract
1 egg
⅓ cup milk

1. Line a nine-inch pie pan or false-bottomed quiche pan with pastry.

2. Peel apples. Reserve two or three apples for the top of the tart and finely chop the remainder. You should have about 2½ cups chopped apples.

3. Mix chopped apples with vanilla and ⅓ cup sugar. Spread the mixture evenly in the pastry lined pan.

4. Halve the reserved apples and remove the cores and stems with a melon baller. Place the halves with the flat sides down on a cutting board and slice in thin, half-moon slices. Lay the slices over the chopped apples in an overlapping circular pattern.

5. Bake the tart in a preheated 400 degree oven for 30 minutes.

6. While apples are baking, prepare the custard. Beat the egg with the remaining one tablespoon sugar and stir in milk. Mix until well blended.

7. Remove the tart from the oven. Pour the custard over the apples and return the tart to the oven for 20 more minutes, until custard is set and apples are a golden brown. Cool and brush with hot apricot glaze. Chill in refrigerator until ready to serve.

Apricot Glaze

2 Tbsp. apricot jam
1 Tbsp. water

1. In a small saucepan, stir jam and water over medium heat until jam is melted. Strain and brush over cooled tart with a pastry brush.

Pumpkin pie made with fresh pumpkin puree has a lighter, more subtle flavor than pie made with canned pumpkin. Pumpkin puree may be stored in the freezer and used in cakes, breads, and soups, too.

Pumpkin Pie

Makes one 9-inch pie

pastry for a 9-inch pie shell
2 *eggs*
½ *cup brown sugar*
1½ *cups evaporated milk*
1½ *tsp. cinnamon*
¾ *tsp. ginger*
1 *tsp. salt*
2 *cups pumpkin puree (see instructions below)*
2 *Tbsp. melted butter*

1. Line a nine-inch pie pan with pastry.

2. Beat eggs. Add brown sugar and mix well. Stir in evaporated milk, cinnamon, ginger, salt, and pumpkin puree. Add melted butter and mix until well blended.

3. Pour filling into pastry lined pie pan and bake in a preheated 375 degree oven for 45 to 50 minutes, until knife inserted in the center of the pie comes out clean. Serve at room temperature with lightly sweetened whipped cream.

How to Cook a Pumpkin:

1. Cut pumpkin in half and scoop out seeds. Cut each half in manageable pieces and place them in a large roasting pan with ¼ inch water on the bottom. Cover the pan with a lid or aluminum foil and bake in a preheated 375 degree oven for 45 minutes to an hour, until tender. Remove from oven and cool.

2. When pumpkin is cool enough to handle, peel and discard the rind. Puree cooked pumpkin in a food processor or blender, or mash with a potato masher. Pumpkin puree will keep several days in the refrigerator, longer in the freezer. Freeze in two or four cup quantities convenient for pie and cake-baking. One pound of pumpkin yields approximately one cup of cooked pumpkin puree.

Raspberries, strawberries, blackberries or a combination of berries are all excellent in this pie. It is made with agar-agar, a thickening agent derived from seaweed that makes a good vegetarian substitute for gelatin. Sometimes called *kanten*, agar-agar may be purchased in the form of sticks or squares in many Oriental food stores.

Summerberry Yogurt Pie

Makes one 9-inch pie

½   *stick* kanten *(agar-agar stick)*
1   *cup fresh raspberry puree*
1   *Tbsp. cornstarch*
¼   *cup honey*
1½   *cups plain yogurt*
2   *eggs whites, beaten until stiff*
½   *cup heavy cream, whipped*
1   *baked graham cracker crust*
   sweetened whipped cream for garnish

1. Break *kanten* in small pieces and combine in a saucepan with ½ cup water. Soak for 30 minutes. Stir over medium heat until *kanten* is dissolved and liquid is smooth.

2. Puree berries in a blender or food processor. Add cornstarch, honey, and ½ cup yogurt, and blend until smooth. Pour mixture into a saucepan and stir over medium heat until it comes to a boil. Boil for 30 seconds to cook the cornstarch. Set aside to cool.

3. Stir remaining 1 cup yogurt into cooled fruit mixture. Fold in beaten egg whites and whipped cream. Fold in melted agar-agar and pour mixture into baked graham cracker crust.

4. Chill pie in refrigerator until set, about 2 hours. Serve garnished with sweetened whipped cream.

This pie has a rich texture similar to cheesecake. It is also delicious made with pure maple syrup instead of honey.

Honey Yogurt Pie

Makes one 9-inch pie

1	*baked graham cracker crust, made with honey*
4	*Tbsp. butter*
⅓	*cup honey*
2	*egg yolks*
1	*tsp. vanilla*
1½	*tsp. grated orange rind*
¼	*cup all-purpose flour*
1⅓	*cups yogurt*
2	*egg whites*

Orange Glaze

½	*cup orange juice*
1	*tsp. cornstarch*
2	*tsp. honey*

1. Cream butter until smooth and beat in honey, egg yolks, and vanilla. Blend in orange rind and flour. Add yogurt and mix until smooth.

2. Beat egg whites until stiff but not dry. Fold into yogurt mixture.

3. Pour filling into baked pie shell and bake in a preheated 325 degree oven for 30 minutes, until light brown on top. Cool and spread with orange glaze. Chill at least 3 hours before serving.

1. Dissolve cornstarch in orange juice in a small saucepan. Add honey and bring to a boil while stirring constantly. Let boil 30 seconds to cook the cornstarch. Strain and spread over top of pie.

This is a creamy, luscious pie with a tangy, lemon bite.

Lemon Ice-Box Pie

Makes one 9-inch pie

1	*baked graham cracker cust*
2	*large eggs*
1	*can sweetened condensed milk*
⅝	*cup lemon juice*

1. Beat eggs and mix with sweetened condensed milk. Stir in lemon juice just until blended. Do not beat. Pour filling into cooled pie shell and chill in refrigerator until set, about 3 hours.

2. When filling is set, spread sour cream topping over pie. Bake in a preheated 300 degree oven for 10 minutes. Remove from oven and chill until ready to serve.

Sour Cream Topping

1½	*cups sour cream*
1	*tsp. vanilla*
4	*tsp. sugar*

1. Mix together until well blended.

A chocolate crust is the perfect complement for the lime filling in this pie. It is also excellent served frozen.

Lime Pie

Makes one 9-inch pie

Crust:

2	squares unsweetened chocolate
¼	cup butter
1½	cups graham cracker crumbs
¼	cup sugar

Filling:

1	can sweetened condensed milk
3	egg yolks
⅔	cup lime juice
3	egg whites

1. Melt chocolate with butter in a double boiler. Mix with graham cracker crumbs and sugar until well blended.

2. Press evenly into the bottom and sides of a nine-inch pie pan. Bake in a preheated 350 degree oven for 5 to 7 minutes. Cool.

1. Mix sweetened condensed milk with egg yolks until well blended. Stir in lime juice.

2. Beat egg whites until stiff but not dry. Fold into filling. Pour into cooled pie shell and bake in a preheated 250 degree oven for 10 minutes.

3. Chill in refrigerator until set, about 3 hours. Garnish with lightly sweetened whipped cream.

This is an old-fashioned American favorite that is never out of style. Use large pecan pieces.

Pecan Pie

Makes one 9-inch pie

	pastry for a nine-inch pie shell
3	eggs
¾	cup brown sugar
1	cup dark corn syrup
3	Tbsp. melted butter
1	tsp. vanilla
1½	cups broken pecans

1. Preheat oven to 400 degrees.

2. Line a nine-inch pie pan with pastry.

3. Beat eggs. Stir in brown sugar and corn syrup. Add melted butter, vanilla, and pecans and mix until blended. Pour into pie shell.

4. Reduce oven temperature to 325 degrees and bake pie for one hour. Serve warm or at room temperature with lightly sweetened whipped cream.

A much acclaimed dessert from the menu of Rudi's in Big Indian, New York, this pie has an ultra-rich mocha filling and a chocolate nut crust.

Coffee Toffee Pie

Makes one 9-inch pie

Crust:

1¼ cups homemade or
       packaged pastry mix
¼   cup brown sugar
¾   cup chopped walnuts
1   ounce finely chopped
       semi-sweet chocolate
1   tsp. vanilla

1. Mix all ingredients together until well blended. Press into the bottom and sides of a nine-inch pie pan. Bake in a preheated 350 degree oven for 10 to 12 minutes, until golden brown. Cool.

Filling:

¼   lb. butter, at room
       temperature
1   square unsweetened
       chocolate, melted
       and cooled
1   Tbsp. instant coffee,
       dissolved in a little
       hot water
¾   cup sifted confectioner's
       sugar
2   eggs

1. Cream butter and add melted chocolate and coffee. Mix until smooth. Add confectioner's sugar and beat until light.

2. Add one egg and beat with an electric mixer for 3 minutes. Add remaining egg and beat 3 more minutes, until light and fluffy. Pour into baked pie shell and chill until firm, 2 to 3 hours. Serve topped with coffee whipped cream and garnished with chocolate curls.

Coffee Whipped Cream

1   cup whipping cream
2   tsp. instant coffee
2   Tbsp. sugar

1. Add sugar and instant coffee to cream and let stand in the refrigerator for 10 minutes to melt coffee crystals. Beat until mixture holds soft peaks.

This adaptation of the Russian Easter cake *paskha* is so rich that it must be doled out in thin slices.

Russian Cheesecake

Serves 12 to 14

2 pounds cream cheese
1 pound unsalted butter
3 egg yolks
1½ cups confectioner's sugar, sifted
2 tsp. vanilla
¾ cup walnut pieces
¾ cup chopped, mixed, dried fruit, such as apricots, dates and prunes

1. Let cream cheese and butter stand to room temperature.

2. Beat butter until smooth, add cream cheese and beat again. Beat just until mixture is creamy; do not aerate.

3. Mix in egg yolks. When well blended, add confectioner's sugar and vanilla and mix well. If you are using a mixer, fold in nuts and dried fruit by hand.

4. Line a clean, 2-quart earthenware flowerpot with cheesecloth. Pour in filling, level off, and fold cheesecloth over the top. Refrigerate overnight until firm. Sorry, but this process cannot be speeded up very successfully by putting the cake in the freezer.

5. Turn flowerpot upside down on a plate and turn out cake. If cake doesn't fall out easily, pull on the cheesecloth. The cake should be very firm. Remove cheesecloth and cut in thin slices.

Originally created as an alternative dessert to those made with white sugar, this cheesecake has a luscious flavor all its own. The creamy, nutty texture is enhanced by the richness of pure maple syrup.

Maple Nut Cheesecake

Serves 12 to 16

Crust:

6 Tbsp. melted butter
1½ cups graham cracker crumbs
¼ cup brown sugar

Filling:

1¾ lbs. cream cheese
4 eggs
¾ cup pure maple syrup
1 tsp. vanilla
2½ Tbsp. flour
½ cup coarsely chopped pecans

1. Mix butter with graham cracker crumbs and sugar until blended. Press into bottom and sides of a 9-inch spring form pan and bake in a preheated 350 degree oven for 10 minutes.

1. Beat cream cheese until smooth. Add eggs one at a time, beating after each addition. Stir in maple syrup, vanilla, and flour and mix until smooth. Fold in pecans and pour into prepared pan. Bake in a preheated 350 degree oven for 40 to 45 minutes.

2. When cheesecake has cooled slightly, brush the top with 1 Tbsp. maple syrup and sprinkle with 1 Tbsp. finely chopped pecans.

Note: To keep cheesecake from cracking as it cools, place a pan of water in the bottom of the oven during baking.

Carob powder is made from carob tree pods, also called Saint John's bread. It is often used as a healthful substitute for chocolate and in my estimation, it is a disappointing one. Combined here with peppermint extract, however, carob has a pleasant and interesting flavor in its own right.

Carob Mint Cheesecake

Makes one 9-inch cake

Crust:

- 4 *Tbsp. butter*
- 1 *Tbsp. honey*
- 1½ *cups graham cracker crumbs*

Filling:

- 2 *8-ounce packages cream cheese, at room temperature*
- 1 *cup sour cream or yogurt*
- 4 *Tbsp. butter*
- 2 *Tbsp. carob powder*
- 1 *tsp. peppermint extract*
- ½ *cup honey*
- 2 *Tbsp. cornstarch*
- 2 *eggs*

1. Melt butter with honey and mix with graham cracker crumbs until well blended. Press into bottom and sides of a nine-inch cake pan. Bake in a preheated 350 degree oven for 5 to 8 minutes, until crust starts to brown. Cool.

1. Beat cream cheese until smooth and beat in sour cream or yogurt.

2. Melt butter and stir in carob powder to make a smooth paste. Add to beaten cream cheese with peppermint extract, honey, and cornstarch. Mix well.

3. Beat in eggs one at a time.

4. Pour filling into prepared pan and place in a larger baking pan. Pour in enough boiling water to come half way up the sides of the cake pan. Bake in a preheated 350 degree oven for 50 minutes to an hour, until top starts to brown. Turn oven off and let cake cool in the oven with the door open for one hour. Refrigerate six hours or overnight.

Note: For an even richer version of this cheesecake, top with sweetened sour cream. (See Lemon Ice-Box Pie recipe.)

Good, fresh coconut is a special treat. Unlike the sugar-coated packaged coconut available in supermarkets, grated fresh coconut will not keep more than a few days in the refrigerator. Extra may be frozen for later use in baking.

Fresh Coconut Layer Cake

Makes one 8 or 9-inch layer cake

enough coconut milk
   and milk to equal
   one cup
1 cup grated fresh coconut
½ cup butter
1½ cups sugar
4 eggs, separated
2 cups cake flour
2 tsp. baking powder
1 tsp. vanilla

1. Pierce the "eyes" of a fresh coconut with a metal skewer and let coconut milk drain into a cup. Strain. Add enough milk to coconut milk to make one cup.

2. Place the drained coconut in a 400 degree oven for ten minutes. Remove and crack open with a hammer. The coconut meat should separate easily from the husk. The brown "skin" on the coconut meat can be peeled with a vegetable peeler. Grate the peeled coconut.

3. Cream butter with sugar and beat in egg yolks.

4. Sift flour and baking powder together and add alternately to creamed mixture with milk/coconut milk. Stir in vanilla.

5. Beat egg whites until stiff but not dry, and fold into cake batter. Gently fold in coconut and pour into two greased and floured layer-cake pans.

6. Bake in a preheated 350 degree oven for 25 minutes, until cake is golden brown and a toothpick inserted in the center comes out clean. Cool and ice with coffee icing. Sprinkle cake with more grated, fresh coconut.

Coffee Icing

¼ lb. butter
1 lb. confectioner's sugar
1 tsp. instant coffee,
   dissolved in a little
   hot water
1 to 2 Tbsp. milk

1. Cream butter until smooth. Beat in half the sugar and the dissolved instant coffee. Add remaining sugar and enough milk to make the icing a good spreading consistency.

This is a homey cake with a coarse texture.

Honey Layer Cake

Makes one 9-inch layer cake

3   eggs
1   cup honey
4   Tbsp. melted butter
1   cup whole wheat flour
1   cup unbleached white
       flour
1   tsp. baking powder
1   tsp. baking soda
2   tsp. cinnamon
½   cup orange juice
½   cup chopped walnuts

1. Beat eggs until thick and light. Beat in honey and melted butter.

2. Sift dry ingredients together and add to egg mixture alternately with orange juice. Mix until well blended. Fold in nuts.

3. Pour batter into two greased and floured 9-inch cake pans. Bake in a preheated 350 degree oven for 20 to 25 minutes, until cake is golden brown and a toothpick inserted in the center comes out clean. Cool and ice with cream cheese icing. Sprinkle top of cake with more chopped walnuts.

Cream Cheese Icing

1   lb. cream cheese, at room
       temperature
¼   cup honey, or to taste
1   tsp. vanilla

1. Beat cream cheese until smooth and creamy. Add vanilla and honey and beat again. Spread on cooled cake.

This is a simple cake with a lovely, tart plum topping.

Plum Cake

Makes one 9-inch cake

¼   lb. butter
½   cup sugar
3   egg yolks
1   tsp. grated lemon rind
1   tsp. vanilla
1   cup all-purpose flour
½   tsp. baking powder
3   egg whites
¾   lb. plums, pitted and cut
       in sixths

1. Cream butter and add sugar. Beat until smooth. Beat in egg yolks, lemon rind, and vanilla.

2. Sift flour and baking powder together and add to creamed mixture. Stir until blended.

3. Beat egg whites until stiff but not dry. One half at a time, gently fold into batter.

4. Spread batter in a greased and floured 9-inch cake pan. Arrange plums on top in a circular pattern. Bake in a preheated 375 degree oven for 30 minutes, until plums are soft and a toothpick inserted in the center of the cake comes out clean. Cool and sprinkle with powdered sugar.

This is a foolproof chocolate layer cake that is dark and moist. The surprise ingredient is mayonnaise—which is, remember, a combination of eggs and oil.

Dark Chocolate Cake

Makes one 8-inch layer cake

1 cup mayonnaise
1 cup water
1 cup sugar
1 tsp. vanilla
½ cup cocoa
2¼ cups all-purpose flour
⅛ tsp. salt
1½ tsp. baking soda

1. Mix mayonnaise, water, sugar, and vanilla together until well blended.

2. Sift cocoa, flour, salt, and baking soda together. Stir into liquid ingredients and mix just until blended.

3. Pour batter into two greased and floured 8-inch cake pans. Bake in a preheated 375 degree oven for 20 to 25 minutes, until a toothpick inserted in the center comes out clean. Cool and ice with double fudge icing.

Double Fudge Icing

1¼ cups sugar
1 cup heavy cream
5 squares unsweetened chocolate
¼ lb. unsalted butter, broken into bits
1 tsp. vanilla

1. Bring sugar and cream to a boil. Reduce heat and simmer for 5 minutes. Stir occasionally to keep the cream from boiling over. Remove from heat.

2. Finely chop or grate the chocolate. Stir into cream until completely melted. Stir in butter and vanilla. When butter is melted, refrigerate icing until cold.

3. With an electric mixer or wooden spoon, beat icing until thick and of a good spreading consistency.

Carrot cake has become increasingly popular in recent years. I like this favorite version plain, but you may wish to bake it in layers and add a cream cheese icing.

Carrot Cake

Makes one 10-inch tube cake

2	cups sugar
1¼	cups salad oil
2	cups all-purpose flour
2	tsp. baking powder
2	tsp. cinnamon
1	tsp. baking soda
1	tsp. salt
4	eggs
3	cups grated raw carrots
1	cup chopped pecans
¾	cup raisins

1. Mix sugar and salad oil together in a bowl.

2. Sift flour, baking powder, cinnamon, baking soda, and salt together. Add to sugar mixture alternately with eggs. Beat well after each addition.

3. Fold in carrots, pecans, and raisins. Pour into a greased and floured 10-inch tube or bundt pan. Bake in a preheated 350 degree oven for 50 to 55 minutes, until a toothpick inserted in the center comes out clean.

The surprise ingredient is what makes this cake so moist.

Carob Surprise Cake

Makes one 10-inch tube cake

¾	cup butter
2	cups brown sugar
3	eggs
2	tsp. vanilla
2	cups grated zucchini
2	cups all-purpose flour
¼	cup carob powder
2½	tsp. baking powder
1½	tsp. baking soda
1	tsp. salt
1	tsp. cinnamon
½	cup milk
1	cup chopped pecans

1. Cream butter with brown sugar until smooth. Beat in eggs one at a time. Stir in vanilla and grated zucchini.

2. Sift flour, carob powder, baking powder, baking soda, salt, and cinnamon together. Stir into creamed ingredients alternately with milk. Stir in nuts.

3. Pour batter into a greased and floured 10-inch tube or bundt pan. Bake in a preheated 350 degree oven for 50 to 60 minutes, until a toothpick inserted in the center comes out clean.

Pumpkin Spice Cake

Makes one 9-inch tube cake

¾ cup butter
1½ cups brown sugar
3 eggs
½ tsp. vanilla
1½ cups cooked, pureed
    pumpkin
2 cups all-purpose
    flour
1 tsp. baking powder
1 tsp. baking soda
1 tsp. salt
1 tsp. cinnamon
1 tsp. ground cloves
1 cup chopped pecans

1. Cream butter and brown sugar together. Beat in eggs and vanilla. Stir in pumpkin puree.

2. Sift flour, baking powder, baking soda, salt, cinnamon, and cloves together. Stir into liquid ingredients and mix until well blended. Fold in pecans.

3. Pour batter into a greased and floured 9-inch tube or bundt pan. Bake in a preheated 375 degree oven for 50 to 55 minutes, until a toothpick inserted in the center comes out clean.

The combination of a fruit sherbet and ice cream always brings to mind the creamsicle of childhood 'Good Humour' days. Boysenberry and honey make a particularly fine combination with angel food cake. This cake is best made the day before you are planning to serve it.

Angie's Ice Cream Cake

Makes one tube cake

1 10-inch angel food cake
1 pint honey ice cream
1 pint boysenberry sherbet
1 cup whipping cream
1 Tbsp. sugar
1 tsp. vanilla

1. Turn angel food cake so that the wider part of the cake is on the bottom. With a serrated knife, cut a ½-inch slice from the top of the cake and set aside. This will be the lid for the finished cake.

2. Make a deep, circular incision ½ inch from the outside rim of the cake. Do the same around the inner rim of the cake. Make diagonal cuts between these lines and hollow out the middle section, so that you have a channel to hold your filling. Leave about ½ inch on the bottom of the cake.

3. Fill the bottom of the cavity with half the honey ice cream. Cover this with all the boysenberry sherbet and add a final layer of honey ice cream. Top the cake with the lid and freeze until very firm, at least six hours and preferably overnight.

4. Just before serving, whip the cream with the sugar and vanilla and spread over the cake.

This impressive looking cake is actually Greek in origin.

Serves 16 to 20

Copenhagen Nut Cake

approximately 1 lb.
   phyllo dough
¾ to 1 cup melted butter
8 egg yolks
½ cup sugar
½ lb. finely chopped
   walnuts (about
   2 cups)
½ lb. finely ground
   almonds (about
   1½ cups)
2 Tbsp. flour
1 tsp. baking powder
1 tsp. cinnamon
1 tsp. vanilla
1 Tbsp. dark rum
8 egg whites

1. Butter a 9-inch spring-form pan. Line it with 8 sheets of buttered phyllo. Let the ends hang over the sides of the pan and off-set the sheets so that they extend all around the rim.

2. Beat egg yolks with sugar until thick and light. Stir in walnuts, almonds, flour, baking powder, cinnamon, vanilla, and rum. Beat whites until stiff and fold into mixture, one half at a time. Pour batter into phyllo-lined cake pan.

3. One at a time, brush 5 more sheets of phyllo with melted butter. Fold each in half, butter again, and place on top of cake. When all five layers have been placed over the cake, fold the overhanging edges in toward the center. This will look messy, but once baked, will turn a beautiful, golden brown and look pretty. With a pastry brush, generously brush more butter over the top of the cake.

4. Place the cake pan on a cookie sheet and bake in a preheated 350 degree oven for 50 minutes to an hour, until dark, golden brown. Remove from oven and drench with sugar syrup. Let cool to room temperature before removing from pan.

Sugar Syrup

3 cups sugar
1½ cups water
½ cup honey
3 Tbsp. lemon juice
1 tsp. grated lemon rind

1. Bring all ingredients to a boil. Reduce heat and simmer for 15 minutes. Pour over cake while still warm.

This dense, moist cake is the cornerstone of the excellent reputation of Rudi's Bakery in Bloomington, Indiana.

Rudi's Poppy Seed Cake

Makes one 9-inch tube cake

½   cup butter
½   cup shortening
1½ cups sugar
5   egg yolks
1   tsp. vanilla
2   cups cake flour
¼   tsp. salt
1¼ tsp. baking soda
1   cup sour cream
½   cup poppy seeds
5   egg whites

1. Cream butter and shortening with sugar. Beat in egg yolks and vanilla.

2. Sift flour, salt, and baking soda together and add to creamed mixture alternately with sour cream. Stir in poppy seeds.

3. Beat egg whites until stiff but not dry. Fold into batter one half at a time. Pour batter into a greased and floured 9-inch tube pan. Bake in a preheated 350 degree oven for 45 to 50 minutes, until a toothpick inserted in the center comes out clean. Serve plain or iced with cream cheese icing.

A Tao Restaurant favorite.

Poppy Seed Cake Fudge Sundae

For one serving

1   piece poppy seed cake
1   large scoop vanilla
     ice cream
     plenty of hot fudge sauce
     a few slices of banana
     for garnish

Here is a chocolate sauce guaranteed to devastate.

Chocolate Sauce

Makes 1 to 1½ cups

½   cup heavy cream
¼   cup granulated sugar
½   cup apricot jam
4   squares unsweetened
     chocolate, finely
     chopped or grated

1. Bring cream and sugar to a boil in a saucepan. Stir in jam and cook, stirring, until jam has melted. Remove from heat, add chocolate, and stir until chocolate is melted. If apricot jam is excessively lumpy, strain through a sieve. Serve hot.

Based on a Japanese dessert, this jello lacks the 'bounce' of jello made with gelatin, but it does have a nice, fresh fruit taste. It is made with agar-agar, a thickening agent made from seaweed that makes a good vegetarian substitute for gelatin. If you like this version, try it with some other fruits.

Raspberry or Strawberry Jello

Serves 6 to 8

  2 *sticks* kanten
       (agar-agar squares)
1½ *cups water*
       honey or sugar to taste
2½ *cups fresh raspberry or*
       strawberry puree
  2 *Tbsp. lemon juice*
  1 *sliced banana*

1. Break *kanten* in small pieces and soak in a saucepan with the water for 30 minutes. Add sugar, bring to a boil and stir to dissolve *kanten*. Stir in fruit puree, lemon juice, and banana slices. Pour into a 9-inch square pan and chill until set. Cut in squares or fancy shapes and serve.

This simple yet extremely rich dessert may be prepared in advance and assembled at the last moment.

Chilled Zabaglione with Strawberries

Serves 6 to 8

  6 *egg yolks*
 ½ *cup sugar*
 ¾ *cup Marsala or sweet*
       sherry
  1 *cup heavy cream*
  1 *pint strawberries*
       sweetened whipped
       cream for garnish

1. Use a large double boiler or a stainless steel bowl that fits snugly over a six quart pot. Combine egg yolks, sugar, and Marsala or sherry in the top of the double boiler. With a balloon whisk, beat constantly over simmering water until mixture is thick and has almost tripled in volume. Chill in refrigerator.

2. Beat heavy cream until it forms soft peaks. Fold into chilled Marsala mixture.

3. Halve strawberries and arrange in dessert dishes or wine glasses. Just before serving, ladle chilled zabaglione over them. Garnish with sweetened whipped cream and a few chocolate shavings.

Assemble this dessert at the last minute and serve in pretty glass dishes or wine glasses.

Strawberries Romanoff

Serves 4 to 6

1½ *pints strawberries*
1 *cup sugar syrup*
¼ *cup Grand Marnier, or to taste*
1 *cup whipping cream*
1 *Tbsp. sugar*
a few drops vanilla or Grand Marnier
candied violets for garnish

1. Slice strawberries and toss gently with sugar syrup and Grand Marnier. Arrange in dessert dishes.

2. Whip cream with sugar and vanilla or Grand Marnier until it holds soft peaks. Fit a pastry bag with a large star tip and fill with whipped cream. Garnish each dessert with a circular swirl of whipped cream and top with one or two candied violets.

Sugar Syrup

Makes 1 cup

¾ *cup sugar*
¾ *cup water*

1. Combine sugar and water in a saucepan and bring to a boil. Boil for 3 or 4 minutes, until sugar is dissolved. Cool.

Use only firm, ripe pears for poaching. No amount of cooking will render a hard, green pear palatable. Small pears are lovely poached whole—peel them, but leave the stems intact. For Pears Helene, serve poached pears with vanilla ice cream and chocolate sauce.

Poached Pears

Serves 4

4 *firm, ripe pears*
2 *cups sugar*
1 *cup water*
1 *Tbsp. lemon juice*
1 *tsp. vanilla*

1. Peel and halve pears. With a melon baller, neatly remove cores and stems.

2. Bring sugar, water, and lemon juice to a boil in a heavy, wide-bottomed pan. Stir in vanilla.

3. Simmer pears in syrup until tender, turning once gently. This takes from 8 to 10 minutes. Remove pears from the syrup with a slotted spoon and cool. Once pears are cooled, they may be stored in the cooled syrup until needed.

Brown sugar, sweet potatoes, pineapple, and rum make an interesting and delicious combination in this souffle. If you like, serve with a custard sauce (such as English Cream) flavored with dark rum.

Serves 6 to 8

1¼ cups milk
⅓ cup brown sugar
4 Tbsp. butter
6 Tbsp. flour
6 egg yolks
1 tsp. vanilla
1 Tbsp. dark rum
2 sweet potatoes, peeled, boiled, and pureed, enough to make one cup
1 cup crushed pineapple
6 egg whites

Souffle Barbados

1. Butter a two-quart souffle mold and coat the bottom and sides with two tablespoons of granulated sugar.

2. In a small saucepan, heat milk and brown sugar together until mixture comes to a boil.

3. In a separate saucepan, melt butter and stir in flour. Mix to a thick paste. Slowly add boiling milk while stirring constantly with a wire whisk. Continue to cook and stir until mixture is thick and pulls away from the sides of the pan.

4. Remove pan from heat and beat in egg yolks one at a time. Stir in vanilla, rum, and sweet potato puree. Mix until smooth. Fold in pineapple.

5. Beat egg whites until stiff but not dry. Gently fold half the beaten egg whites into the yolk mixture. Fold in remaining whites and pour into prepared souffle dish. Bake in a preheated 375 degree oven for 30 to 35 minutes, until souffle is puffed and golden. Sprinkle with powdered sugar and serve immediately.

This is a luscious and unusual version of *creme caramel*. The caramel is in the custard as well as on the outside. It is served surrounded by a vanilla custard sauce.

Creme Caramel

Makes six 5-ounce servings

3 cups milk
1 cup sugar
1 tsp. lemon juice
3 egg yolks
3 whole eggs

1. Bring milk to a boil in a two-quart saucepan. Set aside but keep hot while you make the caramel.

2. In a small, heavy-bottomed saucepan, mix ½ cup sugar with lemon juice. Rub mixture with your fingers so that the sugar is well moistened with lemon. This will keep the caramel from crystallizing while you are making it. With a wooden spoon, stir over medium heat until sugar melts and turns a dark caramel color. Spoon a few drops of caramel (about ½ teaspoon each) into six ovenproof custard cups or ramekins. Carefully stir the remaining caramel into the hot milk. Stir until dissolved.

3. Beat egg yolks, whole eggs, and remaining sugar together in a bowl.

4. With a wire whisk, stir hot milk into egg mixture in a steady stream. Mix until blended.

5. Strain custard and pour into prepared molds.

6. Place the molds in a large baking pan. Pour in enough boiling water to come two-thirds the way up the sides of the molds. Bake in a preheated 350 degree oven for one hour, until a knife inserted in the center of the custard comes out clean. Remove and chill.

7. To unmold custards, carefully run a knife around the edge of the mold. Place a dessert plate face down over the mold, reverse and shake hard one or two times to release the custard from the mold. Surround the *creme caramel* with English Cream and top with lightly sweetened whipped cream.

English Cream (Vanilla Custard Sauce)

Makes 2 cups

1 cup milk
1 cup cream
3 egg yolks
⅓ cup sugar
1 tsp. vanilla

1. Combine milk and cream together in a saucepan and bring to a boil.

2. Beat egg yolks with sugar and vanilla. Stirring constantly with a wire whisk, add boiling milk to egg yolks in a steady stream.

3. Return custard to the saucepan. Stirring constantly, heat until mixture coats the back of a spoon (160 degrees on a candy thermometer). It should appear slightly thicker than heavy cream. Be careful not to overcook the custard or the eggs will curdle.

4. Remove custard from pan and stir in vanilla. Chill. Sauce will thicken as it cools.

This Latin American version of caramel custard is thick and rich. You may bake it in one large mold or in individual serving dishes.

Flan

Serves 6

½ cup sugar
1 tsp. lemon juice
4 egg yolks
1 tsp. vanilla
1¼ cups milk
1 can sweetened
   condensed milk
4 egg whites, beaten until
   frothy

1. In a small, heavy-bottomed saucepan, rub sugar and lemon juice together with your hands. Be sure that the sugar is well moistened with lemon. This will keep the caramel from crystallizing while you are making it. With a wooden spoon, stir over medium heat until sugar melts and turns a dark caramel color. Pour hot caramel into an eight-inch round, flat baking dish and quickly tilt the dish back and forth so that the caramel coats the bottom evenly.

2. Combine egg yolks, vanilla, milk, and sweetened condensed milk in a bowl. Stir in egg whites and mix until well blended. Pour into caramel-coated dish.

3. Place dish in a larger baking pan and pour in enough boiling water to come half way up the sides of the dish. Bake in a preheated 350 degree oven for 45 minutes to an hour, until a knife inserted in the center of the custard comes out clean. Chill several hours or overnight.

4. To serve, run a knife around the rim of the custard and invert it on a serving plate. Cut in wedges.

This sweet, warm dessert adds an authentic touch to an Indian meal. A dough made from curd and powdered milk is shaped into balls, deep fried, and simmered in a cardamon flavored syrup.

Gulab Jamen

Serves 4 to 6

2 cups *whole milk*
2 Tbsp. *or more lemon juice*
1 cup *instant powdered milk*
3 Tbsp. *flour*
1 Tbsp. *shortening*
pinch *baking soda*
2 cups *sugar*
3 cups *water*
crushed seeds from 2 cardamon pods
oil for frying

1. The object of this first step is to make curds and whey. Bring milk to a rolling boil and stir in lemon juice. Milk should curdle and visibly separate. If this does not happen right away, stir in a little more lemon juice. Strain through a piece of cheesecloth and reserve the watery part (whey) for use in soup stock or for making Indian *naan* bread. Set curds aside to cool.

2. When sufficiently cool, combine curd with instant powdered milk, flour, baking soda, and shortening. Knead until mixture is no longer sticky. Moisten with a little milk or yogurt if necessary.

3. Coat your hands lightly with shortening and shape the dough in small balls, about the size of a walnut.

4. Combine sugar, water, and crushed cardamon seeds in a large, flat pan. Bring to a boil, reduce heat and simmer for 5 minutes.

5. Heat two inches of oil in a heavy saucepan or deep fryer. When a pinch of dough dropped into the hot oil rises quickly to the surface, the oil is ready for frying. Fry three or four balls at a time, turning often with a slotted spoon, until they are a dark, golden brown. Remove with a slotted spoon and drain on paper towels.

6. As soon as all the *gulab jamen* have been fried, drop them in the simmering sugar syrup. Return the syrup to a boil and simmer for three minutes. Remove pan from heat and cool the *gulab jamen* briefly in the syrup. Serve three or four balls in their syrup per person. Serve warm.

Indian Rice Pudding

Serves 6 to 8

1   cup rice
5½ cups milk
⅓   cup raisins
¾   cup sugar
5   Tbsp. finely chopped
      almonds
4   or 5 cardamon pods

1. Cover rice with water and soak for two hours. Drain.

2. Combine soaked rice with 4 cups milk in a saucepan. Simmer, covered, until most of the milk has been absorbed, 45 minutes to an hour.

3. Stir in raisins, sugar, and remaining 1½ cups milk. Simmer gently, stirring occasionally, for 25 to 30 minutes, until pudding starts to thicken.

4. Break open cardamon pods and crush the seeds with a rolling pin. Stir crushed cardamon and chopped almonds into the pudding. Remove from the pan and chill.

Warning! This is very sweet.

Serves 6

1¾ cups brown sugar
1¾ cups water
1   Tbsp. butter
½   tsp. vanilla
½   cup chopped dates
½   cup chopped walnuts
1   cup flour
2   tsp. baking powder
½   cup milk

Date Nut Pudding

1. Combine 1½ cups brown sugar, water, and butter in a saucepan. Bring to a boil, stirring until sugar dissolves. Remove from heat and stir in vanilla.

2. Mix remaining ¼ cup sugar, dates, walnuts, flour, and baking powder together in a bowl. Stir in milk and mix until well blended.

3. Pour sugar syrup into a greased, 9-inch square pan. Drop the date batter into the syrup by spoonfuls. Bake in a preheated 350 degree oven for 30 minutes, until brown on top. Cool and serve in ice cream dishes garnished with unsweetened whipped cream.

Glossary of Ingredients

Agar-Agar   A neutral-tasting product made from seaweed that is used as a thickening agent. Sold in transparent sticks or strands, it dissolves in boiling water and can be used to make a fairly stiff jelly.

Anaheim pepper   A long, thin, hot to mild, fresh green chili that is readily available in the West and Southwest. Also called California chili, the Anaheim pepper can be substituted for fresh poblano chiles.

Ancho chili   A dark, red, dried chili that is generally mild. Average size is three inches wide and four inches long. It is one of the most frequently used dried, red chiles in Mexican cookery.

Bel-Paese   A delicately flavored, Italian, semi-soft cheese.

Bran   The outer part of the grain that is separated from the flour in the milling process. Unless otherwise specified, bran refers to wheat bran in most recipes.

Bulghur   Also called burghul and cracked wheat, bulghur is a fine, cracked wheat cereal used in Middle Eastern cooking.

Capers   The pickled bud of the caper bush, a wild plant found in southern France and throughout the Middle East.

Cardamon   The aromatic seeds of a spice belonging to the ginger family, used frequently in Indian cooking.

Carob powder   The powder made from carob tree pods, also called St. John's bread, often used as a chocolate substitute.

Chick peas   Garbanzo beans.

Chick pea flour   A finely ground flour made from chick peas used in Indian cooking. Often sold as "gram" flour.

Chili oil   An oil flavored with hot chiles, used as a seasoning in Chinese cooking.

Chili paste   A bean paste flavored with garlic and hot chiles, used as a seasoning (sparingly) in Chinese cooking.

Chinese sesame oil   A strongly flavored oil made from white sesame seeds, used as a seasoning (sparingly) in Chinese cooking.

Coriander   A dark, green herb that looks a little like Italian broad-leaf parsley, and has a distinctive earthy, bittersweet flavor. The leaves are frequently used in Mexican, Indian, and Asian cooking and are available, fresh, in most markets that cater to these cuisines. The Spanish name is *cilantro*.

Coriander seeds Small, round seeds that look like peppercorns and are ground or crushed for use as a spice. The seeds should not be substituted for fresh coriander leaves. Instead, they are used as an ingredient for curry powder, or as a seasoning for baked goods, and smell of a blend of citrus, anise, and cumin.

Cous-cous A golden grain made from finely crushed wheat and used in the North African dish of that name.

Cracked wheat A cereal made from cracked wheat berries. Very finely cracked wheat is used often in Middle Eastern cooking and called bulghur.

Curry powder A combination of spices ground to a powder and used in Indian cooking. The strength of the curry powder is determined by the amount of chili (or cayenne pepper) used. Most curries consist of cumin, coriander seeds, cloves, pepper, cinnamon, fennel, and ginger. The exact mixture may vary from cook to cook, or region to region.

Dumpling wrappers Ready-made circles of dough used for making Chinese or Japanese pastries, available fresh or frozen in many Oriental groceries.

Egg-roll wrappers Ready-made squares of dough used for making egg rolls.

Egg sheets Square sheets of very thin omelet, used in Japanese cooking.

Egg strips Strips cut from egg sheets, used as garnish in Japanese cooking.

Farmer's cheese A mild cheese closely related to cottage cheese and pot cheese, sometimes firm, sometimes dry and crumbly.

Feta cheese A white, crumbly, and often salty, Greek cheese made from sheep's milk and preserved in brine.

Fontina cheese A mild, Italian cheese.

Ginger, fresh A gnarled, tan root that is sliced, grated, or finely chopped for use in Oriental cooking. It must be stored in the refrigerator.

Ginger, red pickled A Japanese condiment made from ginger root.

Green chiles, canned Mild to slightly hot green chiles readily available in most Latin American sections of large supermarkets. They may be poblano or Anaheim chiles and are simply called "green" chiles.

Heavy cream Whipping cream.

Jalapeno pepper Often available fresh in California and the Southwest, this small, hot, green chili is also widely available canned or in jars *en escabeche* (pickled).

Japanese rice A short-grained rice that is moist and

somewhat sticky when cooked. Look for the brands Cal-rose, Japan Rose, Zenith, and Lucky Rose.

Kampyo   Japanese dried gourd strips.

Kanten   Sticks of agar-agar.

Kasha   Buckwheat groats, used in Russian cookery. If not already toasted, stir kasha over medium heat in a dry frying pan until golden brown before cooking.

Masa harina   A flour made from dried corn and treated with lime, used for making tortillas and tamales in Mexican cooking. Quaker brand instant masa harina is widely available. Do not substitute corn meal.

Mirin   A sweet *sake* (rice wine) used only for cooking. Sherry makes an acceptable substitute.

Miso   A dark or light soybean paste used in Japanese cooking. Light (or white) miso has a milder flavor than dark (brown or red) miso.

Mung bean   A bean grown primarily for sprouting. Mung bean sprouts are used in salads, egg rolls, and other Oriental dishes.

Mushrooms, dried   Mushrooms from Japan, China, and Italy that must be soaked in water for about 30 minutes to reconstitute. Although expenisve, they stretch a long way and add a distinctive flavor to a dish.

Nori   Thin sheets of dried seaweed used in Japanese cooking. See nori rolls.

Pastina   Tiny pasta used in soups.

Pequin pepper or chili   A small, hot dried, red pepper used in Mexican and Latin American cooking.

Pernod   A French, anise flavored aperitif.

Phyllo   A paper thin pastry used in Greek cookery, similar to strudel dough. Available ready-made in one pound boxes in many gourmet food shops.

Pignoli nuts   Small kernels from pine cones that resemble almonds in flavor. Also called pine nuts.

Pita   Syrian flat bread.

Poblano chili   A large, dark green chili with a mild to hot flavor. Widely available canned, available fresh in California and the Southwest.

Rice wine vinegar   A slightly sweet Japanese white rice vinegar, milder than American distilled white vinegar or cider vinegar. It is also available seasoned for making sushi.

Saffron   The dried stamens of crocus blossoms which impart a beautiful, dark orange color and a distinctive flavor. Costly because of the number of blossoms to make one pound of saffron (75,000). Spain produces the best quality saffron.

Sake Japanese rice wine.

Saimin Hawaiian name for *ramen* (Japanese instant noodles).

Semolina A fine-grained golden cereal made from durum wheat, called *semolino* in Italian. Semolina should not be confused with the white, quick-cooking breakfast cereal called farina or cream of wheat.

Serrano pepper A small, very hot, green chili, primarily available canned *en escabeche* (pickled).

Shitake Japanese dried mushrooms.

Split red lentils A quick-cooking, red lentil used in Indian and Middle Eastern cookery.

Sushi Japanese cold, vinegared rice.

Tahini A paste made from sesame seeds with a nutty flavor and of the consistency of peanut butter, used in Middle Eastern cookery.

Tamarind The fruit of the tamarind tree. The pods contain an acidic pulp that is used as a flavoring in Indian, Middle Eastern, and West Indian cooking and also to make a tart, cold drink. Tamarind concentrate can be purchased where Indian specialty foods are sold.

Tofu Bean curd or soybean cake. A staple of Oriental cooking that is high in protein and low in cost. Fresh soybean cake will keep in the refrigerator for one week. Cover with water and change the water daily.

Tomatillo Small, green, Mexican tomato with a delicate flavor. Primarily available canned in Latin American specialty food shops.

Won-ton wrappers Squares of dough available ready-made, fresh, or frozen (about 70 squares to a one pound box) for making Chinese won-tons.

Index